0 kilometres   20

0 miles   20

Apostolos
Andreas

Dipkarpaz
(Rizokarpaso)

Aigialousa
(Yenierenkoy)

Trikomo (Iskele)

NORTH CYPRUS

Famagusta
(Gazimağusa/
Ammochostos)

Agia Napa

Larnaka

North Cyprus
Pages 128–157

South Nicosia
Pages 116–127

Southern Cyprus
Pages 64–87

EYEWITNESS TRAVEL

CYPRUS

TRAVEL

CYPRUS

Main Contributors

Grzegorz Micuła and Magdalena Micuła

Produced by Hachette Livre Polska sp. z o.o., Warsaw, Poland

Senior Graphic Designer
Paweł Pasternak

Editors
Agnieszka Majle, Robert G. Pasieczny

Main Contributors
Elżbieta Makowiecka, Grzegorz Micuła, Magdalena Micuła

Cartographers
Magdalena Polak, Michał Zielkiewicz

Photographer
Dorota and Mariusz Jarymowicz, Krzysztof Kur

Illustrators
Michał Burkiewicz, Paweł Marczak, Bohdan Wróblewski

Typesetting and Layout
Elżbieta Dudzińska, Paweł Kamiński, Grzegorz Wilk

Printed and bound in China by L. Rex Printing Co., Ltd.

First American Edition, 2006
Published in the United States by DK Publishing,
345 Hudson Street, New York, New York 10014

16 17 18 19 10 9 8 7 6 5 4 3 2 1

Reprinted with revisions 2008, 2010, 2012, 2014, 2016

Copyright © 2006, 2016 Dorling Kindersley Limited, London
A Penguin Random House Company

Published in Great Britain by Dorling Kindersley Limited.
A catalog record of this book is available from the Library of Congress

ISSN 1542 1554

ISBN: 978-1-46544-095-2

Floors are referred to throughout in accordance with American usage;
ie the "first floor" is at ground floor level

MIX
Paper from
responsible sources
FSC
www.fsc.org   FSC™ C018179

The information in this
DK Eyewitness Travel Guide is checked regularly.
Every effort has been made to ensure that this book is as up-to-date as
possible at the time of going to press. Some details, however, such as
telephone numbers, opening hours, prices, gallery hanging arrangements
and travel information are liable to change. The publishers cannot accept
responsibility for any consequences arising from the use of this book, nor for
any material on third party websites, and cannot guarantee that any website
address in this book will be a suitable source of travel information. We value
the views and suggestions of our readers very highly. Please write to:
Publisher, DK Eyewitness Travel Guides, Dorling Kindersley, 80 Strand, London
WC2R 0RL, Great Britain, or email: travelguides@dk.com.

Front cover main image: Pafos, Akamas Peninsula, Akamas Natural Park

 Sanctuary of Apollo Ylatis, near Kourion

Contents

Introducing
Cyprus

Cypriot saint Agios Mamas, the Byzantine
Museum in Pafos

Beach in the bustling resort of Agia Napa in
southeast Cyprus

Ruins of the Sanctuary of Apollo Ylatis, near Kourion

Picturesque Kyrenia harbour, one of the most beautiful in Cyprus

Popular Cypriot dessert *mahallepi*– a creamy pudding

Kyrenia Castle *(pp152–3)*

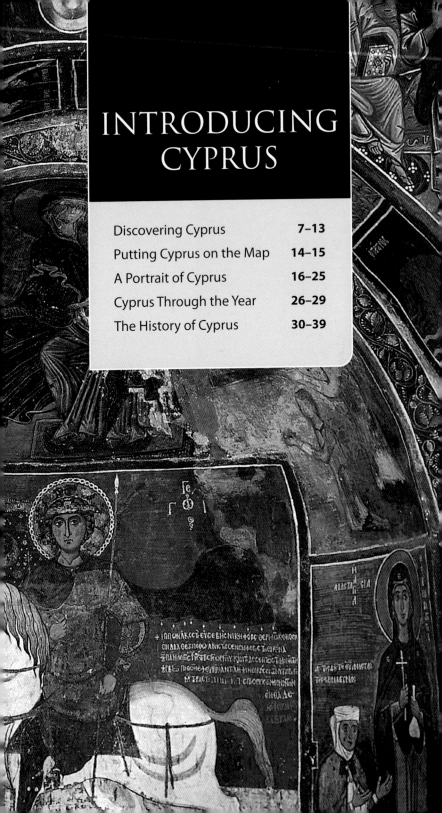

INTRODUCING CYPRUS

DISCOVERING CYPRUS

The following itineraries cover the highlights of Cyprus, and are of varying lengths: mix and match these to create your ideal Cypriot holiday. First are a couple of two-day tours of the island's most walkable towns, Nicosia and Pafos. Next, a three-day driving tour of the UNESCO World Heritage-listed frescoed churches of the Troodos mountains. Of the week-long itineraries, one covers West Cyprus – essentially the hinterland of Pafos – with its hill villages, pristine beaches, country monasteries and chapels, and natural beauty spots. The other is end-to-end North Cyprus, taking in its many monuments, towns and beaches.

Agios Neofytos Monastery
Founded by the hermit monk Neofytos in the 12th century, the *enkleistra* (hermitage) was carved out the mountain by Neofytos himself. The monastery contains fine Byzantine frescoes dating from the 12th to 15th centuries.

A Week in West Cyprus

- Squeeze through the frescoed, cut-from-living-rock *encleistra* of Agios Neofytos monastery.

- Contemplate the sensual, water-sculpted sides of the unspoilt Avakas Gorge.

- Learn about sea-turtle nesting at the Lara Bay hatchery station.

- Discover the elegant stone-built villages of the Akamas peninsula.

- Sample Cyprus' cleanest sea, the supposed bathing spot of the goddess Aphrodite, at Chrysochou Bay.

- Marvel at intricately painted archaic amphorae in the Marion-Arsinoe Archaeological Museum.

- View the cedar groves of Cedar Valley.

- Pick up a bottle of the monks' own wine at the Chrysorrogiatissa monastery.

- Purchase fine lacework and woven wall-hangings in Fyti.

Avakas Gorge
This deep ravine of towering limestone cliffs, with the river Avgas runing through it, is popular with both rock climbers and hikers.

◀ Detail of the interior of Asinou Church in the Troodos mountains

Kyrenia Castle
Built on the site of a Roman fort by the Venetians, the castle affords magnificent views of the harbour below.

Apostolos Andreas

Dipkarpaz
Nangomi (Golden) Beach

Agios Thyrsos
Sipahi

Mediterranean Sea

Kantara Castle

yrenia Girne)
Kyrenia (Girne) beaches
Bellapais
Antifonitis Monastery
Buffavento Castle
NORTH CYPRUS
Trikomo (İskele)

Nicosia Lefkoşa)
St Barnabas Monastery
Royal Tombs
Salamis
Famagusta

LARNAKA

Larnaka Bay

Bellapais Abbey
These romantic ruins date back to the 13th century, when the Gothic abbey housed Augustinian monks fleeing Jerusalem.

A Week in North Cyprus

- From Kyrenia's imposing castle, gaze over the picturesque port.
- Savour Lusignan Gothic style at Bellapais abbey.
- Visit the royal apartments of St Hilarion Castle.
- Study the north's best-preserved Byzantine frescoes in site at the Panagia Theotokos church, Trikomo.
- Walk on the stunning geometric mosaic flooring at Agia Trias basilica in Sipahi.

- Stretch out on Golden Beach (Nangomi), the island's longest and wildest, on the Karpasia peninsula.
- Explore the colonnades, Roman theatre, mosaics and baths of ancient Salamis.
- Peruse the Gothic architecture of old Famagusta, especially Lala Mustafa Pasha mosque.

0 kilometres 25
0 miles 25

Key

— A Week in West Cyprus
— A Week in North Cyprus

Two Days in Pafos (Paphos)

Pafos (pp52–7) offers ancient sites, worthwhile museums, a well-loved shore promenade and a lively bazaar.

- **Arriving** Pafos (PFO) airport lies 15 km (9 miles) to the southeast; take a bus, taxi or hire car to/from town.

Day 1
Morning Your first stop is the Roman mosaics in **Kato (Lower) Pafos** (pp56–7), then stroll along the harbourfront to the old fort for views from its roof, or head north to the restored Roman odeon, then east across Apostolou Pavlou to the **Agia Solomoni catacombs** (pp54–5), with their sacred pool. From there, thread through the Kato Pafos back streets to medieval **Agia Kyriaki church** (p54), before stopping for lunch.

Afternoon Take a swim at one of the pocket **beaches** (p55) along the municipal promenade leading east from the old port. Then change direction to follow the shoreline walkway north for an hour to the subterranean **Tombs of the Kings** (p54), off the road to Coral Bay.

Day 2
Morning Explore the **Agora** (p52), the covered bazaar, and the lanes between Agora and Kanari streets in Ktima, best on Saturday when there's a street

The stone church of Agia Kyriaki, built in the 12th century and still in use today

produce market. Downhill at the base of the escarpment is the **Mehmet Bey Ebubekir Hamam** (p52), with panels detailing the old public baths of Cyprus. Have lunch at a traditional bazaar taverna on Votsi Street.

Afternoon Continue into Moutallos, with its time-warped 1960s houses and the **Grand** mosque (p52). Return to the centre of town to visit the **Byzantine and Ethnographic museums** (both p53). From the nearby municipal gardens, it's a short bus ride southeast to the **Archaeological Museum** (p55). Finish the day with a traditional meze.

Two Days in Nicosia (Lefkoşa)

Old, walled Nicosia has experienced a revival, with numerous restaurants and boutiques lining its pedestrianized streets.

- **Arriving** Larnaka airport is 45 km (27 miles) southeast of Nicosia, with bus services to the edge of the city and ample hire-car facilities.

Day 1
Morning Allow 2 to 3 hours for the **Cyprus Museum** (pp126–7), one of the Mediterranean's great collections of ancient art, with special distinction in Bronze Age, Geometric and archaic artifacts. Follow this with lunch at one of the city's growing number of quality new restaurants, just southeast.

Afternoon Enter the old walled town via Plateia Solomou and head east across Ledra Ave for the excellent **Leventis Museum** (p125). From here, stroll north past the ornate **churches of Tripiotis and Faneromeni** (p126) and the **Araplar Mosque** (p126), before turning east towards the **Municipal Arts Centre** (p122), aka "the Powerhouse", as it used to be an old Electricity Authority building. Admire the exhibits, then head south for a peek

The Gothic façade of Selimiye Camii mosque (Aya Sofya Cathedral)

inside the **Omar mosque** (p123) before dining at one of the old quarter's traditional tavernas.

Day 2
Morning Enter old Greek Cypriot Nicosia from its far eastern corner, into Chrysaliniotissa, with its tottering Ottoman-era houses. Explore the **Chrysaliniotissa church** (p124) from c.1450, then meander southwest to reach the Municipal Cultural Centre in **Famagusta Gate** (p124), home to superb Byzantine art rescued from desecrated churches in North Cyprus. If time permits, peek inside the nearby **Hadjigeorgakis Kornesios House** (p123) with its ethnographic displays. Then go to the **Ledra Street checkpoint** (p125) between the two sectors of Nicosia – don't forget your passport. Have lunch at one of the restaurants around the **Selimiye Mosque** (pp132–3), after admiring this Gothic place of worship inside and out.

Afternoon West of the mosque, the craft shops of the well-restored Ottoman **Büyük Han** (p132) beckon. Nearby, the **Mevlevi Tekke** (p134) museum unveils the former monastery of the Whirling Dervishes. From here, stroll southwest to the central mosque of **Arabahmet district** (p135), North Nicosia's answer to Chrysaliniotissa. Finally, head back to the Ledra–Lokmacı crossing for a night on the town in livelier South Nicosia.

Painted Churches of the Troodos

This itinerary explores the frescoes and murals of churches in and around the Troodos mountains, most of which are on the UNESCO World Cultural Heritage list. Stay overnight in Agros, Kakopetria, or Kalopanagiotis to minimize driving.

- **Duration** This is a three-day tour.
- **Transport** A car is necessary for this itinerary.

The beautifully painted interior of Panagia Forviotissa (tis Asinou)

Day 1

Morning Take the E110 road up from the A6 motorway at Limassol to Kalo Chorio, bearing right for the small **Chapel of St Mamas** *(p115)* in Louvaras village. Continue uphill on the E110 to Potamitissa village for Pelendri village and its grander 14th-century church of **Timios Stavros** *(p102)*. Retrace your route to Potamitissa, continuing east to **Agros** *(p115)* for lunch.

Afternoon Head north via Chandria to Lagoudera and the **Panagia tou Araka** *(pp104–5)*, with its superb late-12th-century frescoes. If time and daylight permit, head one valley

east, via Platanistassa village where the key-keeper lives, to visit remote **Stavros tou Agiasmati** *(p105)* church and more vivid frescoes. Return to Agros for the night.

Day 2

Morning Return to the ridge road at Chandria, then head west via Karvounas junction, Troodos resort and Prodromos, descending to Pedoulas and the late 15th-century **Church of the Archangel Michael** *(p93)*. Continue to Moutoullas village and the oldest painted church in these mountains, **Panagia tou Moutoulla** *(p93)*. Arrive at the scenic **Kalopanagiotis** village *(p93)* further down the valley in time for a spot of lunch.

Afternoon Cross the river to take in the rambling **Agios Ioannis Lambadistis monastery** *(pp92–3)*, the frescoes in its triple church recently restored by students from London's Courtauld Institute, and the excellent icon museum adjacent. Retrace your tyre treads to Pedoulas and the useful link road east to **Kakopetria** *(p103)*, a good place to spend the night.

Day 3

Morning Start the day with a pilgrimage to **Agios Nikolaos tis Stegis** *(pp102–3)* on Kakopetria's outskirts. Next, head to the nearby village of Galata, where you'll be shepherded around three churches, including **Panagia tis Podithou** *(p103)*, with frescoes by master Simeon Axenti. Stop here for some lunch.

Afternoon Drive north towards Nicosia on the fast B9 road, turning off at Koutrafas for access to **Panagia Forviotissa (tis Asinou)** *(p104)*, perhaps the finest of the UNESCO-listed churches, with frescoes of similar date to Agios Nikolaos tis Stegis. Proceed from here to Nicosia, pausing en route at Vyzakia to admire the Venetian-style frescoes in its **Church of the Archangel Michael** *(p104)*.

The UNESCO-listed ancient church of Panagia tis Podithou

A Week in North Cyprus

- **Arrival/departure** Ercan airport, northeast of Lefkoşa (North Nicosia), or Larnaka airport in the south for a greater selection of flights.

- **Transport** This tour is best undertaken with a hire car.

Day 1: Kyrenia and Bellapais

Kyrenia (Girne) (pp150–53) has long been the crown jewel of Cypriot tourism. The huge castle with its two museums, and the medieval Venetian port, are in-town highlights; after lunch, head up to **Bellapais village** (p149), graced by an exquisite Lusignan-era abbey. Bellapais and adjacent villages have a variety of restaurants for dinner. Spend the night in Bellapais or Kyrenia proper.

Day 2: Vouni and Soloi

Still using Kyrenia or Bellapais as a base, head west, then southwest via Morphou to the ancient sites of **Soloi** (pp156–7), with its mosaic-floored basilica, and the enigmatic hilltop citadel of **Vouni** (p157). Have a swim and some lunch at one of the tavernas nearby at Yedidalga or Yeşilirmak before returning to Kyrenia or Bellapais.

Day 3: Castles and Kyrenia Beaches

Climb up from the Kyrenia area to the fairy-tale Byzantine-Lusignan **St Hilarion Castle** (p149), best viewed in the early morning. Return to sea level and drive east for a swim or – if nesting season – a spot of turtle-watching at **Algadi beach**. Contact the Society for Protection of Turtles (www.cyprusturtles.org) for more information. Afterwards, drive up the good road to Beşparmak pass and take the track west from there to **Buffavento Castle** (p148) in time to take in the dramatic sunset views.

Day 4: Into the Karpasia (Karpas) Peninsula

Head east from the Kyrenia area, leaving the coast road briefly to take in the damaged but still worthwhile 12th-century frescoed monastery of **Antifonitis** (p148). Continue east to Kaplıca and the sharp climb up to **Kantara Castle** (p144), the gateway of Karpasia. Once on the peninsula trunk road, pause at **Sipahi village** (p145), where vast mosaics cover the Agias Trias basilica floor. After a restorative lunch near **Agios Thyrsos** (p145), there's time for a swim nearby before reaching abundant accommodation just outside **Dipkarpaz** (p145), your base for the next couple of nights.

Day 5: Exploring the Karpasia Peninsula

After taking in the half-ruined Levantine-fantasy church of **Agios Philon** (p145), with its flanking palm trees, pack a picnic and take the peninsula trunk road beyond Dipkarpaz to the northeastern-most cape of Cyprus, the cave-riddled **Kastros** (p145). On the return journey, stop to pay your respects at the rambling **Apostolos Andreas monastery** (p145), and spread your towel and picnic lunch at **Nangomi (Golden) Beach** (p145), the island's longest, and another haven for nesting sea turtles. Meander back to Dipkarpaz, dining at one of the excellent fish tavernas outside the village.

Day 6: Salamis and Around

With an early start, a southwesterly drive out of

Salamis, the largest archaeological site on Cyprus

Dipkarpaz brings you to Trikomo (İskele) and its **Panagia Thetokos** church (p144), sheltering the only intact Byzantine frescoes in North Cyprus. Further along the main coastal road, the sprawling site of ancient **Salamis** (pp138–9), and the beach fringing it, demand a few hours of your time until lunch. Nearby, the Bronze Age **Royal Tombs** (p136), and the **St Barnabas monastery** (p137) with its catacomb and museum, will fill the afternoon. Overnight at a beachfront hotel.

Day 7: Famagusta

Spend the day in the walled city of **Famagusta** (pp140–43), admiring the **Citadel** (p142), the façade of the **Lala Mustafa Pasha mosque** (p140) (originally a Lusignan Gothic cathedral) and the **churches of the Knights Templar and Hospitaller** (p141), before a late lunch in the *medrese* next to the mosque. Drive back to Ercan airport, or cross back into Southern Cyprus for Larnaka airport.

The formidable ruins of Bellapais abbey

For practical information on travelling around Cyprus, see pp202–3

A Week in West Cyprus

- **Arrival/departure** Pafos (PFO) airport.
- **Transport** A car is needed for this itinerary.

Day 1–2: Pafos
See the Two Days in Pafos itinerary on p10.

Day 3: Around Pafos
Pause in Empa for its imposing **Panagia Chryseleoussa** *(p51)*, sporting expressive, if damaged, 15th-century frescoes. Next, continue inland to **Agios Neofytos monastery** *(p51)*, where the eponymous saint dwelt in the intriguing, rock-cut *enkleistra*. After lunch, stop in **Geroskipou** *(p50)* village to admire the six-domed, vividly frescoed **Agia Paraskevi** *(p50)* church. Its frescoes – of similar date to those at Empa – were recently consolidated. Continue along the B6 highway to the ancient site and museum of **Palaipafos (Old Pafos)** *(pp48–9)*, a powerful city-state in ancient times. Undergoing continuing excavations here is the **Sanctuary of Aphrodite** *(p49)*. Finally, continue southeast to **Petra tou Romiou** *(p48)* for a late swim, and admire the sunset over this noted beauty spot. Then, return to modern Kouklia village next to Palaipafos for supper at one of its many tavernas, and overnight in Pafos.

Day 4: Safari to the Akamas Peninsula
Take the initially paved coast road beyond Coral Bay to the mouth of the **Avakas Gorge** *(p58)*, whose spectacular narrows take just over 2 hours return to hike from the parking area. Have lunch at one of the nearby snack bars before forging north on a much rougher track to **Lara** *(p58)* and its two flanking beaches – the northerly one is idyllic and has a sea-turtle research and protection station. After a swim, backtrack slightly to the narrow but paved track up to **Ineia** *(p58)* and other Akamas

The arched Venetian bridge of Roudia

peninsula villages, spending the night in **Drouseia** or **Kathikas** *(both p58)* after tastings at one (or more) of the local wineries.

Day 5: Chrysochou Bay
From Drouseia or Kathikas, descend the fast ridge road to the **Polis** *(p62)* area and enjoy a swim at one of the best beaches in West Cyprus. A 15-minute walk from town is one of the peninsula's marked nature trails from the **Baths of Aphrodite** *(p59)*, with fine views of Chrysochou Bay and Cape Arnaoutis. Spend the night on the resort strip here between Polis and the Baths of Aphrodite.

Day 6: Polis and Beyond
Stroll the tiny old town of Polis, stopping at diminutive **Agios**

Agios Neofytos monastery, located in what once was a secluded valley

Andronikos *(p62)* church to view its fine frescoes, then take in the excellent **Marion-Arsinoe Archaeological Museum** *(p62)*. (Keys to Agios Andronikos are available here if the church is unattended.) Afterwards, your course lies northwest along a rugged, wild coast to **Pomos** *(p47)* with its fish tavernas and pocket beaches, detouring halfway at **Gialia** *(p47)* to explore a 12th-century Georgian monastery excavated in 2005–07. Spend the night at **Lysos** *(p47)*, in the foothills above Polis.

Day 7: The Pafos Forest
From Lysos, head east into the wild, forested **Tilliria** *(p92)* region, visit **Stavros tis Psokas** *(p92)* forestry station and the famous cedar groves of **Cedar Valley** *(p92)*, before veering southwest to **Panagia** *(p63)*, birthplace of Archbishop-President Makarios III *(see p39)*. Just 2 km south, the **Chrysorrogiatissa monastery** *(pp62–3)* has exceptional woodwork and offers quaffable products from its very own Monte Royia winery; there are more wineries in the area, such as Vouni Panagia. After a late lunch here, search out the historic medieval **bridge of Roudia** *(p63)*, built by the Venetians, before heading north to **Fyti** *(p47)*, famous for its lacework and woven wall-hangings. From here it's a scenic drive back to Lysos.

Putting Cyprus on the Map

Situated in the eastern Mediterranean Sea, Cyprus is its third largest island (after Sicily and Sardinia), covering an area of 9,250 sq km (3,571 sq miles) with a 720-km- (447-mile-) long coastline. Divided since the 1974 war into the Greek Cypriot-governed Republic of Cyprus in the south and the Turkish-sponsored Turkish Republic of North Cyprus in the north, both regions share Nicosia as a capital. The rocky Pentadaktylos mountain range runs along the north, while the central part of the island is dominated by the mighty massif of the Troodos mountains. The wildest and least accessible areas are the Akamas and Karpasia (Karpas) peninsulas.

↗ *Taşucu*

Cape Apostolos Andreas

K A R P A S I A

(Dipkarpaz)
(Rizokarpaso)

Aigialousa
(Yenierenköy)

Galateia
(Mehmetcik)

Akanthou
(Tatlısu)

Trikomo
(İskele)

C Y P R U S

O   Kythrea
(Değirmenlik)   Lefkonoiko
(Gecitkale)
R   *Pediaios*

Nicosia
International   *Famagusta Bay*

Tymvou
(Kırklar)   Vatili (Vadili)   *Gialias*   A

Lysi

Famagusta
(Gazimagusa/
Ammochostos)

S   Paralimni

Agia Napa

A2   A3   B3   Xylofagou   *Cape Gkreko*

Aradippou   Larnaka

A5   *Larnaka Bay*

B5   Larnaka
International

Key

═══ Motorway

▭▭▭ Main road

═══ Minor road

▭▭▭ Border

Europe   *North Sea*   SWEDEN   ESTONIA
DENMARK   LATVIA   RUSSIAN
REP OF   LITHUANIA   FEDERATION
IRELAND   UNITED
KINGDOM   NETH   POLAND   BELARUS
BELGIUM   GERMANY
CZECH   UKRAINE
REPUBLIC   SLOVAKIA
FRANCE   AUSTRIA HUNGARY   MOLD
SWITZ   SLOV   ROMANIA
Atlantic   ITALY   CROATIA   *Black Sea*
Ocean   BOSNIA   SERBIA
HERZ.   MONTEN   BULGARIA
SPAIN   KOS
MAC
PORTUGAL   ALBANIA   TURKEY
GREECE

ALGERIA   TUNISIA   *Mediterranean*   CYPRUS   SYRIA
Sea   LEBANON
MOROCCO   ISRAEL

For map symbols *see back flap*

A PORTRAIT OF CYPRUS

The legendary birthplace of Aphrodite, Cyprus enjoys a hot, Mediterranean climate moderated by sea breezes. Visitors bask in the sun on its many beaches, but within an hour's drive can find themselves in the mountains, enjoying the shade of cool herb- and resin-scented cedar woods, villages set amid orchards and peaceful vineyards, as though time stands still here.

Cyprus is an idyllic destination for romantics, with so many old castles, ancient ruins and secluded mountain monasteries to explore. The exploration of these historic sights is enhanced by plentiful sunshine – over 300 days of it a year. Cyprus also has a great number of scenic beaches, and the warm waters encourage bathing and relaxation.

Tucked away in the shady valleys are monasteries with ancient icons of the Virgin, one of which was supposedly painted by St Luke. The tiny churches, many of which are listed as UNESCO World Heritage Sites, hide unique frescoes – some of the most magnificent masterpieces of Byzantine art.

In the Pafos district, valleys overgrown with pine and cedar forests provide a home to the moufflon – a shy mountain sheep. Its image can be seen on Roman mosaics in Pafos.

Cypriot meadows are at their loveliest in springtime, when covered with motley carpets of colourful flowers: anemones, cyclamens, hyacinths, irises, peonies, poppies and tulips, among others. Orchid-lovers will find over 50 species of these beautiful flowers growing in the sparsely populated regions of the island – in the Akamas peninsula, in the Troodos mountains and on the Pentadaktylos mountain range. The island lies on a route for bird migration. Thousands of birds, including

A symbol of Cyprus – a carob tree against the backdrop of a sapphire-blue sea

◀ Anchored catamaran along the coastline at Konnos beach, Protaras

Beautifully preserved ruins of the Gothic Bellapais abbey, built during the Lusignan era

flamingos, cormorants and swans, can be seen wintering on the salt lakes at Larnaka and Akrotiri.

Historic Divisions

The winds of history have repeatedly ravaged this beautiful island. Cyprus has been ruled in turns by Egyptians, Phoenicians, Persians, Romans, Byzantines, Crusaders, Franks, Venetians, Turks and the British. Each of these cultures has left its mark on the architecture, style, cuisine, language and the mentality of the island's inhabitants.

Above all, the island has been shaped by the conflict between the Greeks and the Turks. The Greeks first arrived over 3,000 years ago. The Turks began to settle here following the conquest of the island by Sultan Selim II in 1571.

People and Society

Cypriot society has been composed of two completely separate cultures since the division of the island in 1974 into the Turkish-occupied North and the Greek-speaking Republic of Cyprus in the south. Greek Cypriot society

has always been highly traditional, particularly among country people. This is partly due to the power of the Orthodox Church. Life proceeds at a slow pace in the villages, centering around traditional coffee shops where men spend hours playing backgammon and discussing politics.

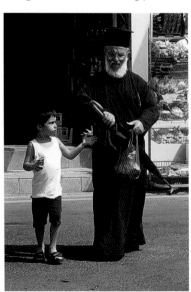

An Orthodox priest out shopping

Village women excel in sewing and embroidery. There has been gradual change, however, with many villages becoming deserted as their residents move to towns, where life is generally easier and the standard of living higher, but this decline is slowly being reversed; old houses are frequently bought by artists, often foreigners, in search of tranquillity. In Fikardou, two abandoned houses have been turned into a museum of village life, and awarded the Europa Nostra medal for the preservation of architectural heritage. Overall, the Republic of Cyprus is highly urbanized with a modern economy supported by the abundance of local businesses, hotels and restaurants. Life in the cities of Larnaka, Nicosia, Pafos and Limassol proceeds at a speedy pace.

In the Turkish North, life proceeds at a far gentler pace, partly due to the international boycott that has afflicted tourism and hampered development since 1974. The North is quite separate from southern Cyprus in both atmosphere and landscape. It is far less affluent and more sparsely populated, and Islam is the main religion.

The Cape Gkreko area – one of the most beautiful areas in Cyprus

A lace-maker at work

hosts and historic sights. Following the Turkish invasion of Cyprus and the displacement of tens of thousands of its people, it seemed that the island would never recover. Over 40 years on, the southern part of the island has seen great prosperity. After the 1974 invasion, hundreds of thousands of refugees from the North found new homes and began new lives. Since then, national income has increased severalfold. The economy is flourishing, based on tourism, maritime trade and financial services, despite the island being hit hard in the Eurozone crisis of 2013. The same cannot be said of the northern part of the island, where the standard of living is much lower, caused by the isolation of North Cyprus.

Modern-day Cyprus

The Republic of Cyprus lives off tourism. Its towns are bustling and – like the beaches – full of tourists. Tourist zones have been established in Limassol, Larnaka and Pafos, and around Agia Napa.

This small island provides everything for the holiday-maker, from beautiful scenery to delicious food, excellent hotels, gracious

Bustling Ledra Street in South Nicosia, dotted with restaurants and boutiques

Landscape and Wildlife

The Cypriot landscape is surprisingly varied. Besides high mountains covered with pine and cedar forests, and the rugged crags of Kyrenia, the central part of the island is occupied by the fertile plain of Mesaoria. The crowded beaches of Limassol, Pafos and Agia Napa contrast with the less developed coastal regions of the Karpasia (Karpas) and Akamas peninsulas. In spring, the hills and meadows are covered with colourful flowers. The forests are the habitat of the moufflon – mountain sheep – while the Karpasia peninsula is home to wild donkeys.

A flock of goats grazing freely – a typical sight in the Cypriot landscape

The Coast

Besides beautiful sandy and pebble beaches, the coastline features oddly shaped rocks jutting out of the sea and rugged cliffs, which descend steeply into the water. The northern part of Famagusta Bay and the Karpasia and Akamas peninsulas contain virtually empty sandy beaches where loggerheads and green turtles come to lay their eggs. The exposed Jurassic rocks near Coral Bay, northwest of Pafos, are being destroyed by erosion.

Lizards, particularly the ubiquitous sand lizard, can be seen almost everywhere. The largest Cypriot lizard, Agama (*Agama stellio cypriaca*), can reach up to 30 cm (12 in) in length.

Rocky coastlines are created wherever mountain ranges reach the sea. The rocky coast near Petra tou Romiou (Rock of Aphrodite) is being worn away over time by erosion.

Sandy coastlines are found at Agia Napa, Famagusta Bay and the Karpasia peninsula, but the loveliest beaches are on the Akamas peninsula.

Rock Formations

The Troodos mountains, in the central part of Cyprus, are formed of magma rock containing rich deposits of copper and asbestos. The Kyrenia mountains (the Pentadaktylos range), running to the Karpasia peninsula in the northeast part of the island, are made of hard, dense limestone. The lime soils in the southern part of the island, near Limassol, are ideally suited for the growing of vines.

Salt lakes – near Larnaka and on the Akrotiri peninsula – are a haven for pink flamingos, wild ducks and the Cyprus warbler (*Sylvia melanthorax*).

Copper mine at Skouriotissa

Mountains

The island features two mountain ranges, separated by the fertile Mesaoria plain. The volcanic Troodos massif in central Cyprus, dominated by Mount Olympus at 1,951 m (6,258 ft) above sea level, is covered with pine and cedar forests. The constant mountain streams in the Troodos mountains even have waterfalls. Spring and autumn bring hikers to the cool forests and rugged valleys, while winter brings out skiers. The Kyrenia mountains (the Pentadaktylos or "Five-Finger" range) in North Cyprus rise a short distance inland from the coast. The highest peak is Mount Kyparissovouno, at 1,024 m (3,360 ft).

The Troodos mountains are largely forested but vines are grown on the southern slopes and apple and cherry orchards abound in the valleys.

In springtime wild flowers carpet the hillsides and meadows of the island with a colourful, fragrant display.

The Cypriot moufflon is a spry mountain sheep, living wild in the forests of Pafos, in the western part of the island.

Mountain streams flow year-round, bringing cooling water to lower ground.

Other Regions

The island's interior is occupied by the vast, fertile Mesaoria plain, given mainly to grain cultivation. The northern area around Morfou (Güzelyurt) is full of citrus groves, and to the south, in the region of Larnaka, runs a range of white semi-desert mountains stretching for kilometres. The sun-drenched region of Limassol, with its limestone soil, is a patchwork of vineyards, which yield grapes for the production of the sweet Commandaria wine.

The Akamas peninsula is a remote region in the west of Cyprus. It features the island's most beautiful wild, sandy beaches (*see pp59–61*).

Donkeys can be seen in the Karpasia peninsula. These ageing domesticated animals have been turned loose by their owners.

Pelicans with wing-spans up to 2.5 m (8 ft) visit the island's salt lakes. Some stop for a few days, others remain longer. These huge birds can also be seen at the harbours of Pafos, Limassol and Agia Napa, where they are a tourist attraction.

The Karpasia peninsula is a long, narrow strip of land jutting into the sea. Its main attractions are its wild environment and historical sights (*see pp144–5*).

Cypriot Architecture

The long and rich history of Cyprus is reflected in its architecture, and some true gems can be glimpsed amid the ocean of nondescript modern development. The island has a number of Neolithic settlements, as well as Bronze Age burial chambers, ruins of ancient buildings (including vast Byzantine basilicas), medieval castles, churches and monasteries. From the Ottoman era, relics include mosques and caravanserais. The British left behind colonial buildings. In villages, particularly in the mountains, people today still live in old stone houses.

Brightly painted houses in Lefkara village, a beautiful example of traditional Cypriot architecture

Ancient Architecture

The Greeks, Phoenicians, Romans and Byzantines who once ruled over Cyprus left behind numerous ancient buildings. Archaeologists have uncovered the ruins of ancient Kourion, Amathous, Kition, Soloi, Salamis and Pafos with temples, theatres, basilicas, bathhouses and palaces. These ancient ruins include fragments of the old defence walls, sports stadiums, gymnasiums, and necropolises. Some Roman theatres are still in use today for shows and festivals.

The palaestra in Salamis (see pp138–9) is surrounded by colonnades and statues. It was devoted to the training of athletes and to staging sporting competitions.

Kourion, a beautiful, prosperous city, was destroyed by an earthquake in the 4th century AD (see pp70–71).

Medieval Architecture

During the 300 years when Cyprus was ruled by the Crusaders and the Lusignans, many churches were built, including the opulent cathedrals in Famagusta and Nicosia. Added to these were charming village churches and chapels, Gothic monasteries and castles. The Venetians, who ruled the island for over 80 years, created the magnificent ring of defence walls around Nicosia and Famagusta, whose mighty fortifications held back the Ottoman army for almost a year.

Angeloktisi Church in Kiti is one of a number of small stone churches on the island whose modest exteriors often hide magnificent Byzantine mosaics or splendid frescoes (see p80).

This beautifully carved capital crowns the surviving column of a medieval palace in South Nicosia.

Bellapais, with its ruins of a Gothic abbey, enchants visitors with its imposing architecture (see p149). International music festivals are held here (see p26 and p28).

Islamic Architecture

Following the conquest of Cyprus by the army of Selim II, new structures appeared, including Turkish mosques (minarets were often added to Gothic cathedrals), bath houses, caravanserais and covered bazaars. In many villages you can still see small mosques with distinctive pointed minarets.

Büyük Han in North Nicosia is a magnificent example of an Ottoman caravanserai, with a *mescit* (prayer hall) in the courtyard *(see p132)*.

The Hala Sultan Tekke *(see p81)* is the country's most sacred Muslim site. It comprises a mosque and a mausoleum with the tomb of Umm Haram, aunt of the Prophet Mohammed.

The Colonial Period

British rule on the island from the 19th to 20th centuries marked the beginning of colonial-style architecture, including churches, government offices, courts of law, army barracks, civil servants' villas, bridges and other public buildings. The British administration also admired the Greek Classical style, and commissioned, designed and built a great number of Neo-Classical buildings.

The Faneromeni High School in South Nicosia *(see p126)* is an example of a Neo-Classical public building. When it was founded in 1852, it was seen as a connection to the students' Greek roots.

The Pierides Museum in Larnaka is a typical example of colonial architecture, with shaded balconies resting on slender supports *(see p82)*. Its flat roof and wooden shutters complement the image of a colonial residence.

Modern Architecture

Following independence in 1960, the architectural style of Cypriot buildings, particularly of public buildings such as town halls, offices, banks and hotels, became more modern and functional. Most of these buildings were erected in Nicosia and in Limassol, which has since become the international business capital of Cyprus. The majority of modern buildings lack architectural merit.

Limassol's modern architecture is largely limited to functional office buildings constructed of glass, concrete and steel, located in the eastern business district of town.

Traditional Homes

For centuries, Cypriot village houses, particularly in the mountains, were built of stone, offering the benefit of staying cool in summer and warm in winter. While some new homes imitate the traditional style, most are built of breeze blocks and reinforced cement.

A modern stone building reminiscent of a traditional village home

Christianity and the Greek Orthodox Church

Christianity gained an early foothold in Cyprus, when saints Barnabas and Paul introduced the religion to the island in the 1st century AD. For 500 years the Church remained relatively unified. However, subsequent divisions led to the emergence of many parallel Christian creeds. The Great Schism of 1054 marked the split between East and West, resulting in the emergence of the Orthodox and Roman Catholic Churches. One of the groups of the Eastern Orthodox Church is the Greek Orthodox Church, and the majority of Greek Cypriots are devoutly Orthodox. Most of the churches in the south are still consecrated and can be visited; in the North, most have been converted into mosques or museums.

Byzantine frescoes, some of the most splendid in existence, decorate the walls of small churches in the Troodos mountains. Ten of them feature on UNESCO's World Heritage List.

The late Father Kallinikos from St Barbara's Monastery (*Agia Varvara*) was regarded as one of the greatest icon painters of recent times. His sought-after icons are sold at the monastery (*see p80*).

Neo-Byzantine churches are topped by a grooved cupola with a prominent cross. They have distinctive arched windows and portals.

Saint Nicholas

Saints' days are celebrated by placing an icon of the saint on a small ornamental table covered with a lace cloth.

Saint Barnabas and Saint Paul

Two saints are associated with Cyprus – Barnabas (a citizen of Salamis, and patron saint of the island), and Paul. Together, they spread Christianity to Cyprus in AD 45. Paul was captured and tied to a pillar to be flogged. It is said that the saint caused his torturer to go blind. Witnessing this miracle, the Roman governor of Cyprus, Sergius Paulus, was converted to Christianity. Barnabas was stoned to death in AD 61.

St Paul's Pillar in Kato Pafos

Icons with images of Christ or the saints, depicted in traditional Byzantine style, play a major role in the Orthodox Church. They are painted on wood, according to strictly defined rules.

The Royal Doors are found in the central part of an iconostasis. They symbolize the passage from the earthly to the spiritual world. The priest passes through them during the service.

The Iconostasis is a "wall of icons" that separates the faithful from the sanctuary.

Royal Doors

Monasticism

Cypriot monasteries, some of them hundreds of years old, are scattered among the mountains. These religious communities of bearded monks live in accordance with a strict regime. Built on inaccessible crags or in shadowy green valleys, they were established in the mountains to be closer to God and further from the temptations of this world. The monasteries hide an extraordinary wealth of frescoes, intricate decorations and magnificent iconostases. The best known of the Cypriot monasteries is Kykkos – the Royal Monastery *(see pp94–5)* which is a place of pilgrimage for the island's inhabitants.

Two monks in the courtyard of Kykkos Monastery

Divine Liturgy

This is a liturgy celebrated in commemoration of the Last Supper. In the Greek Orthodox Church the service lasts longer than in the Catholic Church and there is no organ, only a choir. The service consists of two parts: the "catechumen liturgy", during which psalms and the Gospel are read; and the "liturgy of the faithful" – the main Eucharist when all worshippers (even children) receive Holy Communion in the form of bread and wine.

Icons on either side of the Royal Doors depict Mary and Jesus. The second from the right usually depicts the patron saint of the church.

CYPRUS THROUGH THE YEAR

Cypriots hold strongly to their traditions, which are manifested in the celebration of numerous religious festivals. The Orthodox Church, to which most Greek Cypriots belong, has a great influence on their lives. Besides local village fairs and public holidays, the festivities include athletic events and even beauty contests. Added to this, every village has its own *paniyiri* – the patron saint's day celebration – the

equivalent of church fairs, when the villagers celebrate them with copious food, drink, dancing and song.

In North Cyprus, the main Muslim feasts include Şeker Bayramı, which ends the 40 days of Ramadan; Kurban Bayramı, which is held to commemorate Abraham's willingness to sacrifice his son (rams are slaughtered and roasted on a bonfire); and Mevlud, the birthday of Mohammed.

Olive trees flowering in the spring

Spring

This is the most beautiful season on the island. The slopes of the hills begin to turn green and the meadows are carpeted with a profusion of colourful flowers, though in places it is still possible to ski. The main religious festival held in spring is Easter.

March
International Skiing Competition *(mid-Mar)*, Troodos. Since 1969, competitive ski races have been held on the slopes of Mount Olympus *(see p96)*.
Evangelismós, Feast of the Annunciation *(25 Mar)*. Traditional folk fairs are held in many places around the island, such as the villages of Kalavasos *(see p78)*, and in Nicosia *(see pp116–27)*.
Easter *(varies – Mar to May)*. A

week before Easter, the icon of St Lazarus is paraded through Larnaka. In all towns on Maundy Thursday, icons are covered with veils, and on Good Friday

Winners of the May Cyprus International Rally in Limassol

the image of Christ adorned with flowers is carried through the streets. On Easter Saturday, icons are unveiled and in the evening an effigy of Judas is burned. Easter Day is celebrated with parties. Orthodox Easter is based on the Julian calendar, and may occur up to five weeks after Easter in the West.

April
Wild Flower Festival *(Mar & Apr)*. This celebration of nature's blooms is held every Saturday and Sunday in many towns throughout southern Cyprus. **International Spring Concerts** *(Apr & May)*, Bellapais. Performances by musical ensembles, singers and choirs are held in the Gothic abbey *(see p149)*.

May
Anthistiria Flower Festival *(mid-May)*, Pafos, Limassol. The return of spring is celebrated with joyful processions and shows based on Greek mythology.
Orange Festival *(mid-May)*, (Morfou) Güzelyurt *(see p156)*. Held annually since 1977 in celebration of the orange harvest, there are two weeks of parades, folk concerts and art exhibitions.
Cyprus International Rally *(May)*. Three-day international car rally, starting and ending in Limassol *(see pp72–5)*.
Chamber Music Festival *(May–Jun)*, Nicosia *(see pp116–27)* and Pafos *(pp52–5)*. Top international orchestras and ensembles travel from far and wide to perform here.

Average daily hours of sunshine

Hours

12
10
8
6
4
2
0

Jan Feb Mar Apr May Jun Jul Aug Sep Oct Nov Dec

Average Hours of Sunshine

In June and July, the amount of sunshine reaches nearly 13 hours per day. These months mark the peak holiday season. December, January and February have the fewest hours of sunshine, but the winter sun is pleasant and warm.

Hours

12
10
8
6
4
2
0

Locals at the Wild Flower Festival in Larnaka

Summer

Summer is rich in cultural events, especially art festivals, fairs and music concerts. Tourist resorts, hotels and attractions vie with one another to organize attractive cultural events for their guests. There are numerous

The popular Limanaki Beach in Agia Napa, Southern Cyprus

folk fairs held in the mountain villages, particularly in August. This is also the hottest and sunniest time of the year.

June
St Leontios' Day *(mid-Jun)*, Pervolia village. Traditional religious fair.

Pancyprian Choirs Festival *(late Jun)*, Kato Pafos *(see pp56–7)*. During this festival, choirs perform in the ancient Roman Odeon.

Pentecost-Kataklysmos Fair (Festival of the Flood); *7 weeks after Easter)*. Coinciding with Pentecost, this is celebrated over several days with processions and sprinkling each other with water to symbolize cleansing.

July
International Music Festival *(Jun–Jul)*, Famagusta *(see pp140–43)*.

Ancient Greek Drama Festival *(Jul)*, Limassol, Kourion *(see pp70–71)*, Pafos ancient Odeon *(see pp56–7)*, Nicosia and other locations. Theatre festival with Greek dramas.

Xarkis Festival *(mid-Jul)*, Lofou village *(see pp98–9)*. Concerts and workshops are held to celebrate the Cypriot tradition.

Fengaros Music Festival *(Jul–Aug)*, Kato Drys village near Lefkara *(see p79)*. Many international bands perform at this three-day celebration of various forms of music.

August
Pomos Jazz Festival *(early Aug)*, Pomos, a 15-minute drive from

Pomegranate from the environs of Larnaka

Polis *(see p62)*. A two-day jazz music event with local and international bands held at the Paradise Bar.

Assumption of the Virgin Mary *(15 Aug)*. Traditional fairs in Kykkos *(see pp94–5)* and Chrysorrogiastissa monasteries and in the Chrysospiliotissa church *(see p110)* in Deftera.

Commandaria Festival *(late Aug)*. Food, wine, music and theatre at Kalo Chorio north of Limassol to mark the beginning of the grape harvest.

Dionysia *(late Aug)*, Stroumbi near Pafos. Cypriot and Greek dances and music. An all-night party with local wine and food.

Public Holidays in South Cyprus

New Year's Day (1 Jan)

Fóta Epiphany (6 Jan)

Green Monday (varies)

Greece Independence Day (25 Mar)

Good Friday (varies)

Easter Monday (varies)

Pentecost-Kataklysmos (varies)

Greek Cypriot National Day (1 Apr)

Labour Day (1 May)

Assumption (15 Aug)

Cyprus Independence Day (1 Oct)

Ochi Day (28 Oct)

Christmas Eve (24 Dec)

Christmas Day (25 Dec)

Boxing Day (26 Dec)

Average monthly rainfall

Rainfall

The lowest rainfall occurs in July and August, the highest between November and February. Thunderstorms are rare in the summer. In the mountain regions, however, clouds may be thicker and rain more frequent than in the coastal areas.

Autumn

After the summer heat, autumn brings cooler weather. With the end of the peak holiday season many resorts slow down. The Cypriots celebrate successful harvests, with particular prominence given to the grape-gathering festivals. Many towns and villages hold local fairs. The Wine Festival in Limassol attracts hordes of visitors.

Troodos mountains in their autumn colours

September

Wine Festival *(early Sep)*, Limassol *(see pp72–5)*. Wine-tasting and dancing in the Municipal Gardens.

Aphrodite Opera Festival *(Sep)*, Pafos *(see pp52–5)*. One of the main cultural festivals, with a cast that includes major international singers.

Agia Napa International Festival *(mid-Sep)*, Agia Napa *(see p86)*. This beautiful seaside resort becomes a gathering place for folk musicians and

Autumn harvest of grapes in the wine-growing village of Vasa

dancers, theatre groups, opera ensembles, traditional and modern singers, and magicians.

Elevation of the Holy Cross *(14 Sep)*. One of the oldest religious feasts in the Greek Orthodox Church calendar. Traditionally, men tucked basil leaves behind their ears on this day.

International North Cyprus Music Festival *(Sep–Oct)*, Bellapais *(see p149)*, and **Ta Kypria International Festival** *(Sep-Oct)*, in various locations. Both of these festivals feature performances by international artists: musical virtuosos in the first one, while drama, dance and other forms of art are the major attractions in the second event.

Participant in the Elevation of the Holy Cross

October

Afamia Grape and Wine Festival *(early Oct)*, held in Koilani village *(see p98)* in the Limassol region.

Agios Ioannis Lampadistis *(early Oct)*, Kalopanagiotis *(see p93)*. Traditional folk festival combined with a fair.

International Dog Show *(mid-Oct)*, Pafos *(see pp52–5)*; with the Kennel Club.

Agios Loukas *(mid-Oct)*. Traditional village fairs in Korakou, Koilani *(see p98)* and Aradippou.

Turkish National Day *(29 Oct)*.

November

Feast of Archangels Gabriel and Michael *(mid-Nov)*. Festival and fair in the St Michael monastery southwest of Nicosia *(see p110)*, in the village of Analiontas.

Cultural Winter *(Nov– Mar)*, Agia Napa *(see p86)*. A cycle of concerts, shows and exhibitions organized by the Agia Napa Municipality and Cyprus Tourism Organization.

TRNC Foundation Day *(15 Nov)*. Celebrating the foundation, in 1983, of the Turkish Republic of Northern Cyprus, which is recognized only by Turkey.

St Andrew's Day *(30 Nov)*. Many pilgrims from southern Cyprus visit the monastery of St Andrew *(see p145)*.

Average monthly temperature

Temperature
In the summer, temperatures may reach up to 40° C (104° F). Many people enjoy visiting the island out of the high season. Only the higher sections of the Troodos mountains, which are covered with snow in winter, record temperatures below freezing.

Winter

The winters in Cyprus are mild, and the days are usually sunny. At times winter brings rain, but snow is limited to the upper reaches of the Troodos mountains. Many cultural events are organized by local authorities at this time. Christmas is traditionally celebrated within the family circle.

December

Winter Solstice *(22 Dec)*. The Solstice is observed at Amathous *(see p78)*, the Sanctuary of Apollo *(see p68)*, the Sanctuary of Aphrodite *(see pp48-9)* and Agios Tychonas in Limassol *(see pp72–5)*.
Christmas *(25 Dec)*. All over Cyprus family celebrations are held after attending church.
Carols Evening *(25 Dec)*. This occurs in the central square in Agia Napa *(see p86)*. Events include carol singing, rides in Santa's sleigh and food markets with traditional Cypriot dishes.

Welcoming the New Year *(31 Dec)*, in all towns. In Agia Napa *(see p86)*, free wine is served in the town's main square.

January

New Year (Agios Vassilios) *(1 Jan)*, formally celebrated with the exchange of presents.
Fóta, the Epiphany *(6 Jan)*. Greek Orthodox churches hold processions and bless water. In coastal towns and villages, young men compete with each other to retrieve a crucifix hurled into the water.
St Neofytos' Day *(late Jan)*. A traditional fair held in the Agios Neofytos monastery *(see p51)* near Pafos.
Şeker Bayrami (Sugar Festival) *(varies)*, North Cyprus. A religious feast and a family occasion marking the end of Ramadan, the annual Muslim fast.

February

Carnival, Limassol *(see pp72–5)*. Ten days of wild revelry preceding Lent end with **Green Monday**, which in Limassol features parades and fancy-dress balls.

Salt excavation from the salt lake near Larnaka

Presentation of Jesus to the Temple *(mid-Feb)*. Traditional fair in the Chrysorrogiatissa monastery *(see p62)*, in the Pafos district.
Kite-flying Competition *(late Feb)*, Deryneia *(see p87)*.

Public Holidays in North Cyprus

New Year's Day (1 Jan)
Children's Day (23 Apr)
Labour Day (1 May)
Youth and Sports Day (19 May)
Peace and Freedom Day (20 Jul)
Social Resistance Day (1 Aug)
Victory Day (30 Aug)
Turkish National Day (29 Oct)
TRNC Foundation Day (15 Nov)
Şeker Bayramı (varies)
Kurban Bayramı (varies)
Birth of the Prophet Mohammed (varies)

Winter sports on the slopes of the Troodos mountains

THE HISTORY OF CYPRUS

Lying at the crossroads of the eastern Mediterranean, Cyprus has long been a prize coveted by surrounding lands: Egypt and Aegia, Persia and Greece, Rome and Byzantium, and finally Venice and Turkey. Its rich copper deposits ensured the island's continuing worth to the prehistoric world. In fact the word copper derives from the ancient Greek name for the island – *Kypros*.

The location of Cyprus, at the point where the Eastern and Western civilizations met, determined its history to a large extent. Many rulers tried to conquer the island that occupied such a strategic position. Cyprus has been ruled in turn by the Egyptians, Mycenaeans, Phoenicians, Assyrians, Persians, Ptolemies, Romans, Byzantines, Crusaders, Franks, Venetians, Turks and British.

Stone Age

Not much is known about the earliest inhabitants, who lived in coastal caves and did not leave much trace of their habitation. Recent evidence from archaeological discoveries at Aetokremmos (Eagle Cliff), however, indicates that Cyprus has been inhabited since at least 8000 BC. The settlements of Petra tou Limnitis and Tenta existed here in the Neolithic era (late Stone Age), around 7000–6000 BC.

The first permanent settlements appeared in the 6th millennium BC. These early settlers are thought to have come from Asia Minor. They built round or oval huts of broken stone, covered with branches and clay. A settlement of this type was discovered in the area of Choirokotia. The inhabitants engaged in primitive farming, livestock rearing (one species of sheep was domesticated at that time) and fishing. The scarce flint stones and obsidian were used to make tools, and vessels were gouged out of limestone. Burial practices included weighing down the bodies with stones, in the belief that this would stop the dead disturbing the living.

From this period until around 4500 BC there is a gap in information about the activities on the island. Archaeologists have discovered traces of settlements in the vicinity of Çatalköy (Agios Epikitotos), in the North, and Sotira in the South, where they found early "combed pottery" – the oldest ceramics in Cyprus. This pottery was produced by dragging a comb-like tool over the wet vessel to create straight or wavy lines.

After 4000 BC the Chalcolithic era ushered in the first small-scale use of metal – copper – in addition to the widespread use of stone.

8000 BC	5000 BC	4000 BC	3500 BC	3000 BC
c.6000 BC Choirokotia is Cyprus' earliest known settlement	**5250 BC** Existence of monochromatic and linear-pattern painted ceramics	**After 4000 BC** Chalcolithic settlements start to emerge in the western part of the island		
c.8000 BC evidence of Neolithic-era (Stone Age) human habitation			**3400–2300 BC** The earliest copper mines are established; copper vessels and steatite (soapstone) images of female idols are produced	

Howling Man *from Pierides Museum in Larnaka (5500–5000 BC)*

◀ Richard the Lionheart, who conquered Cyprus in 1191

Neolithic settlement of Tenta

The Copper and Bronze Ages

The transitional period between the Stone and Bronze ages was known as the Chalcolithic era (after the Greek words for copper and stone: *chalkos* and *lithos*); it saw the small-scale use of copper for tools and implements. Most Chalcolithic villages were established in the previously unsettled western part of Cyprus. Figurines of limestone fertility goddesses from Lempa and cruciform figurines in picrolite (blue-green stone) from Yala indicate the growing cult of fertility.

The Troodos mountains contained large deposits of copper, and thanks to this the power of Cyprus began to increase in the third millennium BC. Cyprus became the largest producer and exporter of copper in the Mediterranean basin. The technology of bronze-smelting had by then spread throughout the entire Mediterranean basin. Copper, the main component of bronze, became the source of the island's wealth.

Trade with Egypt and the Middle East developed during this period. Along with vessels of fanciful, often zoomorphic shapes, human figurines and statuettes of bulls associated with the cult of fertility

were produced. By the start of the second millennium BC, there were towns trading in copper. The most important of these was the eastern harbour town of Alasia (modern-day Egkomi). At that time, cultural influences brought by settling Egyptian and Phoenician merchants intensified.

Flourishing trade necessitated the development of writing. The oldest text found in Cyprus is a Minoan incised clay tablet from the ruins of Alasia (16th century BC), a form of writing which came about through links with the Minoan civilization of Crete.

During the 16th and 15th centuries BC, the most important towns were Kition (modern-day Larnaka) and Egkomi-Alasia. Despite diverse influences (from Egypt, Mesopotamia, Phoenicia and Persia), it was Greek culture that would dominate.

Choirokotia, one of the earliest settlements

c.2500 BC Early Bronze Age, with the earliest bronze smelting occuring in Mesaoria

2000–58 BC The island is ruled by Mycenaeans, Egyptians, Phoenicians, Assyrians and Persians

Statuette of an idol, 1900 BC

2500 BC	2350 BC	2200 BC	2050 BC	1900 BC	1750 BC

c.2500 BC Red polished ceramics spread across the island; growth of the cult of fertility (its symbol a bull)

Ceramic pot from Vounous, 2500–1900 BC

1900–1650 BC Middle Bronze Age; settlements appear in the south and east of the island, as a result of overseas trade

Around the 12th century BC, marauders known as the "sea peoples" invaded Cyprus, destroying Kition and Alasia. They settled in Maa (Paleo-kastro) in the west of the island, among other places. But with the mass arrival of Mycenaeans in the 11th century BC, balance was restored. The Greek

Ruins of Phoenician-populated Kition

language, customs and culture were widely adopted, and a flourishing cult of Aphrodite developed. The Temple of Aphrodite in Palaipafos rose in status and soon became the main shrine of the goddess in the ancient Greek world. Mycenaean culture left a permanent imprint on the future development of Cypriot culture.

Female figurine from the Temple of Aphrodite

Around 1050 BC, an earthquake devastated Cyprus, heralding the island's Dark Ages. Kition and Alasia were reduced to rubble, and their inhabitants relocated to Salamis.

Iron Age

The first millennium BC ushered in the Iron Age throughout the entire Mediterranean area, although it in no way diminished the demand for copper from Cyprus. During this time, Cyprus was divided into kingdoms, ruled by local kings. The most important were Salamis, Marion, Lapithos, Soli, Pafos, Tamassos and Kourion. By the 9th century

BC the wealth of Cyprus lured Phoenicians from nearby Tyre, who established a colony at Kition. The joint influences from the Phoenicians, Mycenaeans and the Cypriots fuelled this era of outstanding cultural achievement, with the building of new towns and the development of metallurgy.

In and around the 8th century BC Amathous (east of modern-day Limassol) began to develop, and Kition (modern-day Larnaka) became a major trading hub and the centre of the cult of the Phoenician goddess, Astarte.

Archaic Era

In about 700 BC, Cyprus fell into the hands of the Assyrian kings, who did not wish to rule but merely demanded payment of tributes. This period saw the creation of Ionian-influenced limestone statues, pottery decorated with images of people and animals, and votive terracotta figurines.

Amathous, one of the oldest Cypriot towns

---

c.1400 BC Mycenaean merchants and craftsmen begin to settle on the island

12th century BC Invasion by the "sea peoples"

Gold jewellery 1650–1150 BC

1600 BC	1450 BC	1300 BC	1150 BC	1000 BC	850 BC

16th century BC The earliest Cypro-Minoan writing on a tablet found in the ruins of Alasia

c.1050 BC A violent earthquake destroys Cypriot towns, including Alasia and Kition

c.1000 BC Phoenicians arrive from Tyre and settle on the southern plains

Sarcophagus from Pierides Museum in Larnaka

Classical Period

In the early 6th century BC, Cyprus was ruled by Egyptians, but their influence on local art was negligible. The most distinctive architectural features of the period are the subterranean burial chambers, resembling houses, unearthed in Tamassos. In 546 BC, Egypt was conquered by the Persians, under whose control Cyprus fell. The small Cypriot kingdoms were forced to pay tributes to the Persians and to supply battleships in the event of war. Cyprus became a battleground for the Greek-Persian Wars.

Although the kingdoms were not at first involved in the Persian Wars (499–449 BC), strife akin to civil war erupted. Some kingdoms declared themselves on the side of the Greeks, while others supported the Persians (especially the Phoenician inhabitants of Kition and Amathous, as well as Marion, Kourion and Salamis). In the decisive battle at Salamis (480 BC), insurgents were defeated and the leader, Onesilos, was killed. The Persians went on to conquer

other kingdoms. These included Palaipafos and Soloi (in 498 BC). Having quashed the revolt, the pro-Persian king of Marion built a palace to watch over Soloi.

By the start of the 5th century BC, Cyprus had ten kingdoms, the existing ones having been joined by Kyrenia, Idalion, Amathous and Kition, while Soloi submitted to the rule of the king of Marion. The Athenian general Kimon, who was sent to the island, failed to conquer Cyprus, despite a few minor victories, and was killed during the siege of Kition.

Despite the difficult political situation, the influence of Greek culture on Cyprus grew considerably. This was especially noticeable in sculpture; hitherto the portrayal of gods and men had been stiff, endowed with an obligatory "archaic smile", and now it became more naturalistic.

Hellenistic Era

When Alexander the Great attacked the Persian Empire in 325 BC, the Cypriot kingdoms welcomed him as a liberator, providing him with a fleet of battleships for his victorious siege of Tyre. The weakening of Phoenicia resulted in greater revenues from the copper trade for Cyprus. But the favourable situation did not last. After Alexander's death in 323 BC, Cyprus became a battleground for his successors – the victor was the Greek-Egyptian Ptolemy I Solter. Kition, Kyrenia, Lapithos and Marion were destroyed and Nicocreon,

Marble statue of Apollo from Lyra, 2nd century AD

800 BC Phoenicians settle in Kition

570 BC Egyptians assume control of Cyprus

546 BC Start of Persian rule

Jug (5th century BC)

294 BC Island falls under the control of the Egyptian Ptolemys

700 BC	600 BC	500 BC	400 BC	300 BC

8th century BC Assyrians leave control of the island to Cypriot kings, demanding only an annual tribute

c.500 BC Ionian cities revolt against the Persians

Lion from a tomb stele (5th century BC)

381 BC Evagoras, King of Salamis, leads revolt against the Persians

333 BC Alexander the Great occupies Cyprus

Ruins of Kambanopetra basilica in Salamis

the King of Salamis who refused to surrender, committed suicide. Cyprus became part of the Kingdom of Egypt, and its viceroy resided in the new capital – Nea Pafos. Cultural life was influenced by Hellenism, with the Egyptian gods joining the pantheon of deities.

Roman Rule and Christianity

In 58 BC, Cyprus was conquered by the legions of Rome. The island was given the status of a province ruled by a governor,

Saranda Kolones in Kato Pafos

who resided in a magnificent palace in Nea Pafos. The largest town, port and main trading centre was still Salamis, which at that time numbered over 200,000 inhabitants. The imposing ruins of Salamis bear testimony to its prosperity, while the Roman floor mosaics in Pafos are among the most interesting in the Middle East. The flourishing city of Kourion was the site of the temple and oracle of Apollo – which continued to be of religious significance. Roman rule lasted in Cyprus until the end of the 4th century AD.

Mosaic from the house of Theseus in Kato Pafos

Christianity came to Cyprus with the arrival from Palestine of the apostle Paul in AD 45. He was joined by Barnabas, who was to become the first Cypriot saint (see p24). In the same year they converted the Roman governor of Cyprus, Sergius Paulus. The new religion spread slowly, until it was adopted as the state religion by Emperor Constantine. His edict of 313 granted Christianity equal status with other religions of his empire. St Helena, the mother of Constantine the Great, stopped in Cyprus on her way back from Jerusalem, where she had found fragments of the True Cross. She founded Stavrovouni monastery, which is said to house a fragment of the cross.

Eros and Psyche (1st century AD)

58 BC Rome annexes Cyprus

1st century BC Cyprus hit by violent earthquakes

| 200 BC | 100 BC | AD 1 | AD 100 | AD 200 | AD 300 |

313 Edict of Milan grants freedom of worship to Christians throughout the Roman Empire, including Cyprus

AD 45 The apostles Paul and Barnabas arrive as missionaries to spread Christianity to Cyprus

115–16 Jewish rebellion put down by Emperor Hadrian. Salamis destroyed

In 332 and 342, two cataclysmic earthquakes destroyed most of the Cypriot towns, including Salamis and Palaipafos, marking the end of the era.

St Hilarion Castle boasts an idyllic viewing point

Byzantine Period

The official division of the Roman realm into an Eastern and Western Empire in 395 naturally left Cyprus on the eastern side of the divide, under the Byzantine sphere of influence.

The 5th and 6th centuries were flourishing times. The centres of pagan culture linked to the cults of Aphrodite and Apollo (Pafos and Kourion) lost importance, while the role of Salamis increased. Renamed Constantia, it became the island's capital. New towns also arose, such as Famagusta and Nicosia, and vast basilicas were built.

Beginning around 647, the first of a series of pillaging raids by Arabs took place. In the course of the raids, which continued over three centuries, Constantia was sacked and many magnificent buildings were destroyed.

In 965, the fleet of the Byzantine emperor Nicephorus II Phocas rid the island of Arab pirates and Cyprus again became safe. But not for long. From the 11th century, the entire Middle East became the scene of new warfare. Anatolia, Syria and, above all, the Holy Land were captured by the Seljuk Turks. Byzantium was incapable of resisting the onslaught, and Crusades were organized in Europe to recover the Holy Land and other lost territories.

Christ Pantocrator from the church of Panagiatou tou Araka

Crusades and Lusignan Period

The first successful recovery of the Holy Land from the Muslims took place with the capture of Jerusalem (1099). Successive crusades continued throughout most of the 12th and 13th centuries. European knights set up the Kingdom of Jerusalem, but surrounded as it was by Turkish emirates, it was unable to survive. Further crusades were launched but mainly suffered defeats. The Sultan Saladin conquered nearly the entire Kingdom of Jerusalem in 1187. The next crusade was organized in 1190. One of its leaders was

---

Pendant from the early Byzantine period

488 Following the discovery of the tomb of St Barnabas, Emperor Zenon confirms the independence of the Cypriot Church

688 Emperor Justinian II and Caliph Abd al-Malik sign a treaty dividing control of the island

| 300 | 450 | 600 | 750 | 9(|

395 Partition of the Roman Empire; Cyprus becomes part of the Eastern Roman Empire

David in the Lion's Den, *a 7th-century AD relief*

Richard I (the Lionheart), King of England, whose ships were forced onto Cyprus by a storm. The local prince, Isaac Komnenos, who had proclaimed himself King of Cyprus, plundered the ships and tried to imprison the sister and fiancée of Richard. In reprisal, Richard smashed the Komnenos artillery on the Mesaoria plain and chased his enemy, capturing him in Kantara Castle.

As spoils of war, Cyprus passed from hand to hand. Richard turned it over to the Knights Templar, and they in turn sold the island to the knight Guy de Lusignan, who started the Cyprian Lusignan Dynasty and introduced the feudal system to Cyprus. A period of prosperity for the nobility ensued, partly due to trade with Genoa and Venice, although local Cypriots experienced terrible poverty. Magnificent cathedrals and churches were built, and small churches in the Troodos mountains were decorated with splendid frescoes. The state was weakened by a devastating raid by the increasingly powerful Genoese in 1372, who captured Famagusta. Finally, the widow of James, the last Lusignan king, ceded Cyprus to the Venetians in 1489.

Venetian Rule

Venetian rule over Cyprus lasted less than a century. The island was a frontier

A costume from Venetian times

fortress, intended to defend the Venetian domains in the eastern Mediterranean from the Ottoman Empire. The most formidable fortifications around ports and towns date from this period (including Kyrenia and Famagusta). Still, these were no match for the overwhelming power of the Ottoman Empire. When the Ottoman army of Sultan Selim II landed on Cyprus in 1570, one town after another fell to the invaders. Nicosia was able to defend itself for just a few weeks; when it fell, the Turks slaughtered 20,000 people. The defence of Famagusta lasted longer – 10 months – and was one of the greatest battles of its time. The Venetian defenders did not survive to see the arrival of the relief army, and were forced to capitulate. The Ottoman commander, Lala Mustafa Pasha, reneged on his promises of clemency and ordered the garrison to be slaughtered, and its leader Bragadino to be skinned alive.

A 16th-century map of Cyprus

The Ottoman Era

This was the start of 300 years of Turkish rule. The conquerors destroyed most of the monasteries and churches, turning others into mosques. They abolished the hated feudal system, and divided land among the peasants. The Orthodox clergy were allowed to adopt some Catholic churches and monasteries, and later the archbishop was recognized as the Greek community's representative.

The Turks brought their compatriots to settle on the island, and quashed the regular rebellions. In 1821, after the beginning of the Greek War of Independence, the Ottoman governor ordered the execution of the popular Archbishop Kyprianos and many other members of the Orthodox clergy.

In the mid-19th century, Great Britain came to play an increasingly important role

Selimiye Mosque in North Nicosia

in the Middle East. In exchange for military aid in its war with Russia, the Ottoman Empire handed over occupation and administrative rights of Cyprus to Britain in perpetuity in 1878, though the island continued to be an Ottoman possession.

British Rule

Cyprus' strategic location was vital in defending the sea routes to India and in safeguarding British interests in the Middle East. During their rule, the British introduced the English justice system, reduced crime and built roads and waterworks. Following the outbreak of World War I, when Turkey declared itself on the side of Germany, Britain annexed Cyprus.

After World War II, Greek Cypriots pressed for *enosis* (unification with Greece), which was

Hoisting of the British flag in Cyprus

Hadjigeorgakis Kornesios mansion, South Nicosia

1570 Cyprus invaded by Ottoman Turks

1754 The sultan confirms the Orthodox archbishop as a spokesman for the Greek Cypriots

The hanging of Archbishop Kyprianos

| 1600 | 1650 | 1700 | 1750 | 1800 |

1571–1878 Ottoman era

1660 Ottoman authorities recognize the legitimacy of the Archbishop's office with the Greeks

Büyük Han in North Nicosia

1779 Establishment of the dragoman (intercessor between the Turks and the Greeks)

1821 Bloody suppression of the Greek national uprising by the Turks strongly opposed by the Turkish minority. Rising tensions led to the establishment of the organization EOKA (National Organization of Cypriot Fighters) in 1954 by Archbishop Makarios and Greek general George Grivas. Its aim was to free Cyprus from British control. In 1958, Turkish Cypriots founded the Turkish Resistance Organisation (TNT), which provided a counterbalance to EOKA.

Archbishop Makarios, first president of the Republic of Cyprus

The 1955–9 EOKA liberation struggle led the British to grant independence to Cyprus. A constitution was drafted that, among other things, excluded *enosis* and *taksim* (partition of Cyprus between Turkey and Greece, favoured by Turkish Cypriots). Britain, Greece and Turkey signed a treaty that obliged them to ensure Cyprus' independence. Archbishop Makarios, who had been interned by the British, returned to Cyprus in triumph and was elected President of the Republic of Cyprus. Independence was officially declared on 16 August 1960.

Independent Cyprus

In December 1963, animosity between Greek and Turkish Cypriots erupted into warfare. The Greek-Cypriot army intervened and the Turkish air force bombarded Tylliria. In 1964, United Nations troops arrived to restore peace between the warring parties, however the mission failed and troops remain to this day.

On 15 July 1974 a coup d'état, encouraged by Athens and staged by rebel units of the Cypriot National Guard (led by Greek army officers), ousted Makarios. This provided the Turkish government in Ankara with a pretext to send troops to Cyprus. After a short battle, the invading army controlled the north, and the resettlement of the population began. The "Green Line" buffer zone still divides the Turkish-occupied North from the South, and continues to be patrolled by UN troops.

In November 1983 the Turks declared the Turkish Republic of Northern Cyprus (TRNC), which is recognized only by Turkey. In April 2004 a referendum preceding Cyprus' entry into the European Union failed to unify the island. The leaders, President of the Republic of Cyprus Nico Anastasiades and President of the TRNC Mustafa Akıncı, make repeated attempts at reunification by participating in frequent rounds of talks.

Referendum on the reunification of Cyprus (2004)

General George Grivas

78 Great Britain takes over the administration of Cyprus

1925 Cyprus becomes a British colony

1950 Makarios is elected Archbishop

1960 (16 August) Proclamation of independence. Archbishop Makarios III becomes President of the Republic of Cyprus

1850 **1900** **1950** **2000** **2050**

1914 Outbreak of World War I; Great Britain annexes Cyprus

1963–4 Fighting erupts between Greek and Turkish Cypriots; UN troops arrive

1974 Coup d'état against President Makarios. Turkish invasion of North Cyprus

1983 TRNC is declared

2013 Eurozone crisis

2010 Festivals mark 50 years of independence

2008 Southern Cyprus adopts the euro

2004 Referendum on reunification

CYPRUS REGION BY REGION

Cyprus at a Glance

Cyprus has a wide variety of historic sights. Visitors can find everything from Neolithic settlements and ancient towns to medieval cathedrals and small mountain churches decorated with exquisite frescoes, castles built by the Crusaders and Venetian fortresses, and modern buildings and museums. The island abounds in picturesque towns and villages, beautiful coastal areas, and scenic mountains, with diverse wildlife and friendly people.

Nicosia is the world's only divided capital city. A highlight of its southern part is the Byzantine-style Archbishop Makarios Cultural Centre, housing an impressive collection of icons *(see p122)*.

Agios Nikolaos tis Stegis, a UNESCO World Heritage Site, is one of the many small churches hidden in the sheltered valleys of the Troodos mountains that feature magnificent frescoes *(see p102)*.

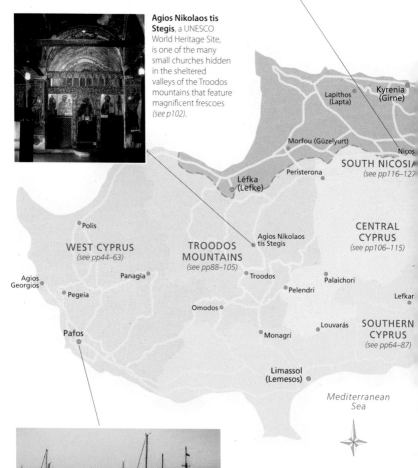

Lapithos (Lapta)

Kyrenia (Girne)

Morfou (Güzelyurt)

Nicos

SOUTH NICOSIA *(see pp116–127)*

Peristerona

Léfka (Lefke)

Polis

WEST CYPRUS *(see pp44–63)*

TROODOS MOUNTAINS *(see pp88–105)*

Agios Nikolaos tis Stegis

CENTRAL CYPRUS *(see pp106–115)*

Agios Georgios

Panagia

Troodos

Palaichori

Pelendri

Lefkar

Pegeia

Omodos

Pafos

Louvarás

SOUTHERN CYPRUS *(see pp64–87)*

Monagri

Limassol (Lemesos)

Mediterranean Sea

Pafos, divided into Kato Pafos (Lower Pafos) and Ktima, is full of history. With its picturesque harbour, it is also one of the most beautiful towns in the Mediterranean *(see pp52–7)*.

◀ Aerial view of rooftops in the hilltops of Cyprus

Buffavento Castle in the Kyrenia mountains was one of three castles, along with Kantara and St Hilarion, that defended Cyprus against attacks along the north coast (*see p148*).

Aigialousa
(Yenierenkoy)

0 kilometres   15

0 miles   15

Bogazi
(Boğaz)

Trikomo (Iskele)

ffavento
stle
Kythrea

NORTH CYPRUS
(*see pp128–157*)

Salamis

Famagusta
(Gazimağusa/
Ammochostos)

Lysi

Idalion

Kellia

Agia Napa

Larnaka

Pyrga

Kiti

Salamis was the island's most important port and trading town for almost a thousand years, and also its capital. Now it is one of the largest archaeological sites (*see pp138–9*).

In Larnaka the remains of the 18th-century Kamares Aqueduct stand beside the Larnaka–Limassol highway. Known as the Kingdom of Kition in ancient times, today Larnaka is a large port town with a thriving tourist zone (*see pp82–5*).

Famagusta, a city surrounded by Venetian defence walls, contains Gothic churches that have been transformed into mosques with minarets (*see pp140–43*).

WEST CYPRUS

West Cyprus is a varied region, made up of mountains, historical sights and a lovely coastline. It was once the most neglected part of the island, remote from the main cities and harbours. Now it is becoming a popular attraction due to its wild natural environment. Lovers of antiquities are sure to be enchanted by the Roman mosaics in Pafos, while mythology buffs can see the place where the goddess Aphrodite emerged from the sea at Petra tou Romiou.

Pafos' Hellenistic, Roman and Byzantine relics are among the most interesting on the island, especially the Roman mosaics.

The modern town is divided into a bustling tourist zone on the coast, with dozens of luxury hotels, taverns, pubs and restaurants, and Ktima – the old town of Pafos – which is only a short drive inland but a world away from the tourist zone.

This region has a slightly milder climate than the rest of the island, as witnessed by the banana plantations north of Pafos. There is practically no industry here and it has the most extensive forest areas in Cyprus, including the famous Cedar Valley inhabited by wild moufflon. The Akamas peninsula, with its rugged hills overgrown with forests, is home to many species of wild animals, and the beautiful beaches provide nesting grounds for sea turtles. This is a paradise for nature lovers and is one of the best places to hike in Cyprus. Movement around the peninsula is hindered by the lack of roads, but there are trails for use by walkers.

This is the land of Aphrodite, goddess of love, who is said to have been born in the south of the island by the rocks jutting out of the sea in the Petra tou Romiou area, which are named after her. North Akamas, on the bay of Chrysochou, is the goddess's bath, which she used after her amorous frolics with Adonis.

Boats and yachts moored in Pafos harbour on a sunny day

◀ Sunset over Petra tou Romiou beach

Exploring West Cyprus

The best place to begin exploring West Cyprus is Pafos, which has a large concentration of hotels and a developed tourist infrastructure. Here you will also find a wealth of historic relics that have made Pafos a UNESCO World Heritage Site. They range from Bronze Age dwellings (Maa Paleokastro at Coral Bay), royal tombs dating from the Hellenistic era and Roman floor mosaics to Byzantine castles and churches. Pafos forest is home to wild moufflon. Cape Lara, to the northwest of Pafos, has beautiful beaches, and further on is the Akamas peninsula.

Lempa is a favourite place with watersports enthusiasts

Getting There

The easiest way to arrive is by air to the international airport southeast of Pafos, where a motorway links the town with Limassol, offering easy access to the southwest coast. It is also possible to get from Limassol via a parallel road running along the coast and over the southern slopes of the Troodos mountains. However, the mountain roads are not of the best quality, and driving around the Akamas peninsula is best done in a four-wheel-drive vehicle.

Sights at a Glance

1. Petra tou Romiou
2. Palaipafos
3. Geroskipou
4. Pafos *pp52–7*
5. Lempa
6. Agios Neofytos
7. Coral Bay
8. Pegeia
9. Agios Georgios
10. Lara
11. Baths of Aphrodite
12. Akamas Peninsula
13. Polis
14. Marion
15. Panagia Chrysorrogiatissa
16. Xeros Valley
17. Diarizos Valley

Walking in the Akamas Peninsula pp60–61

For hotels and restaurants in this region see p162 and pp170–71

Pomos

Morfou

Gialia

Argaka

Kynousa

Lysos

Agios Georgios church at Cape Drepano, which lies
north of Coral Bay

Fyti

Argakiytis Agius

Thrinia

Pano Panagia

PANAGIA 🏛 **15**
CHRYSORROGIATISSA

Agia Moni

P A F O S

Polemi

Vretsia

Roudia Bridge

Letymvou

Platres

Kallepeia

Pentalia

Panagia tou
Sinti Monastery

Salamiou

Amargeti

Xeros

VALLEY

Diarizos

Episkopi

🍴 **16**

Kelokedara

Kithasi

Agios Savvas
tis Karonos

17

X E R O S

DIARIZOS VALLEY

Agia
Varvara

Fasoula

Anarita

Asprokremmos
Reservoir

Timi

Nikokleia

Pano
Archimandrita

PALAIPAFOS 🏛 **2**

Mandria

Kouklia

Limassol

B6

A6

Pissouri

PETRA TOU ROMIOU **1** 🏖

0 kilometres — 5
0 miles — 5

Key

══ Motorway

▦ Major road

── Secondary road

⋯ Minor road

── Scenic route

--- Track

▦ Regional border

For additional map symbols *see back flap*

Petra tou Romiou, the legendary birthplace of Aphrodite

❶ Petra tou Romiou

Road Map B4. 25 km (16 miles) southeast of Pafos.

The area between Pafos and Limassol includes what is probably the most beautiful stretch of the Cyprus coast, dominated by limestone crags rising from the blue sea. At Petra tou Romiou there are three huge, white limestone rocks known collectively as the **Rock of Aphrodite**. In Greek mythology it was here that Aphrodite, goddess of love, beauty and fertility, emerged from the sea foam. She sailed to the shore on a shell towed by dolphins and rested in nearby Palaipafos, where a temple was built to her.

The location of these picturesque rocks is beautiful, with clear blue water beckoning swimmers. The large beach near the rocks is covered with fine pebbles and stones polished smooth by the action of the waves. A word of caution,

however: the road between the car park and the beach is dangerous, and you are advised to use the underground passage.

Nearby you can see trees on which infertile women tie handkerchiefs or scraps of fabric to appeal for help from Aphrodite. They are joined by others who are lonely and unlucky in love, beseeching the goddess of love to help them. A local legend says that swimming around the jutting rock at full moon will make you a year younger with each lap. Other legends lead us to believe that the amorous goddess, after a night spent in the arms of her lover, returned to this spot to regain her virginity by bathing in the sea.

On the slope of the hill above the Rock of Aphrodite, the Cyprus Tourism Organization has built a cafeteria where you can eat while taking in the beautiful view over Petra tou Romiou. Meaning "Rock of Romios", the name Petra tou

Romiou also commemorates the legendary Greek hero Digenis Akritas, also known as Romios. He lived during the Byzantine era and, during an Arab raid by Saracen corsairs on Cyprus, hurled huge boulders into the sea to destroy the Arab ships. According to legend, the rocks here are the stones thrown by Romios.

Environs

A few kilometres east of Petra tou Romiou is the small resort community of **Pissouri**, surrounded by orchards. There is a large resort here, and some smaller hotels, as well as a long, sandy beach. Nearby are two golf courses: Secret Valley and Aphrodite Hills.

❷ Palaipafos

Road Map A4. In Kouklia village, 14 km (9 miles) southeast of Pafos, by the Pafos–Limassol road. 🚌 632 from Ktima Pafos. **Tel** 264 32155. **Open** 8:30am–7:30pm daily (to 5pm early Sep–mid-Apr). 🏛

Just north of the large village of Kouklia are the ruins of the famous Palaipafos (Old Pafos), which was the oldest and most powerful city-state on the island in ancient times. According to tradition, it was founded by Agaperon – a hero of the Trojan Wars and the son of the King of Tegeia in Greek Arcadia. Palaipafos was also the site of the **Temple of Aphrodite**, the most important shrine of the goddess in the ancient world, but now only of specialist interest. Archaeological evidence points

Aphrodite

The cult of Aphrodite arrived in Cyprus from the East; she was already worshipped in Syria and Palestine as Ishtar and Astarte. She was also worshipped by the Romans as Venus. In Greek mythology Aphrodite was the goddess of love, beauty and fertility who rose from the sea foam off the shore of Cyprus. She was married to Hephaestus, but took many lovers, including Ares and Adonis. She was the mother of Eros, Hermaphrodite, Priap and Aeneas, among others. The main centres for her cult of worship were Pafos and Amathous. The myrtle plant is dedicated to her, as is the dove.

Marble statue of Aphrodite from Soloi

to the existence of a much older town on this site, dating back to the Bronze Age. Legend says that Pygmalion, a local king and also a brilliant sculptor, carved many statues, including one of an extraordinarily beautiful woman with whom he fell madly in love. Aphrodite, moved by his love, turned the cold statue into a living woman. Their union produced a son, Pafos, who gave the town its name.

The most famous figure of Pafos was Kinyras, ruler of the city and great priest of Aphrodite, who introduced many religious ceremonies and gave rise to the dynasty that ruled the city for centuries.

A large **centre of worship** devoted to Aphrodite was established here in the 12th century BC, at the end of the Bronze Age. Its foundations and fragments of the walls remain. The sanctuary was destroyed during an earthquake and rebuilt in the 1st century, during Roman times. Here the goddess was represented by a black stone shaped as a cone, symbolizing fertility. For centuries, crowds of pilgrims flocked to Pafos from all over the ancient world. Adorned with flowers, the pilgrims walked into the temple where they were met by the temple courtesans. Aphrodite was worshipped through ritual sexual intercourse between the pilgrims and Aphrodite's priestesses – young Cypriot women who were obliged to

The small stone church of Agios Constantinos and Eleni near Kouklia

offer their virginity to the goddess by giving themselves to a pilgrim man within the temple area. These orgiastic rites were mainly held in the spring, and elements have survived in the form of the spring flower festival – the Anthistiria.

Palaipafos was not always peaceful. It took part in the rebellion of the Ionian cities against the Persians. In 498 BC, the Persians laid siege to the city and, following a fierce battle, forced entry by scaling the ramparts, the remains of which can still be seen. In 325 BC, following a devastating earthquake that destroyed Palaipafos, its last king, Nikikles, moved the city to Nea Pafos (present day Kato Pafos), but Aphrodite's sanctuary retained its importance until the end of the 4th century, when Emperor Theodosius banned pagan cults within

Panagia Chrysopolitissa inscription

the empire. The sanctuary is now a site of excavations by Swiss archaeologists.

Standing on the hill is a Gothic structure known as the **Lusignan Court**, built in the times of the Crusaders and subsequently remodelled by the Turks. It is built on a square floor plan, and leading on to a square yard is an old tower gate. The rooms in the east wing contain a museum that exhibits locally discovered ceramics, stone idols, bronze articles and the black stone worshipped by followers of Aphrodite. On the ground floor there is an impressive Gothic hall with cross vaulting.

In the nearby Roman villa, known as the **House of Leda**, archaeologists have uncovered a 2nd-century AD floor mosaic of the Spartan queen Leda with Zeus in the guise of a swan.

Adjacent to the sanctuary is the small 12th-century church of **Panagia Chrysopolitissa**, which was built over the ruins of an early Byzantine basilica. It is dedicated to the early Christian Madonna, whose cult derives directly from Aphrodite, the pagan goddess of love. As part of a tradition stemming from Cypriot folklore, women came here to light candles to the Virgin Mary – Giver of Mother's Milk. This church contains interesting 14th-century frescoes, and some of the colourful mosaics that covered the floor of the basilica have been preserved.

Ruins of the Sanctuary of Aphrodite

Folk Art Museum in Geroskipou

❸ Geroskipou

Road Map A4. 3 km (1.8 miles) southeast of Pafos. 🚌 601, 606, 612, 613, 631, 632, 633, 634, 636. 🎭 Agia Paraskevi (Jul).

The name Geroskipou means "sacred garden" (*hieros kipos*) in Greek. This testifies to the fact that this former village (now a suburban district bordering Pafos) was built on the site of a forest dedicated to Aphrodite. To this day, it is notable for its many flowers and fruit trees, especially citrus and pomegranate trees – symbols of the goddess.

The main street is lined with workshops producing the local delicacy – *loukoumi* (Cyprus delight). Made from water, sugar and citrus juice, thickened through evaporation, the resulting jelly is cut into cubes and coated with icing sugar. The workshops are open to visitors, who can view the production process and, while there, also buy other sweets including sugar-coated almonds and delicious halva – made of nuts, honey and sesame seeds. The tree-shaded main square of the town is surrounded by colourful shops selling baskets, ceramics and the celebrated *loukoumi*; there are also numerous cafés serving coffee and pastries.

Standing at the southern end of the market square is **Agia Paraskevi**, one of the most interesting Byzantine churches on the island. Built in the 9th century, this stone church features five domes arranged in the shape of a cross. The sixth one surmounts the reliquary,

located under the 19th-century belfry. Originally, the church was a single-nave structure. Its interior is decorated with beautiful 15th-century murals depicting scenes from the New Testament, including the lives of Jesus and Mary, and the Crucifixion. The frescoes were restored in the 1970s.

The vault of the central dome has been decorated with the painting of the *Praying Madonna*. The three images opposite the south entrance – the *Last Supper*, the *Washing of the Feet* and the *Betrayal* – can be dated from the Lusignan period, due to the style of armour worn by the knights portrayed. Opposite are the *Birth and Presentation of the Virgin*, the *Entry into Jerusalem* and the *Raising of Lazarus*.

Another attraction, close to the market square, is the 19th-century historic house once home of the British Consul, Andreas Zamboulakis. Now

The historic stone church of Agia Paraskevi in Geroskipou

the building houses the **Folk Art Museum**, containing a collection of local folk costumes, textiles, embroidery and toys, as well as decorated gourds, furniture and domestic items.

🔼 **Agia Paraskevi Church**
Tel 26 961 859. **Open** Apr–Oct: 8am–1pm, 2–5pm Mon–Sat; Nov–Mar: 8am–1pm, 2–4pm Mon–Sat.

🏛 **Folk Art Museum**
Leondiou. **Tel** 26 306 216. **Open** summer: 9am–5pm daily; winter: 8:30am–4pm daily. 🎨

❹ Pafos

See pp52–7.

Reconstructed Chalcolithic houses in Lempa's Experimental Village

❺ Lempa

Road Map A4. 4 km (2½ miles) north of Pafos. 🚌 607, 642 from Ktima Pafos.

Set among citrus groves between the villages of Chlorakas and Kissonerga just a short distance from the sea, Lempa is home to the **Cyprus College of Art**. The artists, craftsmen and students here have studios in restored village houses. The road to the college is lined with sculptures. The independent pottery workshops are worth visiting.

Lempa was home to the earliest islanders, who settled here more than 5,500 years ago. West of the village centre you can see the **Lempa Experimental Village** – a partially reconstructed settlement dating from the Chalcolithic (Bronze) era (3500 BC). British archaeologists have rebuilt four complete houses from that era. The cylindrical clay dwellings are covered with makeshift roofs.

Agios Neofytos monastery, founded in the 12th century

🏛 **Cyprus College of Art**
Tel 99 452 757. 🆆 artcyprus.org

🔲 **Lempa Experimental Village**
Open dawn–dusk daily.

Environs
In the centre of the nearby village of Empa, 2 km (1 mile) southeast of Lempa, is the 12th-century monastery church of **Panagia Chryseleoussa**. Inside it are the remains of frescoes that were initially destroyed by an earthquake in the mid-1900s, and later damaged by a bad restoration job.

❻ Agios Neofytos

Road Map A4. 9 km (5 ½ miles) north of Pafos 🚌 604. **Open** 9am–1pm, 2–6pm daily (to 4pm Nov–Mar). 🎫 🎫 24 Jan & 28 Sep. 🆆 stneophytos.org.cy

This monastery was founded in the 12th century by a monk named Neofytos, one of the main saints of the Cypriot church. He was a hermit and an ascetic, author of philosophical treatises and hymns, who spent dozens of years here. Some of his manuscripts survive, including the *Ritual Ordinance*, a handbook of monastic life, and an essay on the acquisition of Cyprus by the Crusaders.

The future saint dug three cells in the steep limestone rock with his bare hands. The murals covering the walls are reputed to have been painted by Neofytos himself. This, the oldest part of the monastery, is called the *enkleistra* (hermitage). In two of the caves, murals depict the final days of the life of Christ – the *Last Supper*, *Judas' Betrayal* and the *Deposition from the Cross*, featuring Joseph of Arimathea whose face is thought to be a portrait of the saint. The dome, hewn from the soft rock, features the *Ascension*.

The cell of the saint has bookshelves, benches and a desk at which St Neofytos used to work, all carved in the rock, as well as his sarcophagus, presided over by an image of the *Resurrection*.

A pottery woman

The main buildings, which are still inhabited by monks, include an inner courtyard, a small garden with an aviary, and a *katholikon* – the monastery church with a terrace dedicated to the Virgin Mary.

❼ Coral Bay

Road Map A4. 10 km (6 miles) north of Pafos. 🚌 615, 616.

This fine sandy beach between two promontories has a tropical air. All summer long it is covered by rows of sunbeds for hire. It offers soft sand and safe swimming for families, and there is a wide choice of watersports. There are many restaurants, hotels and bars, including a beach bar, as well as a campsite for more thrifty visitors. Live pop concerts are held here on summer evenings. This beach is popular with young Cypriots, especially on summer weekends.

On the northern headland archaeologists discovered **Maa Paleokastro** – a fortified Achaian settlement dating from the Bronze Age. The site now houses the **Museum of the Mycenean Colonization of Cyprus**.

Environs
Opposite the village of Chlorakas on the road to Pafos is the **Church of St George**, which commemorates the landing of General George Grivas at this spot in 1954. The local museum has a boat that was used by EOKA fighters for weapons smuggling.

Several kilometres inland lies the Mavrokolympos reservoir. Above the car park are the **Adonis Baths**, whose main attraction is a 10-m- (32-ft-) high waterfall. The road running along the Mavrokolympos river leads to more waterfalls.

The region also features numerous vineyards and banana plantations.

The picturesque crescent-shaped Coral Bay

❹ Pafos

Pafos is the name given to the twin towns of Pano Pafos (Upper Pafos, known as the Old Town or Ktima by locals) and Nea Pafos or Kato Pafos (Lower Pafos) *(see pp56–7)*. During the Byzantine era, when coastal towns were threatened by Arab raids, the town was moved inland to its present hilltop location. This is now the modern regional centre of trade, administration and culture, while the lower town is the site of fine Roman ruins and the majority of tourist facilities.

Exploring Pafos

Ktima's major historic buildings and interesting sights, except for the Archaeological Museum, are within walking distance of one another. The main shopping street is Makarios Avenue, where you will find a wide choice of jewellery, clothing and footwear. Within the Old Town, the Agora is a colourful bazaar selling food, leather goods, art and handbags. After strolling along the streets of the Old Town it is worth stopping for a rest in the green district, to the south of town, near the acropolis and the Byzantine and Ethnographic Museums. The eastern part of town contains wide avenues lined with classical public buildings, schools and libraries. The western part is a maze of narrow streets and traditional architecture.

⬤ Grand Mosque (Cami Kebir) Namik Kemil.

The Grand Mosque is a relic of the past Turkish presence in this area. Standing in the Mouttalos district, it had been the Byzantine church of Agia Sofia before being turned into a mosque.

The façade of Agios Kendeas church, built around 1930

⬛ Agora
Agoras.

In the centre of the Old Town is an ornamental covered market hall building, dating from the early 20th century. Fresh fruits, vegetables, fish and meat produced in the Pafos region are sold at this municipal market.

🔷 Mehmet Bey Ebubekir Hamam (Turkish Baths)
Militiathou, next to the covered bazaar (Agora).

Among the trees south of the Agora are the Turkish baths. Originally this dome-covered stone structure was probably a church. After serving as the Turkish baths, some of the rooms were used to house the municipal museum, but when this moved to new premises, the building stood empty. A period of neglect followed, but the building has been restored to its former glory. It now houses a coffee shop.

⬆ Agios Kendeas
Leoforos Archiepiskopou Makariou III.

Built in 1930, the exterior is not particularly exciting, but the interior is worth a visit. Here you will find a carved wooden iconostasis, a bishop's throne and many 19th-century icons.

⬛ Town Hall
Plateia 28 Octovriou.

The single-storey Neo-Classical building standing on the edge of the Municipal Gardens, redolent of ancient Greek architecture, houses the Town Hall and Registry Office, a popular wedding venue. Opposite, behind the slender Ionian column in the middle of the square, is the one-storey municipal library.

The Neo-Classical Town Hall and Registry Office of Pafos

⬆ Agios Theodoros (St Theodore's Cathedral)
Andrea Ioannou.

Built in 1896, Agios Theodoros is the oldest church in Ktima and is as important for the Orthodox community as St John's Cathedral (Agios Ioannis) in Nicosia.

Close to the square stands a column commemorating the victims of the Ottoman slaughter of 1821 that claimed the lives of the Bishop of Pafos, Chrysanthos, and other members of the Greek clergy.

A lovely café at the Pafos market, known to the locals as the Agora

Display in the Ethnographic Museum

🏛 Geological Exhibition
Ayios Theodoros 2. **Open** 9am–4pm Mon–Sat (summer).

One of a few places on the island where you can learn about the geology of Cyprus, this is a small private collection of rocks and minerals. On display are sedimentary rocks with fossils; volcanic rocks from the Troodos mountains and the Akamas peninsula; and metallic minerals, particularly copper and asbestos which have been mined here for millennia.

🏛 Bishop's Palace and Byzantine Museum
Andrea Ioannou 5. **Tel** 26 931 393. **Open** 9am–3pm Mon–Fri, 9am–1pm Sat. 🎨

This beautiful Byzantine-style building is the residence of the Bishop of Pafos and the most important ecclesiastical building after Agios Theodoros. It was built in 1910 by Iaskos, the Bishop of Pafos. Bishop Chrysostomos subsequently extended the palace, furnishing it with beautiful

The Dormition of the Virgin Mary, Byzantine Museum

arcades and allocating part of it to the Byzantine Museum. The museum houses a collection of icons, including the oldest on the island – the 9th-century *Agia Marina*, and the 12th-century *Panagia Eloussa* from the Agios Savras monastery. There are also religious books, including a 1472 Bible and a collection of documents produced by Turkish sultans.

🏛 Ethnographic Museum
Exo Vrysis 1. **Tel** 26 932 010. **Open** 10am–5:30pm Mon–Sat, 10am–1:30pm Sun. 🎨

This privately run museum houses collections of coins, folk costumes, kitchen utensils, baskets, ceramics, axes, amphorae and carriages. In the sunken garden is a wood-burning stove from an old bakery and an authentic 3rd-century stone sarcophagus.

Pafos Town Centre

① Grand Mosque
② Agora
③ Loutra (Turkish Baths)
④ Agios Kendeas
⑤ Town Hall
⑥ Agios Theodoros
    (St Theodore's Cathedral)
⑦ Geological Exhibition
⑧ Bishop's Palace and
    Byzantine Museum
⑨ Ethnographic Museum

0 metres   200
0 yards   200

For key to symbols *see back flap*

🏛 Tombs of the Kings

Leoforos Tafon ton Vasileon. 🚌 615.
Tel 26 306 295. **Open** summer:
8:30am–7:30pm daily; winter:
8:30am–5:30pm daily. 🏛

The necropolis is a fascinating
system of caves and rock tombs
dating from the Hellenistic and
Roman eras (the 3rd century BC
to 3rd century AD). Situated
north of Kato Pafos, beyond the
old city walls and close to the
sea, it consists of imposing
tombs carved in soft sandstone.

Eight tomb complexes have
been opened for viewing; the
most interesting are numbers
3, 4 and 8. Stone steps lead to
underground vaults. Some
tombs are surrounded by
peristyles of Doric columns,
beyond which you can spot
burial niches. Others have
been decorated with murals.

The architectural style of many
tombs, particularly those in the
northern section, reveals the
Egyptian influence; they were
inspired by the Ptolemy tombs in
Alexandria. One funerary custom
that has been documented is
that on the anniversary of the
death, relatives of the deceased
would gather around the
tomb for a ceremonial meal,
depositing the leftovers by the
actual sepulchre. Similar customs
prevail to this day in some Greek
Orthodox communities.

Over the following centuries
the tombs were systematically

The 12th-century stone church of Agia Kyriaki

plundered. One of the more
notorious looters was the
American consul from Larnaka,
Luigi Palma de Cesnola
(1832–1904), who plundered
many sites in Cyprus, including
Kourion. The tombs were built
when there were no longer
kings on Cyprus, and
they were probably
used to bury
prominent citizens
of Pafos, civil
servants and
army officers;
nevertheless, due
to their opulence
they became
known as the Tombs
of the Kings.

Inscription on one of the stones
in Agia Kyriaki

During times of persecution
they were used by Christians as
hiding places. Later the site was
used as a quarry. The place has
a unique atmosphere, best
experienced in the morning.

🏛 Agia Kyriaki

Odos Pafias Afroditis.
Open daily.

The 12th-century stone
church of Agia Kyriaki,
with a later small belfry
and dome, is also
known as Panagia
Chrysopolitissa (Our
Lady of the Golden City).
It was built on the ruins
of an earlier seven-aisled
Christian Byzantine
basilica, the largest in
Cyprus. A bishop's palace
also stood nearby. Both
buildings were destroyed
by the Arabs, but the
parts that have survived
include 4th-century
religious floor mosaics.
The road to Agia Kyriaki

leads along a special platform
built over the archaeological
digs, from where you can see
several single columns. One of
them has been dubbed "St Paul's
Pillar". The apostle came to
Cyprus to preach Christianity, but
was captured and led before the
Roman governor,
Sergius Paulus, who
sentenced him to
flogging. St Paul
blinded his accuser,
Elymas, thus con-
vincing Sergius of
his innocence to
such an extent that
the governor
converted to Christianity.

Agia Kyriaki is used jointly by
the Catholic and Anglican communities. The beautiful church
standing nearby, built on a
rock which forms part of the
Kato Pafos defence walls, is
called Panagia Theoskepasti –
"guarded by God". It is
apocryphally told that during
a scourging Arab attack a
miraculous cloud enveloped
the church, concealing it
from the enemy.

🏛 Catacombs of Agia Solomoni and Fabrica Hill

Leoforos Apostolou Palou, Kato
Pafos. **Open** dawn–dusk.

Inside a former tomb is a
subterranean church dedicated
to Solomoni, a Jewess, whose
seven children were tortured
in her presence, and regarded
by the Cypriots as a saint.

In Roman times the site
was probably occupied by a
synagogue, and earlier on by
a pagan shrine. Steep steps
lead down to the sunken
sanctuary. The adjacent cave

The Tombs of the Kings necropolis

contains a tank with what is believed to be miraculous water. Similar catacombs on the opposite side of the street are called Agios Lambrianos.

Beyond Agia Solomoni, to the right, is the limestone Fabrica Hill containing carved underground chambers. They were created during Hellenistic and Roman times but their purpose is unknown.

On the southern slope of the hill, Australian archaeologists have unearthed a Hellenic amphitheatre hewn out of the living rock. Nearby are two small cave churches, Agios Agapitikos and Agios Misitikos. Tradition has it that when dust collected from the floor of Agios Agapitikos is placed in someone's house, it has the power to awaken their love (*agapi* means "love"), while dust collected from Agios Misitikos will awaken hate (*misos*).

Fabric-festooned tree near the Catacombs of Agia Solomoni

A relief from the Hellenistic era, Archaeological Museum

🏛 Archaeological Museum
Leoforos Georgiou Griva Digeni 43.
Tel 26 955 801. **Open** 8am–4pm daily.
🖼 📷 ♿

Housed in a small modern building outside the city centre, along the road leading to Geroskipou, this is one of the more interesting archaeological museums in Cyprus. The collection includes historic relics spanning thousands of years from the Neolithic era through the Bronze Age, Hellenistic, Roman, Byzantine and medieval periods, and up until the 18th century AD.

Particularly interesting are the Chalcolithic (copper age) figurines. There are steatite idols, a skeleton from Lempa, a 3rd-century AD mummy of a girl and an array of Hellenic ceramics, jewellery and glass. There are also ancient sarcophagi, sculptures, a coin collection, clay pots used for hot water and a set of Roman surgical instruments – evidence of the high standard of ancient medicine. There are also numerous exhibits from Kato Pafos and from Kouklia, site of the ancient city-kingdom Paliapafos and the Sanctuary of Aphrodite. The Archaeological Museum is one of the destinations featured on the Aphrodite Cultural Route, an initiative by the Cyprus Tourist Organisation (CTO) that aims to guide visitors to key places of interest associated with the goddess. A booklet with useful information on the route is available from CTO offices.

🛏 Beaches
Pafos itself has only a few small beaches in front of hotels; these offer excellent conditions for watersports. A pleasant municipal beach is situated by Leoforos Poseidonos, at the centre of Kato Pafos, close to the Municipal Gardens. Somewhat out of the way, to the north of the archaeological zone, lies the sandy-pebbly Faros Beach.

Good pebble beaches can be found north of Pafos. About 8 km (5 miles) along the coast is a small beach in the bay of Kissonerga fringed by banana plantations. The loveliest, most popular sandy beach is situated at Coral Bay, 10 km (6 miles) north of town (*see p51*). All the usual beach facilities are offered here, together with most popular watersports.

There are several beaches to the east, including Alikes, Latsi Vrysoudia, and Pahyammos. A beautiful place for bathing is the beach near the Petra tou Romiou, covered with smooth stones. The water here is crystal clear and the environs truly enchanting. Facilities include a restaurant, toilets and a shower near the car park. Come either early in the morning for some quiet reflection or in the evening to enjoy the beautiful sunset.

Coral Bay beach, Paphos, Cyprus

Kato Pafos

The most accessible and inspiring archaeological park on the island, the ruins at Kato (Lower) Pafos were unearthed in 1962, shedding new light on Cyprus under the Roman Empire. In ancient times, this was the capital of Cyprus. Now a UNESCO World Heritage Site, the remains found here span over 2,000 years. The lavish mosaics found on the floors of four Roman villas indicate that this was a place of ostentatious wealth.

★ House of Dionysos
Some 2,000 sq m (21,500 sq ft) of magnificent mosaics can be viewed from wooden platforms.

House of Aion
This villa, with its interesting mosaics, was destroyed by an earthquake. It takes its name from the god Aion, whose image was once to the left of the entrance.

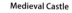

House of Theseus
The palace of the Roman governor contains a set of interesting mosaics portraying the myth of Theseus and Ariadne. The opulent villa discovered underneath dates from the Hellenistic era.

Medieval Castle
The medieval Lusignan castle remodelled by the Ottomans now houses a museum; its flat roof affords a lovely view over the town and the harbour.

KEY

① **The East Tower** was a defence structure, guarding the town against attacks by Arab pirates in the early Middle Ages.

② **Panagia Limeniotissa**, the Byzantine basilica of Our Lady the Protectress of Harbours, was destroyed in the 7th century by Arab raids.

③ **The Hellenic theatre** is located near the Agora.

| 0 metres | 25 |
| 0 yards | 25 |

Lighthouse
The small white lighthouse on top of the hill is not related to the Roman ruins below.

VISITORS' CHECKLIST

Practical Information
Archaeological Park: by Pafos harbour. **Open** 8am–6pm daily (to 5pm Nov–Mar; to 7:30pm Jun–Aug). 🚍 🚌 Aphrodite Festival: opera (Sep).
W pafc.com.cy.
🏰 Medieval castle

★ Roman Odeon
This partly restored small music theatre, built of stone blocks, stands on a hillside overlooking the rest of the site. Summer concerts are held here.

Saranda Kolones
This castle, built by the Lusignans, was destroyed by an earthquake in 1222. It takes its name from the 40 columns found among its ruins.

Plan of Kato Pafos

Key
- 🟦 Building
- Road
- ░░ Footpath
- — Wall

Pegeia Pafos
B20

Ancient Theatre
Agia Solomoni
Cathedral Ruins
Odeon   Agora
Asklepieion
Panagia Chrysopolitissa
House of Dionysos   Saranda Kolones
House of Orpheus
House of Aion
House of Theseus   Panagia Limeniotissa
Geroskipou
E705

Castle   East Tower

0 m   300
0 yards   300

Tree-lined avenue in the village of Pegeia

❽ Pegeia

Road Map A3. 19 km (12 miles) north of Pafos. 🚌 607, 616.

This small, picturesque hillside village, 5 km (3 miles) inland from Coral Bay, is the last sizeable settlement before entering the wilderness of Akamas. Pegeia, meaning "springs", was founded during the Byzantine era. It is famous for its abundant spring water – a great blessing in sun-parched Cyprus.

Soak up the village atmosphere in the pretty cobbled central square with its fountains, and try a bottle of the local Vasilikon wine.

Environs
On the hilltops to the north of Pegeia, at an altitude of some 600 m (1,970 ft), are the villages of the Laona region – **Ineia**, **Drouseia**, **Arodes** and **Kathikas**. Their lofty perches offer sweeping views of the surrounding area. In Ineia you can visit the Ineia Folk Art Museum; the local school in Kathikas houses the Laona information centre.

❾ Agios Georgios

Road Map A3. 🚌 616.

During Roman times **Cape Drepano**, north of Coral Bay, was the site of a late Roman and early Byzantine town and harbour. The remains of a 6th-century early-Christian basilica have been unearthed here, revealing some well-preserved floor mosaics of sea creatures, a semi-circular bishop's throne and several columns.

The coastal cliffs contain several caves that served as hiding places for the local population during enemy raids. Atop one craggy section is the picturesque **Church of St George** (Agios Georgios) built in the Byzantine style in 1928. St George, its patron saint, champions animals and those who are unlucky in love.

Close by there are some tavernas and fishermen's cottages. The location affords a lovely view over the fishing harbour below, and of the nearby island of Geronisos with its remains of a Neolithic settlement. There are also remains of a small temple that was used during Greek and Roman times.

Environs
North of Agios Georgios is the stunning **Avakas Gorge**. This deep ravine has steep craggy banks, a dozen or so metres high, and the river Avgas runs through the base of it. Avakas Gorge is an environmentally protected area.

The picturesque Church of St George

❿ Lara

Road Map A3.

This sandy crescent is home to two of the most attractive beaches in west Cyprus. To the south lies nearly 2 km (1 mile) of uncrowded sand, while to the north there is a shallow bay with a half-moon stretch of fine white sand frequented by sea turtles.

This is one of the few remaining Mediterranean nesting grounds for the rare green and loggerhead varieties. During breeding season (June to September) staff from the Lara Turtle Conservation Project close access to the beach. However, they arrange occasional night-time walks along the beach, when you can see the turtles struggling ashore.

Although marine animals, sea turtles lay their eggs on dry land, crawling out onto beaches during summer nights to do this. Females lay about 100 eggs at a time, which they bury up in the sand up to half a metre (one and a half feet) deep. After laying, the eggs are carefully removed to a protected area on the beach where they are safe from dogs, foxes and other predators.

After seven weeks the eggs hatch and the hatchlings head immediately for the water. Turtles reach maturity at about the age of 20, and the females return to lay eggs on the same beach where they were born.

The sandy beach at Lara Bay – a nesting ground for rare sea turtles

⓫ Baths of Aphrodite

Road Map A3. 8 km (5 miles) west of Polis, towards Akamas peninsula.
🚌 622, 644.

A path from the car park leads to the Baths of Aphrodite – a pool in a grotto shaded by overgrown fig trees. According to legend it was here that Aphrodite met her lover Adonis, who stopped by the spring to quench his thirst. It is said that bathing in this spot restores youth, but sadly people are no longer allowed in the water.

Walking trails lead from the front of the Cyprus Tourism Organization (CTO) pavilion through the Akamas peninsula. The trails of Aphrodite, Adonis or Smigies will take you to the most interesting corners of the northwestern tip *(see pp60–61)*. Detailed descriptions of the trails can be found in the Nature Trails of the Akamas brochure published by the CTO.

Situated a few kilometres further west is another magnificent spring, the Fontana Amorosa (Fountain of Love). It was once believed that whoever took a sip of water from the spring would fall in love with the very first person they encountered afterwards.

Environs

On the way to the Baths of Aphrodite you will pass Latsi (also known as Latchi), a small

Akamas peninsula – the westernmost point of Cyprus

town with a fishing harbour. It was once a sponge-divers' harbour, and is now also the base for pleasure boats that offer tourist cruises along the Akamas peninsula. Latsi has numerous *pensions* and hotels; the harbour features several restaurants, where you can get tasty and inexpensive fish and seafood dishes. The town has pebble and coarse sand beaches.

⓬ Akamas Peninsula

Road Map A3. 18 km (11 miles) north of Agios Georgios.

Spring flowers

Stretching north of Agios Georgios and Pegeia is the wilderness of the Akamas peninsula. The hillsides and headlands form the island's last undeveloped frontier, a region of spectacular, rugged scenery, sandy coves, clear water and hillsides covered with thick woodlands of pine and juniper. Its name comes from the legendary Akamas, son of Theseus, who arrived here on his triumphant return from the Trojan War and founded the town of Akamatis. Archaeologists are still searching for this site.

The peninsula's westward plain has rocks jutting out of the arid landscape, which is overgrown with tangles of trees and bushes.

In the valleys and ravines the vegetation is lush due to more abundant water. The shoreline is characterized by steep cliffs dropping vertically into the sea, particularly around **Chrysochou Bay**.

Nowadays this area is practically deserted, inhabited only by wild animals and herds of goats, but this was not always so. In ancient times, the region had Greek towns, and later Roman and Byzantine towns, that bustled with life. On **Cape Drepano** you can see the ruins of a Roman harbour and a Byzantine basilica; in **Meleti Forest** you can visit the ruins of a Byzantine church and tombs carved in rocks; and in the **Agios Konon region** archaeologists have discovered an ancient settlement. The Roman settlement, which once stood on the shores of Tyoni Bay, is now submerged in water.

The only way to travel around the wild countryside of Akamas is by a four-wheel-drive vehicle or by a cruise along the coast from **Latsi**.

The westernmost point of the peninsula, and of the entire island, is **Cape Arnaoutis**, where you can see an unmanned lighthouse and the wreck of a ship that ran aground. The cape is a magnet for divers, who will find vertical crags and caves where octopuses hide; fantastic arch-shaped rocks; or even come eye-to-eye with a barracuda.

The Baths of Aphrodite

Walking in the Akamas Peninsula

This is the wildest region of Cyprus, practically uninhabited and covered with forests. Its rich flora (over 500 species, including scores of orchid varieties) and fauna, the diverse geological features, the beautiful coastline and the legends and myths associated with this fascinating country make it a paradise for ramblers and nature lovers. The shortage of surfaced roads means that many places on the peninsula can be reached only on foot.

Locator Map

Baths of Aphrodite

Bays
A challenging section of the Aphrodite trail hugs the peninsula's wild coastline. Here you'll find the most beautiful coves and deserted beaches.

Roads
Some sections of the trails run along dirt tracks; the best way to travel here is in a four-wheel-drive vehicle.

Caves
Water has carved many caves and rock niches in the lime rocks of the peninsula. These provide shelter for animals.

Rocks
Rocks, carved in fantastic shapes by wind and water, are a distinctive feature of the peninsula's landscape.

Neo Chorio

A stone church has survived here. There are plenty of places to stay in the village, as well as a few restaurants. To the south is the Petratis Gorge, famous for its bat grotto.

Lizards

Lizards, particularly the wall lizard, are common on the island. You may be lucky enough to encounter the Agana, the largest Cypriot lizard (30 cm/12 in long).

Goats

Herds of free-ranging goats wander around the peninsula, presenting a threat to the region's natural environment.

Key

=== Main road

=== Other road

••• 1. Aphrodite trail (7.5 km/4½ miles)

••• 2. Adonis trail (7.5 km/4½ miles)

••• 3. Smigies trail (7.5 km/4½ miles)

••• 4. Pissouromouttis trail (3 km/1.8 miles)

••• 5. Kathikas trail (2 km/1.2 miles)

River

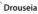

Drouseia

This picturesque hilltop village with its stone houses is increasingly popular among the expatriate community. There is a taverna and accommodation here.

For additional map symbols *see back flap*

The 16th-century church of Agios Andronikos in Polis

⑬ Polis

Road Map A3. 35 km (22 miles) north of Pafos. 🚌 645. 🏔 1,890. 🛈 Vasileos Stasioikou 2, 26 322 468.

This small town, known as Polis Chrysochou (Town of the Golden Land), stands on the site of the ancient city-state of Marion, surrounded by extensive orange groves. Polis provides an excellent base for exploring the Akamas peninsula and the wilderness of Tilliria. In the centre of Polis is the 16th-century **Agios Andronikos** church, featuring some fine frescoes. Under Ottoman rule the church was turned into a mosque. The interior of the **Agios Rafael**, a Byzantine-style church, is decorated with colourful frescoes.

Polis is one of the most attractive and fastest-growing seaside resorts of Cyprus. Popular with both backpackers and families, it offers a range of apartment complexes and a handful of small hotels, along with several campsites, including one on the beach.

Environs

Close to the town are some of the most beautiful beaches on the island, including a sand and-pebble beach stretching eastwards along Chrysochou Bay, a 15-minute walk from Polis. There are also picturesque villages and interesting churches, including the 16th-century Agia Aikaterini and 15th-century Panagia Chorteni.

⑭ Marion

Road Map A3.

Founded in the 7th century BC by Greeks, the city-state of Marion was a major trading centre during the Classical and Hellenistic eras. It owed its rapid development to the nearby copper mines. In 315 BC Marion was destroyed by the Egyptian king, Ptolemy I Soter. His son, Ptolemy II, rebuilt Marion under the name Arsinoe, but the town never regained its former powerful status in terms of trading.

Up until now archaeologists have managed to unearth only a small portion of the ancient town, including a burial ground dating from the Hellenistic period. An interesting collection of

Carved decoration above the entrance to Agios Andronikos in Polis

artifacts discovered at the site can be seen in the **Marion-Arsinoe Archaeological Museum**. Of special note are the amphorae decorated with images of people, animals and birds, as well as with geometric patterns. Growing nearby to the museum is an olive tree, which is over 600 years old, and still bears fruit.

🏛 Marion-Arsinoe Archaeological Museum

Polis. Leoforos Makariou III. **Tel** 26 322 955. **Open** 8am–2pm Mon, 8am–3pm Tue, Thu & Fri, 8am–5pm Wed, 9am–3pm Sat. 🈯

⑮ Panagia Chrysorrogiatissa

Road Map A3. 40 km (25 miles) northeast of Pafos, take a right turn before the village of Stroumpi. 1.5 km (1 mile) south of Pano Panagia. **Tel** 26 722 457. **Open** summer: 9:30am–12:30pm, 1:30–6:30pm daily; winter: 10am–12:30pm, 1:30–4pm daily. Donations welcome. 🈯 15 Aug.

In a beautiful setting 830 m (2,723 ft) above the sea, the Chrysorrogiatissa monastery is dedicated to "Our Lady of the Golden Pomegranate". It features an unusual triangular cloister built of reddish stone.

The monastery was founded in 1152 by Ignatius, who came across an icon with the image of the Virgin Mary. The Virgin appeared and told him to build a monastery. The icon is kept in a special casket. It was supposedly painted by St Luke the Evangelist. Several other icons are also stored here, the most famous being an 18th-century image of Mary and Jesus covered with a cloak. Other

Entrance to the historic Panagia Chrysorrogiatissa monastery

objects include old Bibles, sculptures, manuscripts and crosses. A small Byzantine museum sits on the premises.

Environs

The **Agia Moni** church, about 2 km (1.2 miles) from the monastery, is one of the oldest on the island. Dedicated to St Nicholas, it was built in the 4th century on the site of an old pagan temple of the goddess Hera.

Nearby **Pano Panagia** is the birthplace of Archbishop Makarios III, the statesman and politician, who was born here on 13 August 1913. In 1960 the Archbishop was elected president of the republic. He died on 3 August 1977 and was buried at Throni near Kykkos, overlooking his village.

Makarios' Family Home

Pano Panagia. **Open** daily (key available from info centre). Donations welcome.

Tomb of Archbishop Makarios at Throni above Pano Panagia

⓰ Xeros Valley

Road Map B4.

The Xeros river flows from the western slopes of the Troodos mountains through this scenic valley. The river initially flows through Pafos Forest and Cedar Valley (see p92), which is the main home of the cedars of the local *cedrus brevifilia* species. The area, which has been declared a nature reserve, is also home to the moufflon.

A car is needed to explore the valley. Following the old road from Pafos, turn left in the village of Timi, opposite the airport, to reach **Asprokremmos** reservoir, a mecca for anglers, as it is fed by the Xeros river. The valley of Xeros (which in Greek

means "dry") was devastated by the tragic earthquake of 1953. At the heart of the valley, away from the main roads, is the abandoned stone **Panagia tou Sinti** monastery. It can be reached via local roads from the village of Pentalia or Agia Marina. Further on, the road leads through hillside villages and vineyards.

Beyond the village of Vretsia the road steadily deteriorates, but after driving for a few more kilometres you can cross the Xeros river near the historic Venetian **bridge of Roudia**. The deserted village of **Peravasa** marks the start of the road leading south, towards the scenic Diarizos river valley.

⓱ Diarizos Valley

Road Map B3.

Greener and better irrigated than the arid Xeros valley, the Diarizos valley is studded with medieval churches, farming villages and arched Venetian bridges. The clear-flowing river trickles south-west and, like the Xeros, feeds the Asprokremmos reservoir.

The village of **Nikokleia**, near Kouklia (see p48), is an ancient settlement named in honour of King Nikokles, who transferred his capital to what is now Kato Pafos. The village is scenically located on the banks of the river. The old church contains

Sheep in the Diarizos Valley

fascinating icons. On the opposite side of the river, near the village of Souskiou, archaeologists unearthed a Chalcolithic settlement. In it they found pendants and figurines, as well as statues and ancient tombs. In the village of Agios Georgios are rock tombs.

Further northeast are the remains of a former monastery, **Agios Savvas tis Karonos**, built in the early 12th century and restored by the Venetians.

Above Kithasi the road climbs upwards and the views become increasingly beautiful. On the left side of the road is the restored church of **Agios Antonios**. The church in Praitori houses 16th-century icons. Above the village, the road climbs towards the resort of **Platres** and the peaks of the Troodos mountains.

The arid Xeros valley, a scenic, rugged nature reserve

SOUTHERN CYPRUS

The southern region of Cyprus features Neolithic settlements and ancient towns, medieval castles and monasteries, and the island's most beautiful beaches, around Agia Napa. Other attractions include charming hilltop villages and the ports of Limassol and Larnaka. The region is full of reminders of famous past visitors to Cyprus, including Zeno of Kition, Saint Helena, Richard the Lionheart and Leonardo da Vinci.

The coast from Pissouri to Protaras is famous for its beautiful scenery and historic sites. It has the largest ports on the island and many crowded beaches, but just a short distance inland life flows at a gentle, lazy pace.

This southern region was the site of powerful city-states, including Kition (present-day Larnaka), Kourion – of which only magnificent ruins are left – and Amathous.

Among the oldest traces of man on Cyprus are the Neolithic settlements around Choirokoitia and Kalavasos. There are reminders of subsequent settlers, too. There was a Phoenician presence at Kition; there are temples and stadia attesting to the Greek presence; and villas and theatres from the Romans. The Byzantine legacy includes mosaics in vast basilicas, churches with beautiful murals, and monasteries – including the mountain-top Stavrovouni monastery and the cat-filled St Nicholas monastery on the Akrotiri peninsula.

The medieval castle in Limassol was used by the Crusaders; Richard the Lionheart married Berengaria of Navarre and crowned her Queen of England here; and from the Gothic castle in Kolossi knights oversaw the production of wine and sugar cane. A reminder of the Arab raids is the tomb of the Prophet's aunt at the Hala Sultan Tekke, on the shores of the salt lake near Larnaka. The lake itself attracts flamingoes, swans and pelicans.

Scenic village of Kato Lefkara

◀ The popular Nissi beach in Agia Napa

Exploring Southern Cyprus

The best-preserved ancient town in Southern Cyprus is the Greco-Roman Kourion, with a beautifully located theatre, interesting mosaics, baths, a Byzantine stadium and the nearby Sanctuary of Apollo Ylatis. The best beaches for swimming and sunbathing are in Agia Napa and Protaras, with their enchanting clear water and lovely sandy beaches. They also offer the greatest number of attractions for young people. When exploring this part of the island be sure to visit Lefkara, a charming Cypriot village where women produce beautiful lace by hand and men make silver jewellery. Nature lovers often head for the salt lakes around Limassol and Larnaka, and are rewarded with the sight of hundreds of birds.

Stavrovouni monastery, founded by St Helena, mother of Constantine the Great

Sights at a Glance

Doorway of Panagia Chrysopolitissa church in Larnaka

For hotels and restaurants in this region see pp162–3 and pp171–3

Getting There

Most visitors to Cyprus arrive by air, and the biggest airport in the southern part of the island is outside Larnaka, serving a number of international flights. Motorways provide fast and safe travel links with Limassol and Agia Napa, as well as with Nicosia and Pafos. Alternatively, you can travel to Limassol by ship from Piraeus (Greece), Egypt, Israel, and Lebanon. Most of the historic sites of Limassol and Larnaka are best explored on foot. Public transport in the form of buses and taxis between major cities is good, but to reach smaller or more distant places a rental car is the best option for exploring Southern Cyprus.

0 kilometres 10

0 miles 10

The craggy coastline of Cape Gkreko

Key

▬▬ Motorway

▬▬ Major road

▭▭ Minor road

▬▬ Scenic route

– – Track

▬▬ Regional border

▬▬▬ Green Line

For additional map symbols *see back flap*

❶ Cape Aspro

Road Map B4. 4 km (2½ miles) south of Pissouri.

Cape Aspro is the highest point along the virtually deserted coast that stretches from Kourion to Pafos. Most of the coast along this, the southernmost point of the island (excluding the Akrotiri Peninsula), is as flat as a pancake. Towering over the cape is the **Trachonas Hill**, which affords magnificent views over Episkopi Bay, the southern slopes of the Troodos mountains, the small town of Pissouri and the monastery church Moni Prophitis Ilias.

The area around **Pissouri** is famous for its orchards and vineyards; the fertile lime soil yields abundant crops of sweet grapes. The modern amphitheatre, which was built in 2000 with seating for a thousand people, affords a beautiful view over the sea and the southern coast. During the summer, plays and concerts are staged here.

The town of Pissouri has some good accommodation options, ranging from little inns to luxurious hotels; there are also several rustic tavernas that offer typical local cuisine.

The rugged coastal cliffs rise to a height of 180 m (590 ft). They can be seen very clearly from the air, as planes usually approach Pafos airport from this direction. To the east of Cape Aspro is the pleasant and clean sandy-pebbly Pissouri beach with its clear, blue water.

Ruins of the Sanctuary of Apollo Ylatis near Kourion

❷ Sanctuary of Apollo Ylatis

Road Map B4. 3 km (2 miles) west of Kourion. **Tel** 25 934 250. **Open** 8:30am–7:30pm daily (to 5pm winter).

In ancient times the Sanctuary of Apollo Ylatis (also known as Hylates) was an important shrine. Stone fragments and toppled columns mark the site of this 7th-century BC shrine to the sun god Apollo in his role as "Ylatis", or god of the woods and forests. The present ruins date from early Roman times. It was in use until the 4th century AD, when Emperor Theodosius the Great declared a battle against pagans.

The sanctuary was surrounded by a holy garden, containing laurel trees, myrtle

and palms, and was home to deer. When pilgrims arrived through the Curium and Pafian gates, they placed votive offerings by the residence of the Great Priests, which were then sent to the treasury. When the treasury became full, the priests stored the offerings *(tavissae)* in a nearby holy well. This hiding place was discovered centuries later by archaeologists, and the ancient offerings can be seen at the Kourion Archaeological Museum at Episkopi and in the Cyprus Museum in Nicosia.

Close by were baths and a *palaestra* (gymnasium), surrounded by a colonnaded portico and used as a venue for wrestling. Standing in one corner of the *palaestra* is a fragment of a large clay jug, which was used for storing water for the athletes. The remaining buildings of the complex include storehouses and pilgrims' dormitories.

The former pilgrims' inn marked the start of the holy procession route leading to the sanctuary. At the heart of the sanctuary there was a small temple with a pillared portico, devoted to Apollo. As reported by the ancient geographer Strabo, any unauthorized person who touched the altar was hurled from it to the sea, to placate Apollo. The front of the temple, with its two columns, a fragment of the wall and tympanum, has been partially reconstructed.

Earthquakes, the spread of Christianity and Arab raids all played a role in destroying the sanctuary, and now all that remains are the romantic ruins.

Some 500 m (546 yards) east of the sanctuary is a large, well-preserved Roman stadium that could hold 6,000 spectators. Pentathlon events – consisting of running, long jump, discus- and javelin-throwing, and wrestling – were staged here. The athletes appeared naked, and only men were allowed to watch. In the 4th century the stadium was closed, regarded as a symbol of paganism.

The craggy coast of Cape Aspro

❸ Kourion

See pp70–71.

❹ Kolossi

Road Map B4. 14 km (9 miles) west of Limassol. 🚌 17. **Tel** 25 934 907. **Open** 8:30am–7:30pm daily (to 5pm winter). 🅿️

The best-preserved medieval castle in Cyprus is situated south of the village of Kolossi. In 1210 the land passed to the hands of the Knights of St John of Jerusalem, who built a castle here to be used as the Grand Master's headquarters.

At the turn of the 14th and 15th centuries the castle was sacked several times by the Genoese and Muslims.

Kolossi Castle in its present shape was built in 1454 by the Grand Master, Louis de Magnac. It is a three-storey structure, laid out on a square plan, 23 m (75 ft) high with walls over 2.5 m (8 ft) thick. Entry is via a drawbridge, with the entrance further guarded by a machicolation above the gate, which permitted the pouring of boiling water, oil or melted tar over attackers.

The entrance led to the dining room, whose walls were once covered with paintings. You can still see a scene of the Crucifixion with Louis de Magnac's coat of arms underneath. The adjacent room used to be the castle kitchen; stores were kept on the lower floor, and above were the living quarters; you can see stone fireplaces and windows. A narrow staircase leads to the flat roof surrounded by battlements. From here it was possible to supervise the work on the plantations and in the vineyards, and to spot enemy ships in the

The medieval Kolossi Castle, used by the Knights of Jerusalem

distance. Next to the castle is a large vaulted stone building, once a sugar refinery. To the north are the remains of a mill, formerly used for grinding the sugar, and the small 13th-century church of St Eustace, used as the castle chapel by the Knights Templar and the Knights of St John of Jerusalem.

❺ Agios Nikolaos ton Gaton (St Nicholas of the Cats)

Road Map B4. Cape Gata, 12 km (7½ miles) from the centre of Limassol. **Tel** 25 952 621. **Open** 8am–5pm daily.

The monastery of Agios Nikolaos ton Gaton stands on the Akrotiri peninsula, between the salt lake and the military airport. According to tradition it was founded by St Helena, mother of Constantine the Great, who visited Cyprus while returning from the Holy Land. Appalled by the plague of snakes, she sent a ship full of cats to the island to deal with them. The monks fed the cats and rallied them to fight by the

ringing of the bell. Another reference to the cats is the naming of the nearby Cape Gata – the Cape of Cats.

The monastery was founded in 325, but the buildings we see now are the result of remodelling that occurred during the 14th century. At the heart of the monastery is an old church with Gothic walls and Latin coats of arms above the entrance. Candles inside the dark church illuminate the gilded iconostasis and the elongated faces on the icons, which appear to come to life.

A small section of the salt lake on the Akrotiri peninsula

❻ Akrotiri Peninsula

Road Map B4. 🚌 22.

Akrotiri is the southernmost point of Cyprus. Most of the peninsula is occupied by a sovereign British base – Akrotiri-Episkopi, which includes an air force base and a radio communications station. This base, along with a second one at Ohekelia, is a relic of the island's colonial past, when Cyprus was governed by the British.

The central part of the peninsula is occupied by a salt lake (one of the two on the island), a vantage point for watching water birds including swans, flamingoes and pelicans. Running along the east coast is the wide beach known as Lady's Mile, which was named after a mare used by an English army officer for his regular morning ride.

Image of St Nicholas of the Cats

❸ Kourion

Ancient Kourion (or Curium) was a major centre of cultural, political and religious life. It was home to the centuries-old site of the Sanctuary of Apollo and later the seat of a Christian bishop. Perched on a bluff, the town was founded in the 12th century BC by Mycenaean Greeks, and was a large centre in the days of the Ptolemies and the Romans. Its trump card was its defensive location, and the control it wielded over the surrounding fertile land. Kourion was destroyed by two catastrophic earthquakes in the early 4th century.

Achilles' House
This takes its name from the 4th-century mosaic discovered inside the colonnade.

Baptistry and Bishop's Palace
Adjacent to the basilica and close to the bishop's palace was a large baptistry. Its remains include floor mosaics and some columns.

Basilica
The impressive triple-aisle building, erected in the 5th century AD on the site of a pagan temple, was destroyed by Arabs.

Nymphaeum
This imposing complex of stone fountains was built close to the public baths, on the spot where the aqueduct brought water to the city of Kourion.

Map of Kourion

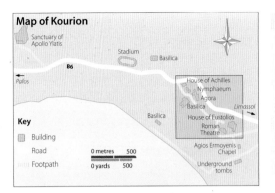

Key

- Building
- Road
- Footpath

0 metres 500
0 yards 500

VISITORS' CHECKLIST

Practical Information
Road Map B4. Kourion
Archaeological Museum:
19 km (12 miles) west of
Limassol. 16 from Limassol.
Tel 25 934 250. **Open** 8:30am–
7:30pm daily (to 5pm winter).
Sanctuary of Apollo
Ylatis: 3 km (2 miles) west
of Kourion. **Tel** 25 934 250.
Open 8:30am–7:30pm daily
(to 5pm winter).

Roman Theatre
The theatre, built in the 2nd century BC, enjoys a magnificent location overlooking the sea as well as boasting excellent acoustics.

Baths
These baths form part of the House of Eustolios, a late 4th-century AD private residence. The best mosaic depicts Ktissis as a woman holding a Roman measure, a personification of architectural art.

KEY

① **The House of the Gladiators** was so named after the discovery of two mosaics depicting gladiator fights.

② **Public baths**

House of Eustolios
Built in the early Christian period, this house had some 30 rooms arranged around a colonnaded courtyard with mosaic floors. The inscription by the entrance reads: "Step in and bring happiness to this house".

❼ Limassol (Lemesos)

Limassol is a major centre of trade, business and tourism, and has the biggest harbour in southern Cyprus. It is probably the most fun-filled city on Cyprus in terms of the number of fairs and festivals held here. The year starts with a riotous carnival; May marks the Flower Festival; and September brings the famous Wine Festival. Hotels, restaurants and nightclubs are clustered mainly along the beach.

Strolling along the seaside promenade

Exploring Limassol

It is best to start from the medieval castle, the town's most interesting historic site. Nearby is the Carob Museum, where visitors can learn about this important Cypriot export. A covered bazaar and a mosque are also close by.

The area has many restaurants with Cypriot and international cuisine, bars and cafés. From here it is not far to the new Limassol Marina, the latest tourist attraction in the town. You can enjoy an extended walk along the seaside promenade, passing the Orthodox Agia Napa cathedral. Just inland from here, is the main shopping street, Aiou

Colourful stalls of fruit and vegetables at the Central Market

Andreou, which runs parallel to the coast.

🏛 Central Market

Saripolou, in the old district near the town hall. **Open** 6am–2pm Mon–Sat.

The Central Market, housed in an arcaded building dating from the British era in the early 20th century, is a great place to shop for handmade reed baskets, olive oil, *loukoumia* (Cyprus delight) and other Cypriot delicacies, as well as fruits, vegetables, cheeses and meats. The stone market hall, its roof supported by metal pillars, is of particular note, featuring two arched gates with Doric columns. The market is surrounded by restaurants and cafés serving local and international cuisine. The stone-paved front square is used as a venue for shows and fairs.

🏛 Cyprus Handicraft Centre

Themidos 25. **Tel** 25 305 118. **Open** 7:30am–2:30pm Mon–Fri (also 3–6pm Thu except Jul–Aug).

At this centre you can buy locally made gifts and souvenirs,

including jewellery, lace, ceramics, mosaics and wood carvings produced by Cypriot craftspeople using traditional methods.

All stock is government-vetted and the fixed prices offer a good gauge of how much visitors should spend on products elsewhere.

🏛 Town Hall

Archiepiskopou Kyprianou.
W limassolmunicipal.com.cy

The town hall is situated in the centre of Limassol, on a narrow street opposite the post office and near Agia Napa Cathedral. It was built to a design by the German architect Benjamin Gunzburg, based on the ancient Greek style of civic architecture.

🏛 Agios Andronikos Church

Agiou Andreou. 🕕 6:30pm (summer), 4:30pm (winter) Sat; prayers Sun (times vary).

The Church of Agios Andronikos and Athanosis (in Greek *athanosis* means immortality) was built in the 1870s in Neo-Byzantine style. For a while it served as the town's cathedral. The church is accessible only from the waterfront. It is separated from the sea by the promenade, near the Agia Napa Cathedral.

Town Hall, dating from colonial times

Seaside Promenade

Perfect for an evening stroll, Limassol's palm-fringed promenade stretches for nearly 3 km (2 miles) along the shoreline, starting at the old harbour and continuing eastward towards St Catherine's Church. It is lined with well-kept greenery and benches, from where you can admire the seascape and watch the ships awaiting entry to the harbour.

🏛 Agia Napa Cathedral

Genethliou Mitella.

On the fringe of Limassol's old quarter, this vast Byzantine-style structure was built in the early 20th century on the ruins of a Byzantine church. It was consecrated in 1906,

For hotels and restaurants in this region see pp162–3 and pp171–3

The Orthodox cathedral of Agia Napa

and today it serves as Limassol's Orthodox cathedral.

This large stone church, sporting a twin-tower façade, is covered with a dome resting on a tambour over the intersection of the nave with the transept.

The cathedral was consecrated with the veil of St Veronica, with the imprinted image of Christ's face (the *veraikon*).

C Grand Mosque

Genethliou Mitella. **Open** times vary. Donations welcome.

The area around the harbour and castle was once inhabited mainly by Turks, and there are some remaining Turkish inscriptions and street names. The Grand Mosque – Cami Kebir – is still used by the handful of Turkish Cypriots in the city, and by Muslim visitors. The city's largest mosque is squeezed between old buildings behind the Turkish Bazaar.

H Limassol Castle

See pp76–7.

Carob Museum

Vasilissis 1, by Limassol Castle. **Tel** 25 342 123. **Open** daily (times vary so call ahead). **W** antisfoundation.org

This museum is located in a renovated former mill close to the medieval castle, in an area that is known for its art exhibitions and stylish cafés.

The Carob Museum shows how the carob is harvested, what it is used for and its relevance to the island's economy. The carob can be used in the production of honey, sweets and chocolate. Derivatives are also used for making paper,

The Grand Mosque with its distinctive pointed minaret

photographic filmplates and medicines. Historic machinery used to store and process the fruit is displayed alongside utensils and useful information.

Rialto Theatre

Andrea Drousioti 19, Heroes Square. **Tel** 77 777 745.

Located at the centre of Heroes Square, the Rialto Theatre hosts film shows, plays, dance and music performances. It serves as the venue for a number of events held throughout the year such as the European Dance Festival, the International Short Film Festival of Cyprus, and concerts featuring international musicians. During summer, the Cyprus Rialto World Music Festival takes place outside the building.

VISITORS' CHECKLIST

Practical Information
Road Map C4. 235,000.
Agiou Andreou 142, 25 362 756. Carnival (Feb–Mar), Flower Festival (May), Wine Festival (early Sep).

Transport
Limassol buses, 25 343 201. New harbour (cruise ships) 3 km (1.8 miles) east of the city. Intercity to Larnaka and Nicosia.

Limassol Town Centre

1 Central Market
2 Cyprus Handicraft Centre
3 Town Hall
4 Agios Andronikos Church
5 Seaside Promenade
6 Agia Napa Cathedral
7 Grand Mosque
8 Limassol Castle
9 Carob Museum
10 Rialto Theatre

0 metres 400
0 yards 400

For key to symbols *see back flap*

Artifacts in the Archaeological Museum

Further Afield

Outside the city centre are a number of sights worth visiting, including St Catherine's Catholic Church, the Municipal Gardens and mini-zoo, the District Archaeological Museum and Folk Art Museum, as well as a theatre, municipal art gallery and – among the best of the local attractions – the wineries. Stretching beyond the municipal beach to the east is the extensive tourist zone, with dozens of hotels, tavernas, pubs, restaurants, souvenir shops and clubs.

🏛 St Catherine's Catholic Church

28 Oktovriou 259. **Tel** 25 362 946.
🏛 6:30pm daily (English & Greek); 8am (Greek), 9:30am (Greek), 11am (Latin) & 6:30pm (English) Sun.

This twin-tower church stands opposite the beach, near the end of Limassol's palm-lined promenade. Consecrated in 1879, it is one of several Catholic churches in this part of the island.

🏛 District Archaeological Museum

At the junction of Kanningos and Vyronos, next to the Municipal Gardens. **Tel** 25 305 157. **Open** 8am–4pm Mon–Fri.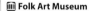

At the entrance to this museum is a mosaic depicting the bath of Eros and Aphrodite. The museum's collection includes artifacts found in excavations of the ancient city-states of Kourion and Amathous, as well as Neolithic tools and jewellery.

The highlights of the collection are the statue of the Egyptian god Bes – the god of harvest depicted in the guise of a dwarf; the statue of Hathor, Egyptian goddess of heaven, music and dance; the statue of Zeus discovered at Amathous; and the head of Zeus from Fasoula, carved from limestone. Other exhibits include collections of glass and terracotta artifacts.

🏛 Municipal Gardens and Mini-Zoo

28 Oktovriou, on the seafront. **Open** summer: 9am–7pm; winter: 9am–4pm.

The charming Municipal Gardens contain ponds and fountains. Shaded by trees, they are full of exotic greenery

Costume from the Folk Art Museum

and flowers. The gardens include an amphitheatre and a small zoo and aviary. The zoo, following a redesign, looks more like a park than a traditional zoo. It consists of farm animals from Cyprus. In early September the Municipal Gardens become the venue for the famous Wine Festival. As well as grape-trampling and folk dances, the crowds are treated to free wine from local producers.

🏛 Folk Art Museum

Agiou Andreou 253. **Tel** 25 362 303. **Open** 8:30am–2:30pm daily.

The Folk Art museum is housed in an attractive historic building dating from 1924. Arranged over six rooms is a good collection of 19th- and 20th-century Cypriot folk art.

The exhibition includes country tools, domestic utensils, wooden chests, traditional folk costumes, jewellery, tapestries and handcrafted products such as net curtains, bedding and bedspreads, which were traditionally stored in *sentoukia* – decorative trunks used as a bride's dowry.

🏛 Cyprus Wine Museum

Pafos St 42, Erimi. **Tel** 25 873 808. **Open** 9am–5pm daily.
🌐 cypruswinemuseum.com

Wine-growing is a long-established tradition in Limassol, which is dotted with vineyards and wineries. The popular sweet dessert wine, Commandaria, is produced in 14 villages in the area. The wine museum offers an ideal opportunity for visitors to learn about the history of Cyprus wine. It is located in Erimi, which initiated the cultivation of grapes and wine production in Europe over 5,500 years ago.

Housed in a restored inn that served as a meeting point for wine merchants from the villages of Limassol and Pafos, the museum exhibits old photographs, documents and audio-visual presentations as well as ancient jars and vases,

The leafy, pleasantly shaded Municipal Gardens

For hotels and restaurants in this region see pp162–3 and pp171–3

medieval drinking vessels and instruments that were used in the wine-making process. There is also a good collection of the different Commandaria wines produced in Cyprus.

Pattichion Theatre

Agias Zonis. **Tel** 25 343 341.

Musicals, drama and ballet productions are staged at the Pattichion, the oldest theatre in Limassol. The theatre was purchased by the Nicos and Despina Pattichi Foundation, then rebuilt and reopened in 1986. It is sponsored by the Limassol Municipality.

The theatre holds up to 760 people; backstage there are dressing rooms for 80 artists. The Pattichion theatre has hosted the Vienna Philharmonic Orchestra, the Athens Chamber Music Ensemble, the Vivaldi Orchestra from Moscow and Jazz Art Ballet from Paris.

Municipal Art Gallery

28 Oktovriou 103. **Tel** 25 586 212. **Open** 7:30am–2:30pm Mon–Fri.

The Municipal Art Gallery houses works by Cypriot painters, including early artists such as Diamantis, Kashialos (whose famous work *Chariot Drawn by Two Donkeys* is displayed), Kanthos and Frangoudis. Contemporary painters are also represented. The gallery, designed by Benjamin Gunzburg (who also designed the Town Hall), was built in the 1930s.

Lady's Mile beach and the new harbour in Limassol

Fasouri Watermania Waterpark

Near Trahoni village, Limassol–Pafos Road. **Tel** 25 714 235. **Open** May–Oct: 10am–5pm daily (to 6pm Jun–Aug). **W** fasouri-watermania.com

This popular water park has many water attractions including swimming pools, slides and artificial waves. Great for families and kids of all ages.

New Port

4 km (2½ miles) west of city centre. **Tel** 25 819 200. **▦** 30.

The New Port in Limassol is the largest in Cyprus. It was enlarged after 1974, when Famagusta port fell under Turkish occupation. Besides the commercial port, it includes a terminal for passenger ferries as well as cruise ships.

The old harbour, situated near Limassol castle, is now used by fishing boats and pleasure craft. The modern yachting marina at the St Raphael resort, is situated around 12 km (7½ miles) east of the city centre, in the tourist zone, near Amathous.

Beaches

Although long and wide, the municipal beach in Limassol is not among the island's most attractive beaches; it is covered with compressed soil and pebbles, and is located near a busy street.

Better beaches can be found further afield. Beyond the new harbour, in the eastern part of the Akrotiri peninsula, is Lady's Mile – a long and relatively quiet sandy beach (*see p69*). To the west, about 17 km (10½ miles) from the city centre, Kourion beach enjoys a lovely location at the foot of the hill where ancient Kourion once stood. You can reach it by public transport from Limassol. Avdimou beach, a further 12 km (7½ miles) along, has nice sand and a pleasant restaurant, although no shade.

The most pleasant sandy beach is found near Pissouri, some 44 km (27 miles) from Limassol. Here you can hire a deck chair and an umbrella, and nearby are several pleasant tavernas and restaurants.

The pre-war building of the Municipal Art Gallery

King Richard the Lionheart

The English king, famed for his courage, was passing near Cyprus on his way to the Crusades when a storm blew one of his ships, carrying his sister and fiancée, to the shore. The ruler of Cyprus, the Byzantine Prince Isaac Komnenos, imprisoned both princesses and the crew. The outraged Richard the Lionheart landed with his army on the island, smashed the Komnenos army, imprisoned Komnenos and occupied Cyprus. In May 1191, in the chapel of Limassol Castle, he married Princess Berengaria. Soon afterwards he sold the island to the Knights Templar.

English king Richard the Lionheart

Limassol Castle

This stronghold at the centre of the Old Town, near the harbour, was built by the Lusignan princes on foundations erected by the Byzantines. Later Venetian, Ottoman and British occupiers strengthened its defences. In 1191 the castle chapel was the venue for the wedding of Richard the Lionheart to Princess Berengaria of Navarre. The Ottomans later rebuilt the castle as a prison. During World War II it served as British army headquarters. Nowadays it houses the Medieval Museum.

Castle Roof
The flat, stone roof of Limassol Castle was once used by its defenders. Today visitors come here to admire the panoramic view – the best in town.

The Reliefs
The section of the museum devoted to Byzantine art houses not only numerous beautiful reliefs and mosaics from the oldest Christian basilicas, but also a number of religious icons.

Grape Press
This grape press is among the stone artifacts in the castle gardens.

Knights' Hall
The first-floor hall, in the south wing of Limassol Castle, houses two suits of armour and a collection of rare antique coins.

Main Hall

The Main Hall houses a large collection of Byzantine, Gothic and Renaissance sculptures, carvings and reliefs. Among them are carved images of the Lusignan kings from the portal of Agia Sofia Cathedral.

VISITORS' CHECKLIST

Practical Information
Irinis. Close to the old harbour.
Tel 25 305 419. **Open** 9am–5pm
Mon–Sat, 10am–1pm Sun.
There are cafés, restaurants and souvenir shops close to the castle, though none inside.

Main Lobby

Leading to the most opulent room, the lobby houses sculptures and coats of arms as well as photographs of Gothic and Renaissance architecture.

Fragment of a Portal
This fragment from Agia Napa Cathedral forms part of the medieval stonemasonry exhibits in the museum collection.

Sarcophagi Chamber

A chamber hidden in the shadowy recesses of the castle contains a collection of sarcophagi and tombstones.

Main Entrance
The castle is entered through a small bastion located on the east side of the castle.

The ruins of ancient Amathous, scenically located along the coast

❽ Amathous

Road Map C4. 12 km (7½ miles) east of Limassol city centre. 🚌 30. **Open** 8am–5pm daily (to 6pm Apr, May, Sep & Oct; to 7:30pm Jun–Aug). 🅿

Located on a high hill east of Limassol are the stone remains of the ancient port of Amathous. Named after its legendary founder Amathus, son of Aerias and king of Pafos, this once major commercial centre was founded between the 10th and 8th centuries BC.

Amathous was the first of the island's city-states. Over the centuries it was inhabited by Greeks, Phoenicians, Egyptians and Jews.

After the arrival of Christianity on Cyprus, St Tychon founded a church here and became the first bishop of Amathous. He became the patron saint of the town.

The town existed until the 7th century AD when, together with other coastal centres, it was destroyed in Arab raids.

In later times the site was used as a quarry; huge stones were transported to Egypt for use in the construction of the Suez Canal. The American consul (and amateur archaeologist) Luigi Palma di Cesnola destroyed large areas of the city while treasure-hunting.

The best-preserved part is the agora (marketplace), with a dozen remaining columns. In the north section are parts of

Large stone vessel from Amathous

the aqueduct system and the site of a bath house. Standing on top of the hill was the acropolis, with temples to Aphrodite and Hercules, the remains of which can still be seen. Close by, archaeologists have unearthed the ruins of an early Christian, 5th-century Byzantine basilica. Fragments of powerful defence walls can be seen on the opposite side of the road.

The coastal part of the town collapsed during an earthquake. Its ruins stretch a great distance into the sea.

❾ Agios Georgios Alamanos

Road Map C4.

The buildings of the Agios Georgios Alamanos monastery can be seen from the Nicosia–Limassol motorway. Although the monastery, just like the new Byzantine-style church,

is not of great architectural merit, it is interesting to watch the local monks painting icons.

In the nearby village of Pentakomo, on the opposite side of the motorway, are surviving stone houses. Close to the church is a pleasant café, where there are occasional concerts and plays.

❿ Kalavasos

Road Map C4. 40 km (25 miles) from Larnaka, 1.5 km (1 mile) from exit 15 on the motorway. 🚌 95 from Limassol, 401 from Larnaka.

Up until the 1970s the inhabitants of this village were involved in mining copper ore from the neighbouring mountains. A symbol of this industrial past is the local steam engine, which was once used here. The Cyprus Agrotourism Company has restored some of the houses for the use of tourists.

Environs
Close by archaeologists have unearthed the Neolithic settlement of **Tenta**. Smaller than the neighbouring Choirokoitia, part of it is covered by a huge tent. The settlement, which was encircled by a defensive wall, featured a roundhouse and beehive huts built from clay and stone.

The nearby village of **Tochni** is one of the most popular agrotourism sites in Cyprus. Situated in a valley, amid olive trees and vineyards, the peaceful village is built around a small church. Picturesque narrow alleys lead to stone houses.

The Neolithic settlement of Tenta

⓫ Choirokoitia

Road Map C4. 40 km (25 miles) from Limassol, 1.5 km (1 mile) from exit 14 on the motorway. 401, 402, 403 from Larnaka. **Tel** 24 322 710. **Open** Apr, May, Sep & Oct: 8am–6pm daily; Jun–Aug: 8am–7:30pm daily; Nov–Mar: 8am–5pm daily.

In the village of Choirokoitia, close to the motorway that runs between Limassol and Nicosia, archaeologists discovered the ruins of a large Neolithic settlement surrounded by a stone wall. One of the oldest settlements in Cyprus, it existed as early as 6800 BC.

It was sited on the slope of a hill, close to the river Maroni. Its inhabitants, who numbered close to 2,000 at the peak of its development, lived in beehive huts built of stone and clay. Many of the houses unearthed by archaeologists contained under-floor graves with gifts and personal effects. The dead were laid to rest in an embryonic position, with heavy stones placed on their chests to prevent them from returning to the world of the living.

The population of Choirokoitia formed a well-organized farming community. They cultivated the fertile local soil, hunted, bred goats, spun and weaved, and produced clay figurines and other objects. The artifacts uncovered at this site include flint sickle blades, stone vases and primitive triangular fertility gods. The women wore beautiful necklaces made of shells or imported red cornelian.

The foundations of several dozens of houses have been unearthed. Some of these have been reconstructed, providing a glimpse into how the earliest Cypriots lived. Many of the items found here are exhibited in the Cyprus Museum in Nicosia.

The settlement was abandoned suddenly, and then repopulated around 4500 BC. These later inhabitants introduced clay pots, some of which have been unearthed. The Choirokoitia archaeological site has been declared a UNESCO World Cultural and Natural Heritage Site.

Lefkara's Lace and Silverware Museum

⓬ Agios Minas

Road Map C4. Close to Lefkara. **Tel** 24 342 952. **Open** May–Sep: 8am–noon, 3–5pm daily; Oct–Apr: 8am–noon, 2–5pm daily.

Agios Minas, a small monastery located in a scenic mountain setting, was founded in the 15th century and renovated in the mid-18th century. Subsequently abandoned, it was taken by a convent in 1965. The nuns are involved in painting icons, growing flowers and fruit, and keeping bees. They sell the delicious honey.

The 15th-century convent church, which was built by the Dominicans, features wall frescoes depicting St George slaying the dragon and the martyrdom of St Minas.

Environs

The nearby village of **Vavla** has lovely stone houses, some of which are being renovated for use by tourists.

⓭ Lefkara

Road Map C4. 40 km (25 miles) from Larnaka. 405 from Larnaka.

This village, set amid picturesque white limestone hills (*lefka ori* means white hills), is famous for the lace-making skills of its womenfolk. In the Middle Ages, Lefkara was a health resort visited by Venetian ladies. While staying here they busied themselves with embroidery, which they taught the local women. One story tells of Leonardo da Vinci supposedly coming to the island in 1481 to order an altar cloth for Milan cathedral. The lace patterns are predominantly geometric, with crosses or diamonds and occasionally flowers, birds or butterflies. While the women busy themselves with embroidery, the local men produce jewellery and other objects from silver and gold.

The village buildings, with their yellow walls and red roofs, stand in attractive contrast with the natural surroundings. At the centre of Lefkara is the 16th-century Church of the Holy Cross containing a carved and gilded wood iconostasis and a precious sacred relic – a fragment of the True Cross on which Christ was crucified. The beautiful stone Patsalos building houses the **Lace and Silverware Museum**.

🏛 **Lace and Silverware Museum**
Pano Lefkara. **Tel** 24 342 326. **Open** 9:30am–5pm daily.

Reconstructed houses at Choirokoitia archaeological site

⓯ Pyrga

Road Map D3. 35 km (22 miles) from Larnaka. 📷 455 from Larnaka.

This village is home to the Gothic **Chapel of St Catherine**, also known as the "Chapelle Royal". Erected by the Lusignan king Janus for his wife Charlotte de Bourbon, the chapel is built of volcanic rock on a square floorplan. It has three doors and, on the altar wall, three Gothic windows. The interior features fragments of the original frescoes. These depict the *Crucifixion*, with King Janus and Queen Charlotte by the cross; the *Raising of Lazarus*; the *Last Supper*; and the Lusignan coats of arms.

Close by is the Marini river on whose banks in 1426 the Egyptian Mamelukes smashed the Cypriot army, capturing King Janus and taking him prisoner to Cairo. The king regained his freedom two years later, after a ransom was paid.

Environs
The village of **Kornos**, to the west, is famous for its oversized ceramic products, such as storage jars.

⓰ Stavrovouni Monastery

Road Map D3. 40 km (25 miles) from Larnaka, 9 km (5½ miles) from motorway. **Tel** 22 533 630.
Open Apr–Aug: 8am–noon, 3–6pm daily; Sep–Mar: 7–11am, 2–5pm daily. 🚫 No women allowed 📅 14 Sep.

Stavrovouni (Mountain of the Cross) monastery was built on a steep, 750-m (2,460-ft)

Agia Varvara (monastery of St Barbara) at the foot of Stavrovouni

Gothic chapel of
St Catherine in Pyrga

mountain. In ancient times the mountain was called Olympus, and it was the site of a temple to Aphrodite.

According to tradition, the monastery was founded in 327 by St Helena, mother of Constantine the Great. On her journey back from the Holy Land, where she found the True Cross of Christ, she stopped in Cyprus and left behind fragments of the precious relic. These can be seen in a large silver reliquary in the shape of a cross. Over the following centuries the monastery fell prey to enemy raids and earthquakes. In 1821, during the Greek independence uprising, it was burned to the ground by the Ottoman governor of Cyprus. The present monastery is the result of 19th-century restoration. The small **church** contains a lovely iconostasis and a wooden cross dating from 1476, carved with

scenes from the life of Jesus. Around the church are the monks' cells and other monastic quarters. The monastery houses a collection of monks' skulls, with the name of the deceased written on each forehead.

Today the monks produce exquisite cheeses and sultanas, and also keep honey bees.

At the foot of Stavrovouni is the **monastery of St Barbara** (Agia Varvara), known for the local monks' icon painting. Their most celebrated artist was Father Kallinikos *(see p24)*.

⓱ Kiti

Road Map D4. 7 km (4½ miles) southwest of Larnaka. **Open** church: 7am–6:45pm daily (from 9:30am Sun).

The **Panagia Angeloktisti** ("Built by Angels") church, in the northwestern end of the village of Kiti, consists of three parts. The first is the 14th-century Latin chapel with the coats of arms of knights above the entrance. The second part is the 11th-century dome-covered church, built on the ruins of an early Byzantine basilica, whose apse has been

The Stavrovouni monastery towering over the district

incorporated into the present building. The 6th-century apse mosaic is the church's main attraction. It depicts Mary holding the Christ Child, flanked by the Archangels Michael and Gabriel, with peacock-feather wings.

The third part of the church is a small 12th-century chapel dedicated to Saints Cosmas and Damian (patron saints of medicine) and decorated with 15th-century murals.

Environs
The 15th-century watchtower, 1 km (half a mile) from Kiti lighthouse, features a statue of a lion – the symbol of the Venetian Republic.

Panagia Angeloktisti church in the village of Kiti

⓱ Hala Sultan Tekke

Road Map D3. 5 km (3 miles) southwest of Larnaka. **Open** 8am–5pm daily (to 6pm Apr, May, Sep & Oct; to 7:30pm Jun–Aug).

On the shores of a salt lake, surrounded by cypress, palm and olive trees, the Hala Sultan Tekke is a major Muslim sanctuary. It includes an octagonal 1816 mosque built by the Ottoman governor of Cyprus, and a mausoleum with the tomb of Umm Haram.

Umm Haram, paternal aunt of the Prophet Mohammed, was killed after falling off a mule while accompanying her husband in a pillage raid on Kition in 649. The mosque has a modest interior and the mausoleum contains several sarcophagi covered with green cloths. After Mecca, Medina and Jerusalem, the Hala Sultan Tekke is among the holiest sites for Muslims.

To the west of the car park, archaeological excavations continue, unearthing a late-

Mosque and Hala Sultan Tekke mausoleum on the shores of the Salt Lake

Bronze Age town. Many items found here originated from Egypt and the Middle East.

Environs
The salt lake, close to the mosque, is one of two such lakes in Cyprus. In winter and early spring it provides a gathering point for thousands of flamingoes, swans, pelicans and other migrating water birds. The lake lies below sea level and in winter is filled with water seeping from the sea through the lime rocks. In summer it dries out, leaving a thick deposit of salt. Until the 1980s it yielded 3–5,000 tons of salt annually.

According to legend, the salt lake was created after Lazarus landed on this shore. Hungry and thirsty, he asked a local woman in the vineyard for a handful of fruit. She tersely refused to give him anything, so the saint, in revenge, turned her vineyard into a salt lake.

⓲ Larnaka

See pp82–5.

⓳ Kellia

Road Map D3. 5 km (3 miles) north of Larnaka. 🚌 442 from Larnaka.

Standing to the west of Kellia, formerly a Turkish Cypriot village that derives its name from the cells of early Christian hermits who once made this their home, is the small **Church of St Anthony** (Agios Andonios), where cells are carved into the rocks.

It was first built in the 11th century, but the subsequent remodelling works have all but obliterated its original shape. The layout resembles a cross inscribed into a square, with the three aisles terminating in an apse and a 15th-century narthex.

Restoration efforts have revealed some beautiful murals. The most interesting of them is the *Crucifixion*, painted on the southeast pillar, one of the oldest paintings on the island. Other notable paintings are on the pillars and on the west wall of the church, including the *Assumption of the Virgin Mary*, *Judas' Betrayal* and *Abraham's Sacrifice*.

Zeno of Kition (Kitium)

Born in 334 BC, this Greek thinker founded the Stoic school of philosophy (named after Stoa Poikale – the Painted Colonnade on the Athenian agora where he taught). Zeno's philosophy embraced logic, epistemology, physics and ethics. The Stoics postulated that a life governed by reason and the harnessing of desires was of the highest virtue, leading to happiness. Stoicism left a deep mark on the philosophy and ethics of the Hellenic and Roman eras.

Bust of Zeno of Kition

St Lazarus Church dating from the 10th century

🏛 Agios Lazaros Church

Plateia Agiou Lazarou. **Tel** 24 652 498.
Open 8am–12:30pm, 2–6:30pm daily
(to 5:30pm Sep–Mar).

The Church of St Lazarus (Agios Lazaros) stands in the southern part of Old Larnaka. It was constructed in the early 10th century on the site of a church dating from 900, which was built to house the saint's tomb.

Its architectural style reveals the influence of both Eastern and Western trends. Following its retrieval from the hands of the Turks in 1589, the church was used by Roman Catholic and Orthodox communities for 200 years, as evidenced by inscriptions on the portico. The interior is built around four vast pillars supporting a roof with three small domes. Its main features are the Rococo pulpit, around 300 years old, and a small icon depicting Lazarus emerging from his tomb. The icon dates from the 17th century and can be seen in the magnificently

Icon from the Byzantine Museum

carved iconostasis. The image is reverently paraded through the church at Easter. On the right side of the central nave is a large gilded reliquary containing the skull of the saint. The crypt houses several stone sarcophagi. One of them supposedly housed the relics of St Lazarus. The tomb bore the Greek inscription: "Lazarus, friend of Jesus".

The graves in the courtyard are mainly of British consuls, civil servants and merchants.

Larnaka has other notable places of worship, including the metropolitan cathedral, Agios Chrysotrios, built in 1853; Agios Ioannis, featuring a beautiful iconostasis from the beginning of the 17th century; and the Roman Catholic church Terra Santa. Also of note is the 19th-century Zahuri Mosque, with its double dome and truncated minaret.

🏛 Byzantine Museum

Plateia Agiou Lazarou.
Tel 24 652 498. **Open**
8:30am–12:30pm, 3–5:30pm Mon–Sat. **Closed** Wed & Sat pm.

Entry to this museum is from the courtyard of Agios Lazaros church. The collection consists of icons and other objects associated with the Orthodox religion, including chasubles and Bibles. A previous, extensive collection

vanished during the turbulent period between 1964 and 1974. It was kept in the fort, which fell into the hands of the Turks. When it was regained by the Greeks, many items had vanished.

🏛 Agia Faneromeni

At the junction of Leoforos Faneromeni and Artemidos.

This subterranean chapel is a two-chambered cave hewn into the rock. Its structure suggests a pagan tomb, probably dating from the Phoenician era. The chapel was famed for its magical properties. The sick would circle it twice, leaving behind anything from a scrap of clothing to a lock of hair in the hope that they were also leaving behind their illnesses. Girls whose boyfriends were far away would come here to pray for their safe return.

🎭 Pattichion Municipal Theatre

Leoforos Artemidos.

The open-air amphitheatre, used for staging events during the July Festival, is situated opposite the Zeno of Kition Stadium, close to the Agia Faneromeni chapel.

☪ Büyük Cami

Leoforus Athenon. **Open** daily.

Standing beyond the fort, at the border between the Greek and Turkish districts, is the Grand Mosque (Büyük Cami). Originally the Church of the Holy Cross, this building now serves Muslim visitors mostly from the Middle East. Modest attire is required, and before entering you must remove your shoes. For a small fee you can climb the narrow, steep stairs that lead to the top of the minaret. From here there is a

---

Saint Lazarus

Lazarus, brother of Martha and Mary, was resurrected by Jesus four days after his death at Bethany. He moved to Cyprus, becoming Bishop of Kition. After his final death he was buried here; his tomb was discovered in 890. Emperor Leo VI helped to build St Lazarus church, in exchange for which some of the saint's relict were transferred to Constantinople, from where they were stolen in 1204. Today they are in Marseille Cathedral.

Painting showing the resurrection of Lazarus

lovely panoramic view of Larnaka and the nearby salt lake. Stretching beyond the fort, right up to the fishing harbour, is a large district that once belonged to the Turks. Its streets still bear Turkish names, but it is now inhabited by Greek Cypriot refugees from the area around Famagusta and the Karpasia peninsula.

The imposing mid-18th-century aqueduct

A variety of yachts moored in Larnaka marina

🚢 Larnaka Harbours

The southern part of town has a small but picturesque fishing harbour. Larnaka marina is situated several hundred metres to the north of the coastal promenade, beyond a small beach. Only boat crews are allowed entry, but you can stroll along the breakwater. Beyond the marina there are cargo and passenger terminals; the passenger terminal is the second largest in Cyprus.

🏰 Larnaka Fort and Medieval Museum

On the seashore, by the south end of the coastal promenade. **Tel** 24 304 576. **Open** 8am–5pm Mon–Fri (to 7:30pm Jun–Aug).

The fort in Larnaka was built by the Ottomans around 1625 on the site of a medieval castle which had been destroyed by Mamelukes two centuries previously. When ships sailed into the harbour (which no longer exists), they were welcomed by a gun salute fired from the castle.

During the Byzantine period, the fort was used as a police

headquarters, prison and execution site. In 1833, it was partially destroyed by a lightning strike. The fort now houses a small Medieval Museum with arms and armour dating from Turkish times, and treasure troves unearthed in Kition and at the Hala Sultan Tekke. The crenellated wall, with guns and cannons, is now a viewing platform. In summer the castle yard hosts concerts, occasional plays and other cultural events.

⚓ Beaches

The sandy municipal beach by the Finikoudes promenade, in the neighbourhood of the marina, owes its popularity to a double row of shade-giving palm trees. There are some good beach bars such as the award-winning Kastella. Another municipal beach is situated to the south of the fishing harbour. Although the beach itself is small, it is popular with locals due to its watersports facilities and the numerous restaurants and cafés in the vicinity.

A cannon at Larnaka's Fort

The best sandy public beach in the area is located some 10 km (6 miles) east of the city and is run by the Cyprus Tourism Organization. About 10 km (6 miles) south of Larnaka, near Kiti, there is a rocky cove with patches of sand; this area is undeveloped and relatively free of people.

A bit further from Finikoudes is Mackenzie beach with watersports facilities, restaurants, beach bars and cafés. Weekends get crowded and there are concerts at night feature local and international artists.

🏛 Aqueduct (Kamares)

3 km (2 miles) from Larnaka.

On the outskirts of Larnaka, by the road leading to Limassol, are the remains of an aqueduct that once supplied the town with water taken from the Thrimitus river. The aqueduct was built in 1745 by the Ottoman governor, Elhey Bekir Pasha, and functioned until 1930. Some 75 spans of the structure still stand; they are illuminated at night.

The popular Finikoudes beach on a pleasant, sunny day

Octagonal fountain in the courtyard of Agia Napa monastery

⑳ Agia Napa

Road Map E3. 🚌 201 Agia Napa
Circle Line. 🚕 3,200. ℹ️ Leoforos
Kryou Nerou 12, 23 721 796.
🎭 Kataklysmos.

Until the 1970s, Agia Napa was
a quiet fishing village with a
scenic harbour. However, following the Turkish occupation of
Varosha – the Greek Cypriot
neighbourhood of Famagusta –
Agia Napa assumed the role of
Cyprus' prime bathing
resort. Now a teeming
holiday resort especially
popular with British,
German, Russian and
Scandinavian young
people, the town
centre has scores of
hotels, nightclubs and
cafés that have given
Agia Napa its reputation
as the second most
entertaining playground in the
Mediterranean, after Ibiza.

An interesting historic relic of
Agia Napa is the 16th-century
Venetian **Monastery of Agia
Napa**, enclosed by a high wall.
According to legend, in the
16th century a hunter's dog led
him to a spring in the woods
where he found a sacred icon of
the Virgin that had been lost
700 years earlier. (A church had
been built here as early as the
8th century, hacked into the
solid rock and named Agia
Napa – Holy Virgin of the Forest).
The spring was thus believed to
have healing powers and the
monastery of Agia Napa was
built on the site. Soon after,
Cyprus fell to the Ottomans and
the Venetian monks fled, but
villagers continued to use the

Fountain detail, Agia
Napa monastery

beautiful **monastery church**.
The only church on the island
with a free-standing belfry, it is
built partly underground in a
natural grotto. The route to its
gloomy, mysterious interior
leads through an entrance
crowned with an arch and a
rosette. Inside is a complex
maze of grottoes, niches and
shrines. Between April and
December, the church cele-
brates Anglican Mass every
Sunday at 11am and
Roman Catholic
Mass at 5pm.

At the centre of the
monastery's arcaded
courtyard is an octa-
gonal Renaissance
fountain decorated with
marble reliefs and
topped with a dome
resting on four
columns. Nearby,
water supplied by a Roman
aqueduct flows from the carved
marble head of a wild boar.

The monastery was restored
in the 1970s and now houses
the **World Council of Churches
Ecumenical Conference Centre**.

The **Thalassa Museum of the
Sea** in Agia Napa is designed

to show the impact of the sea
on the history of the island.
It features a replica of the
"Kyrenia Ship" dating from the
time of Alexander the Great,
which sank off the coast of
Kyrenia some 2,300 years ago.

The majority of the museum's
exhibits come from the private
collection of naturalist George
Tomaritis. They include a range
of preserved marine fauna
as well as a collection of shells
and maritime exhibits.

Beautiful sandy beaches can
be found in the surrounding
area. One of them is **Nissi
Beach**, with its small island.
Neighbouring **Makronissos
Beach** is linked to the town
centre by bicycle routes. Nearby,
on a craggy peninsula, are 19
Hellenistic tombs hacked into
the rock. Two kilometres (1 mile)
west is a sandy beach, **Agia
Thekla**, with a small chapel and
an old church in a rock cave.

🏛️ **Thalassa Museum of the Sea**
Leoforos Kryou Nerou. **Tel** 23 816 366.
Open summer: 9am–1pm Mon,
9am–5pm Tue–Sat, 3–7pm Sun;
winter: 9am–1pm Mon, 9am–5pm
Tue–Sat, closed Sun. 🅿️
🌐 pieridesfoundation.com.cy

㉑ Cape Gkreko

Road Map E3. 🚌 101 from Famagusta
and Paralimni.

This headland at the southeastern tip of Cyprus rises in a
steep crag above the sea. The
neighbouring coves with their
clear water are a paradise for
scuba divers and snorkellers.
The entire area, with its
limestone rock formations,
is a **protected nature reserve**.

Popular sandy beach in Agia Napa

The rugged coast of Cape Gkreko with its limestone cliffs

Archaeologists discovered the remains of two **temples**: the Hellenic temple of Aphrodite, and the Roman temple of Diana. The cape is surrounded by underwater **shipwrecks**, including a Genoese ship once filled with looted treasure, which sank in the 15th century.

Walking along the shore towards Protaras you will come across a rock bridge over a small bay protruding inland, a Roman quarry, and a little further on, the **Agii Anargyri Church** above a grotto hidden in a craggy cliff underneath. The area affords magnificent views over Konnos Bay and the clifftop hotel.

㉙ Protaras

Road Map E3. 🚌 101 from Famagusta and Paralimni. 🛈 Leoforos Protaras Cape Gkreko 356, 23 832 865.

Protaras is a conglomeration of hotels, restaurants, tavernas, bars, cafés and watersports centres, and an excellent place to spend a holiday. In summer, its beautiful sandy beaches such as Fig Tree, which was named one of Europe's best beaches, and the magical Konnos Bay attract crowds of tourists for watersports and cruises on one of the local pleasure boats.

The area is dominated by a rocky hill with the picturesque **Chapel of Prophitis Elias** (the Prophet Elijah) affording a magnificent panoramic view of Protaras and nearby Varosha.

Further north are more beaches including Pernera, Minas and Agia Triada, with a small church, situated in a coastal cove. Near the latter, close to the roundabout on the road to Paralimni, is **Ocean Aquarium**, with crocodiles, penguins and other marine life.

🄰 **Ocean Aquarium**
Paralimni, Protaras Ave. **Tel** 23 741 111. **Open** 10am– 6pm daily.
ⓦ protarasaquarium.com

Environs
The area encompassing Agia Napa, Paralimni and the tourist region of Protaras is known as **Kokkinohoria** (red villages) due to its red soil, which is rich in iron and produces the famous Cyprus potato. The scenery is dominated by windmills that drive pumps, which draw water from deep underground.

After 1974, the village of **Paralimni** became the district's administrative centre. Close to the occupied, northern part of Cyprus, it received many refugees after the invasion and now its population numbers about 11,000.

The village skyline is dominated by three churches. The oldest of these is Panagia (Virgin Mary) dating from the 18th century and lined with porcelain tiles typical of the period. It also houses a small Byzantine museum. Paralimni is famous for delicacies such as smoked pork (pasta) and pork sausages (loukanika).

The neighbouring farming village of **Deryneia** perches atop a hill, right by the "Green Line". From here there

are views of Varosha's abandoned houses, the former tourist district of Famagusta now resembling a ghost town, and the Gothic Cathedral of St Nicholas, which has been turned into a mosque.

Deryneia has three pretty churches–15th-century Agia Marina, 17th-century Agios Georgios and the church of the Panagia.

The village of **Liopetri** is famous for the potatoes that are grown here, as well as the woven baskets used to collect them. You can still see local basket-weavers at work.

The 15th-century village church of Agios Andronikos has a carved iconostasis with beautiful icons and paintings in the apses.

The Akhyronas barn is Cyprus' national memorial. It was here that four EOKA fighters were killed in a battle with the British in 1958.

Potamos Liopetriou, to the south, is the most beautiful fishing village in Cyprus, situated on the shores of a long bay, next to the picturesque church of Agios Georgios and the crumbling walls of the Venetian watchtower. The seaside tavernas serve delicious fresh fish dishes.

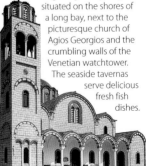
Statue of a diver in Protaras

The 18th-century Panagia church in Paralimni

TROODOS MOUNTAINS

Stretching some 120 km (75 miles) over southwestern Cyprus, the Troodos mountain region is truly astonishing and completely different from the rest of the sun-baked island. In winter and early spring, the peaks are often capped with snow, and the forests fill the cool air with the scent of pine and cedar. The mountain villages and monasteries hidden in the forests seem a world away from the crowded coastal areas, even during the peak holiday season.

The shady valleys and lofty peaks of the Troodos mountains have long been a refuge for people in search of calm and tranquillity, including the monks who came here looking for a place where they could be closer to God and further from temptation.

Mount Olympus, the island's highest peak at 1,950 m (6,400 ft), rises above the other mountains in the mighty massif, crowned with the distinctive radar domes of the British army. In winter, its slopes swarm with skiers eager to enjoy a sport that is rare in this part of Europe.

The southern slopes are perfectly suited to growing the grapes used to produce the island's famous wine, the sweet Commandaria, as well as other varieties.

Almost half of the 144 species of plants unique to Cyprus grow in the Troodos region. The Troodos geopark, located in the central part of the island, has been declared a nature reserve.

Travelling through the Troodos mountains brings visitors into contact with quiet, friendly villages, where the local people produce sweets of fruit and nuts soaked in grape juice (*soujouko*), as well as wine and flavourful goat's cheese (*halloumi*).

No trip to the region is complete without seeing the Byzantine painted churches. The austere architecture of these Orthodox sanctuaries, within remote valleys and glens, hides a wealth of amazingly rich murals (commonly referred to as frescoes) depicting scenes from the Bible.

A church hidden in the mountains – a distinctive feature of the region

◀ The royal Kykkos Monastery in the Troodos mountains

Exploring the Troodos Mountains

Among the highlights of a visit to the Troodos mountains are the many painted churches, some dating from the Byzantine period. Ten of these isolated churches have been listed as UNESCO World Cultural Heritage Sites. The tomb of Archbishop Makarios, the first president of Cyprus, lies near Kykkos Monastery at Throni. The Commandaria region's 14 villages have produced the famous Cypriot dessert wine since the 12th century. The true treasures of the Troodos mountains are their waterfalls hidden among lush greenery – unusual in the eastern Mediterranean.

Theotokos Archangelos Church, one of the many small churches in the region

Sights at a Glance

1. Tilliria
2. Cedar Valley
3. *Kykkos pp94–5*
4. Agios Ioannis Lampadistis
5. Panagia tou Moutoulla
6. Pedoulas
7. Mt Olympus (Chionistra)
8. Troodos
9. Trooditissa
10. Platres
11. Omodos
12. Potamiou
13. Vouni
14. Koilani
15. Lofou
16. Monagri
17. Timios Stavros
18. Pelendri
19. Agios Nikolaos tis Stegis
20. Kakopetria
21. Panagia tis Podithou
22. Panagia Forviotissa
23. Panagia tou Araka
24. Stavros tou Agiasmati

0 kilometres 5

0 miles 5

Getting There

From Larnaka airport, follow the motorway signs toward the Troodos mountains, and then take the B8 road. The B9 road from Nicosia passes through Kakopetria. The best route from Pafos is along the scenic Diarizos Valley. Leave the motorway at Mandria and turn towards Nikoklea. The mountain roads are of good quality, but winding and steep in places.

Winding roads and arid landscape typical of the region

Morfou

Astromeritis

Nicosia

B9

Nikitari   Vyzakia

Evrychou

L E F K O S Í A

rakies

Kalopanagiotis

NAGIA TOU OUTOULLA ⑤

④ AGIOS IOANNIS LAMPADISTIS

⑥ PEDOULAS

Marathassa

Prodromos

② PANAGIA TIS PODITHOU

⑳ KAKOPETRIA

⑲ AGIOS NIKOLAOS TIS STEGIS

Kourdali

Spilia

㉒ PANAGIA FORVIOTISSA

Adbelfi Forest

Xyliatos

Kapoura

Saranti

㉓ PANAGIA TOU ARAKA

㉔ STAVROS TOU AGIASMATI

Mt Adbelfi 1612m

Chandria

Platanistasa

MOUNT OLYMPUS ⑦

⑧ **TROODOS**
Pano Amiantos

Kyperounta

Agridia

Alona

Pitsillia

⑨
TROODITISSA

aminaria

Fini

Troodos

Agros

PLATRES ⑩

L E M E S O S

Pera Pedi

PELENDRI ⑱
⑰ **TIMIOS STAVROS**

⑪ **OMODOS**

POTAMIOU
⑫

⑭ **KOILANI**

Silikou

Trimiklini

B8

Laneia

⑬ **VOUNI**

⑮ **LOFOU**

lalia

⑯ **MONAGRI**

Agios Therapon

Panagia tis Amasgou

↓*Limassol*

Key

— Secondary road
··· Minor road
— Scenic route
– – Track
▪▪▪ Regional border
▪■▪ Green Line
△ Summit

For additional map symbols *see back flap*

❶ Tilliria

Road Map B3.

Tilliria is a desolate region east of Polis, on the northwestern slopes of the Troodos mountains. Its forested hills extend behind the former monastery, Stavros tis Psokas, in the direction of the Turkish enclave of Kokkina, Pyrgos, Kato and the sea. This region has never been inhabited, although people came here to work the long-since defunct copper ore mines. It is ideal for experienced hikers.

In ancient times, Cyprus was overgrown with dense forests, which were cut down to build ships and fire the furnaces in the copper-smelting plants.

Under British rule of the island, action was taken to restore the former character of the Cypriot forests. The extensive Pafos Forest was created in the western region of the Troodos mountains.

The wooded hills of the remote Tilliria region – a hiker's paradise

❷ Cedar Valley

Road Map B3.

This valley, set in the midst of the forest backwoods, contains most of the island's trees of the local *cedrus brevifolia* variety, different from the better known Lebanese cedar. The valley is a nature reserve, and with a bit of luck visitors will see the moufflon – a wild Cypriot sheep. In the early 20th century, when the British declared these animals a protected species, only 15 of them remained in the wild;

now the forests of Cyprus are home to over 1,500 of them. The male displays powerful, curled horns. The moufflon is a symbol of Cyprus and appears on its coins.

Environs
Standing in the midst of the Pafos Forest is the abandoned 19th-century monastery of **Stavros tis Psokas**, now used by the Forestry Commission. It contains a restaurant, several guest rooms and a campsite. The locals claim it to be the coolest place on the island. Close to the campsite is an enclosure containing moufflon.

The Forestry Commission building is the starting point for hiking trails to the nearby peaks of Tripylos and Zaharou. Starting from the car park by the spring and the junction with the road leading towards the sea, you can walk or drive to Mount Tripylos – one of the highest peaks in the district at 1,362 m (4,468 ft), which offers a magnificent panorama of the Pafos and Tilliria hills.

❸ Kykkos

See pp94–5.

❹ Agios Ioannis Lampadistis

Road Map B3. Kalopanagiotis.
Tel 22 952 580. **Open** 9am–12:30pm, 2–5pm daily (Nov–Apr: 9am–noon, 1–4pm). Donations welcome.

The monastery of St John of Lampadou (ancient Lambas) is one of the most interesting in Cyprus and has been awarded

Kalopanagiotis village, scenically located on a mountain slope

UNESCO World Heritage status. The old monastery complex includes three churches covered with one vast roof. The oldest one, dedicated to St Irakleidios, dates from the 11th century and is decorated with over 30 12th- and 15th-century frescoes illustrating key events in the life of Jesus. The painting on the dome depicts Christ Pantocrator. Others show the Sacrifice of Abraham, the Entry into Jerusalem and the Ascension. The 15th-century series of paintings seen on the vaults, arches and walls depicts various scenes from the New Testament.

The second church, of **Agios Ioannis (St John) Lampadistis**, dating from the 11th century, is dedicated to the saint who was born in Lampadou. He renounced marriage in favour of the monastic life, went blind, died at the age of 22, and was canonised soon afterwards. His tomb is inside the church and the niche above contains a silver reliquary with the saint's skull. The church interior is

Monastery buildings of Agios Ioannis Lampadistis

decorated with 12th-century paintings. The richly gilded iconostasis dates from the 16th century. The narthex (portico) common to both churches, which was added in the 15th century, includes a cycle of paintings depicting the miracles of Christ.

The **Latin chapel**, added in the second half of the 15th century, is decorated with 24 magnificent Byzantine wall paintings with Greek texts written in about 1500.

Environs

The mountain village of **Kalopanagiotis** is scenically located in the Setrachos Valley. It has existed since medieval times and has retained its traditional architecture, cobbled streets, and many churches and chapels. The village is now a small spa resort with therapeutic sulphur springs (with beneficial properties for rheumatic conditions and gastric ailments). It is also known for its beautifully carved breadbaskets called *sanidha*. Kalopanagiotis is believed to be descended from ancient Lambas, which produced the local saints, Ioannis and Irakleidios. Nearby is an arched medieval bridge.

❺ Panagia tou Moutoulla

Road Map B3. 3 km (1.8 miles) from Pedoulas. Moutoullas. **Open** vary. Donations welcome.

The village of Moutoulla, situated in a valley below Pedoulas, is renowned for its mineral water spring and its tiny church of **Our Lady of Moutoulla** (Panagia tou Moutoulla) built in 1280.

This is the oldest of the Troodos mountain painted churches. Its most interesting features are the pitched roof and finely carved entrance door. Beyond these doors is another set of equally beautiful doors (wood carving has been a local speciality for centuries). Above them is the image of *Christ Enthroned*, flanked by *Adam and Eve*, and *Hell and Paradise*, with a procession of

Panoramic view of Pedoulas in the Marathassa valley

saints marching into Heaven. The cycle of paintings inside the church, illustrating key events in the life of Jesus and Mary, are similar to the wall paintings in the nearby Church of the Archangel Michael. The most distinctive of these faded paintings include *Mary with the Christ Child* in a cradle, and *St Christopher and St George Fighting the Dragon* with the head of a woman in a crown. There is also a portrait of the church founder, Ioannis Moutoullas, with his wife Irene.

Remains of a wall painting in Panagia tou Moutoulla

❻ Pedoulas

Road Map B3. 🚹 190.

This sizeable village is located in the upper part of the Marathassa valley. The Setrachos River that drains it flows down towards Morfou Bay. Pedoulas is famed for its surrounding orchards, gentle climate, bracing air and bottled spring water, which you can buy in most shops in Cyprus. The most beautiful season

here is spring, when the houses are completely enveloped by a sea of flowering cherry trees.

The most significant site in the village is the **Church of the Archangel Michael** (Archangelos Michail), dating from 1474. It is one of ten mountain churches listed as UNESCO World Cultural Heritage Sites, due to its magnificent interior wall paintings.

The paintings are unusually realistic. The north side of the tiny reading room is decorated with a painting of the Archangel Michael.

The renovated paintings are notable for their realistic images, including the *Sacrifice of Abraham*, the *Baptism in the Jordan River*, the *Kiss of Judas* and the *Betrayal of Christ in the Garden of Gethsemane*. The apse, usually decorated with an image of Christ Pantocrator, includes the Praying Mary (*Virgin Orans*) and the *Ascension*. Seen above the north entrance is the figure of the founder, Basil Chamados, handing a model of the church to the Archangel Michael.

Environs

The neighbouring village of Prodromos, which numbers only 150 inhabitants, is perched on top of a mountain range at an elevation of 1,400 m (4,593 ft). It is the highest village in Cyprus, and also, thanks to its decent accommodation facilities, a good base for starting to explore the Marathassa valley.

❸ Kykkos

This is the largest, most imposing and wealthiest of all the monasteries in Cyprus. Built in the middle of magnificent mountains and forests, away from human habitation, its most precious treasure is the icon of the Most Merciful Virgin, claimed to have been painted by St Luke and credited with the power to bring rain. The holy image is kept in the monastery museum.

12th-century Icon
The most beautiful icon in the museum's collection is this image of the Virgin and Child.

Belfry
The new belfry, with its distinctive architectural style, stands on top of a hill near the monastery.

★ **Museum's Main Hall**
The monastery museum contains some important treasures: gold and silver liturgical vessels, holy books, and embroidered vestments, as well as beautiful and precious icons.

KEY

① **The main wing** of the monastery is home to the monks' cells.

② **The rotunda** has a darkened room housing the museum's most precious exhibits – the ancient, beautiful icons.

③ **A collection of manuscripts, documents and books**

General View
The hills surrounding Kykkos afford memorable views over the small monastery church and belfry, flanked by one-storey buildings with red roof tiles.

Small Courtyard
The church courtyard leads to the monastery buildings that used to house the museum.

VISITORS' CHECKLIST

Practical Information
Road map B3. Monastery, church & museum: **Tel** 22 942 736.
Open Jun–Oct: 10am–6pm daily; Nov–May: 10am–4pm daily. 🅿 🅰 📧 🆆 kykkos.org.cy

★ Royal Doors
Inside the church is a richly decorated iconostasis incorporating the Royal Doors.

Church Entrance
The *katholicon*, or monastery church, is entered via a doorway decorated with lovely mosaics.

Main Monastery Entrance
The small but wonderfully decorated entance is covered in beautiful mosaics.

Main Courtyard
The cloisters running along the edge of the main courtyard are decorated with mosaics depicting the history of Kykkos Monastery.

7 Mount Olympus (Chionistra)

Road Map B3. 45 km (28 miles) north of Limassol. 🚌 bus from Nicosia in the summer.

Chionistra, the traditional name of Olympus, means "the snowy one". The slopes of the 1,950-m (6,400-ft) mountain are covered with umbrella-shaped pine trees interspersed with cedars and junipers. The most beautiful season here is spring, when wildflowers are in bloom. In good weather, the view from the top extends as far as the coast of Turkey.

In winter the mountain is covered with a layer of snow up to 3 m (nearly 10 ft) deep, making Mount Olympus popular with downhill skiers. The ski runs on the southern slopes of Sun Valley are short and easy, while the northern runs are much longer and considerably more difficult. There are also two cross-country trails. Equipment hire and lessons are available.

The nearest hotel and restaurant facilities are in Troodos and Platres.

Ski Station
Open Jan–Mar. 🌐 cyprusski.com

Umbrella pines on the slopes of Mount Olympus

8 Troodos

Road Map B3. 🚌 64 from Limassol. 🚠 15. 🛈 25 421 316. **Open** 8:15am–3:45pm Mon–Fri (2nd week of month: to 3pm Mon–Fri, 9am–2pm Sat). 🚗
🌐 mytroodos.com

This small resort offers a few restaurants, souvenir shops and tourist car parks. In the summer there are horse and donkey rides,

The iconostasis in Trooditissa church with the miraculous icon of Mary

while hikers have a choice of several trails. The **Visitor Centre of the Troodos National Forest Park** has a collection of local natural specimens. There is also a walk along a 300-m- (984-ft-) long botanical-geological trail and a short film about the natural environment of Troodos.

Hidden in the forest a few kilometres south is the former residence of the British governor of Cyprus, now the summer villa of the president of the Republic of Cyprus. The overseer who helped to build it in 1880 was Arthur Rimbaud, the famous French poet.

9 Trooditissa

Road Map B3. 8 km (5 miles) northwest of Platres. **Closed** to the public.

This monastery, originally founded in 1250, is surrounded by pine forests on the southern slopes of the Troodos mountains, a few kilometres west of Platres. During the Iconoclastic Wars of the 8th century, a monk brought an icon of the Virgin Mary which, according to tradition, was painted by St Luke. The icon remained hidden in a cave until 990, when it was discovered, thanks to the miraculous light emanating from it.

The present **monastery church** dates from 1731. Its carved wooden

iconostasis is covered with gold leaf. The miracle-working icon – the magnificent image of the Panagia, Queen of Heaven – is to the left of the Royal Doors, covered with a curtain of silver and gold.

The monastery, whose austere regime is similar to that of Stavrovouni (see p80), is home to a dozen or so monks.

Environs
The nearby village of **Fini** (Foini) is renowned for its traditional handicrafts, now limited to pottery studios and a workshop producing distinctive Cypriot chairs.

The private **Pilavakion Museum**, run by Theofanis Pilavakis, displays vast ceramic jugs for storing olive oil. Adjacent to Iliovasilema bar is a small shop producing the local delicacy – loukoumi (Cyprus delight) that is different from the versions made in Lefkara and Geroskipou.

Between Fini and the monastery, on a small stream running through a deep ravine where British soldiers practise climbing skills, is the picturesque **Chantara waterfall**.

Panoramic view of Fini, known for handicrafts

⑩ Platres

Road Map B3. 37 km (23 miles) northwest of Limassol. 🚌 62 from Limassol. 🔼 350. ℹ️ 25 421 316.

The most famous mountain resort in Cyprus, Platres lies on a steep bank above the Kyros stream. The location and surrounding forests give it an excellent climate, making it a favourite holiday spot for Limassol and Nicosia residents.

Several colonial-style villas serve as reminders of British rule, and the few hotels and restaurants have all been designed in the same style. The town centre consists of a single street with a post office and a square next to the tourist information office, from where buses depart for Limassol *(see p73)*.

Platres is the starting point for several nature trails. One of them is "Caledonia", which passes by the magnificent Caledonia waterfall and ends at Psilo Dendro in Platres. The other trail, "Persefoni", passing through the black pine forest offers amazing views.

⑪ Omodos

Road Map B4. 8 km (5 miles) southwest of Platres. 🔼 300. 🚌 40 from Limassol.

Scattered over the southern slopes of the Troodos mountains are the Krassochoria vine-growing villages, of which Omodos is one. Established in the 11th century, the settlement is famous for its

Courtyard of the Timiou Stavrou Monastery, in Omodos

production of wine, as well as for specialized *papilla* lace-making.

Timiou Stavrou monastery (Monastery of the Holy Cross) stands in the centre of the village. Built around 1150, it acquired its present shape in the 19th century. Timber-roofed monastic buildings surround the three-hall basilica, which contains a carved wooden iconostasis dating from 1813. According to legend, St Helena (mother of Emperor Constantine) left here a piece of the rope with which Christ was tied to the cross. The venerated relic is kept in a vast silver cross-shaped reliquary. Another holy relic, St Philip's skull, is kept in a silver casket.

There are no more monks in the village. The shops and stalls sell local *papilla* lace, silver

Famous Omodos *papilla* lace

jewellery, wine, honey and the ring-shaped *arkatena* bread typical of this village.

Environs

Vasa, a few kilometres southwest of Omodos, is a pleasant village. The Knights Hospitaller of St John, from the Kolossi commandery, were drawn to the village to escape the unbearable summer heat. The knights stayed in the monastery which once stood here. Its 14th-century church, **Agios Georgios**, survives to this day together with its interesting frescoes. The small church museum in Vasa has religious icons and liturgical objects rescued from various abandoned churches.

Vasa has pretty stone houses with red-tiled roofs and a spring flowing with pure mineral water. The village and the surrounding area offer several good restaurants where you can get simple Cypriot dishes.

The Cypriot poet Dimitris Lipertis (1866–1937) has associations with Vasa. The house in which he lived has been made into a small museum.

The nearby archaeological site has yielded several Roman tombs, and the artifacts found in them – including amphorae and jewellery – can be viewed in Nicosia at the Cyprus Museum.

🏛️ **Timiou Stavrou Monastery**
Omodos. **Open** sunrise to sunset daily.

Kingdom of Alashia

For more than 100 years scientists have been searching for the mysterious Kingdom of Alashia. According to texts preserved on clay tablets in el-Amarna, its kings corresponded with the Egyptian pharaohs. Analysis of the texts has established that the copper-rich kingdom was situated at the foot of the Troodos mountains, close to present-day Alassa, where equipment for smelting and processing copper has been discovered.

Tablet from el-Amarna describing Alashia

The Donkey Sanctuary west of Vouni

⑫ Potamiou

Road Map B4. 3.5 km (2 miles) south of Omodos.

This backwoods hamlet, reached via Omodos or Kissousa, is on an architectural par with the neighbouring village of Vouni. In summer its red-roofed stone houses vanish from view, swamped by creeping vines. The pride of the village is its small 16th-century church, Agia Marina, and the ruins of a Byzantine church standing near the Khapotami stream.

⑬ Vouni

Road Map B4. 4 km (2½ miles) south of Koilani.

In the mid-1990s this extraordinarily picturesque, partly deserted village was declared a legally protected historical site. Turned into an

open-air museum, its life now centres around a handful of *kafeneia* (local cafés) and restaurants. As you walk along the cobbled streets, take note of the signboards of the cafés and restaurants. Most of them are beautifully hand-painted.

One of the main attractions is the **Vouni Donkey Sanctuary**, to the west of the village, which is run by the charitable foundation "Friends of the Cyprus Donkey". Mary and Patrick Skinner founded the sanctuary in 1994 with just six donkeys; today they care for about 120 elderly, sick and abandoned animals. During the grape-harvest season, strong and healthy animals are hired out to the local farmers to help them collect the grapes.

Vouni Donkey Sanctuary
Vouni. **Tel** 25 945 488.
donkeysanctuarycyprus.org

⑭ Koilani

Road Map B4.

Another tiny mountain village built on lime soil, Koilani has excellent conditions for growing grape vines and fruit trees. The scenic location, surrounded by lush vineyards, makes up for its shortage of historic sites.

A small two-room **museum** set up behind the Neo-Byzantine church of Panagia Eloussa houses a collection of icons and other religious objects gathered from old churches in the area. For a period during the 17th century, the Limassol archbishopric was based in Koilani.

Close to the village in the valley of the Kyros stream, on the site of a former monastery, is the 12th-century domed **chapel of Agia Mavris**, which was subsequently extended. Its interior, including the domed vault, is decorated with rather unsophisticated wall paintings.

Men whiling away the afternoon in the centre of Koilani

⑮ Lofou

Road Map B4. 26 km (16 miles) northwest of Limassol.

This gorgeous village lies hidden amid the vineyards that cover the hillsides of the Commandaria region. The south-facing slopes and the abundance of water from the nearby Kourris and Kyros rivers produce local grapes that are large and sweet.

Lofou village spreads atop a limestone hill (*lofos* means hill). Its buildings represent the traditional stone-and-timber architecture typical of Cyprus mountain villages.

The Wines of Cyprus

"The sweetness of your love is like Cyprus wine", wrote Mark Antony, offering Cyprus to Cleopatra as a wedding present. To this day various wines, including the sweet Commandaria, are produced on the island and continue to receive international acclaim. Although wines made from known grape varieties, such as Cabernet Sauvignon and Shiraz, are available here, it is worth trying some of the island's indigenous varieties. Maratheftiko, an ancient grape variety grown here, produces full-bodied red wines with rich aromas and flavours. Another indigenous variety, Xinisteri, is used to make floral- and fruity-flavoured white wines.

Wine barrels in Koilani

Towering above the village is the white silhouette of the **Church of the Annunciation**, with a tall, slender belfry. The present church was built in the late 19th century. Inside, among many beautiful icons, is a 16th-century image of the Mother of God.

References to Lofou appear in records dating from the Lusignan period, when it was called Loffu, but the village is probably much older, existing already in the Byzantine era.

Lofou can be reached from the north, via Pera Pedi village, or by a rough track (suitable only for four-wheel-drive vehicles) from Monagri, to the east.

Environs
The attractions of **Silikou** village, situated north of Lofou, include an olive press museum and some interesting examples of 14th-century frescoes in the Timios Stavros church.

⓰ Monagri

Road map B4. 21 km (13 miles) northwest of Limassol.

Rising above the vine covered hills and the Kouris valley are the walls of the **Archangelos monastery**. Built in the 10th century on the ruins of an ancient temple, the monastery was rebuilt in the mid-18th century after a tragic fire. The monastery church features a number of lovely wall paintings, some of them by Filaretos – the creator of the magnificent paintings adorning the cathedral church of John the Theologian (Agios Ioannis) in Nicosia. There are also reminders of Ottoman times, when the new rulers converted the church into a mosque, including the geometric *mihrab* decorations, unique in

View of the hilltop Lofou village

Cyprus. The two Corinthian columns that support the portico probably date from the Roman era. The church has a carved, painted iconostasis.

Environs
A few kilometres downstream from Monagri, on the west bank of the river, is the 12th-century convent church of **Panagia tis Amasgou**, one of several Byzantine churches in the Kouris valley, near Limassol. It features beautiful but unrestored frescoes, created between the 12th and 16th centuries. These can be viewed, thanks to the generosity of the resident nuns.

The **Kouris dam**, down the river, is one of the largest structures of its kind in Cyprus. The reservoir collects rainwater used for domestic supplies and for irrigating fields and vineyards.

Situated along the main road leading from Limassol to the Troodos mountains is **Trimiklini** village. Hidden behind its church is a charming, tiny old stone chapel in a cemetery.

On the east side of the road, amid vineyards, lies another vine-growing village, **Laneia** (Lania). Its well-preserved and lovingly maintained old houses are set along narrow winding streets. Standing in the village centre is a white church with a tall belfry and next to it are two pretty cafés. Laneia and its surrounding villages are home to local artists.

🏠 **Archangelos Monastery**
Monagri. **Tel** 25 362 756.
Open by prior arrangement.

🏠 **Panagia tis Amasgou**
Tel as above. **Open** as above.

Neo-Classical school building in Lofou

⓱ Timios Stavros

Road Map B3. 8 km (5 miles) southwest of Agros. **Open** times vary. Donations welcome.

The design of Timios Stavros (Holy Cross) church is different from that of other Cypriot churches. Standing on the lakeshore, at the southern end of the village, this three-aisled edifice was built on a square plan and topped with a slender dome on four columns.

Opposite the entrance are the portraits of the church's founders, as well as their coats-of-arms, and the figure of the apostle Doubting Thomas. The painting to the right depicts the lineage of Jesus. The series of 14 preserved paintings above the pulpit illustrates the life of Mary, including the *Nativity* and the *Presentation of Jesus at the Temple*, with figures dressed in Lusignan-period costumes.

The iconostasis includes a silver reliquary containing fragments of the True Cross, for which the church is named.

⓲ Pelendri

Road Map B3. 8 km (5 miles) southwest of Agros, 32 km (20 miles) from Limassol. 🚌 60, 66 from Limassol.

In the Middle Ages, this village on the southern slopes of the

Fragment of a painting in Timios Stavros church

Troodos mountains was the seat of Jean de Lusignan, son of Hugo V (the Franconian King of Cyprus).

At the centre of the village is the **Panagia Katholiki** church, dating from the early 16th century, which has Italian-Byzantine-style paintings.

It is worth taking the nature trail **Moni-Fylagra** that starts from the Trimiklini-Pelendri road, passes through pine forests and ends at the Fylagra river.

⓳ Agios Nikolaos tis Stegis

Road Map B3. 3 km (2 miles) southwest of Kakopetria. **Tel** 22 922 583. **Open** 9am–4pm Tue–Sat, 11am–4pm Sun. Donations welcome.

This stone church, built in the form of a cross, supports a double roof, giving it the name St Nicholas of the Roof. The oldest section of the building dates from the 11th century; the dome and narthex were added a hundred years later, and in the 15th century the entire structure was covered with a huge ridge roof. This outer roof was designed to protect the building from snow, which falls here occasionally.

The church once served as the chapel of a monastery, no longer in existence. Inside, you can

see some of the oldest wall paintings anywhere in the Troodos mountain churches. Painted over a period of about 500 years, between the 11th and the 15th centuries, they demonstrate the evolution of Orthodox religious art, making this church an excellent place to study the development of Byzantine wall painting.

Along with paintings from the early Byzantine period, known as "hieratic" or "monastic" styles influenced by the art of Syria and Cappadocia, you can also see typical Komnenos and Paleologos art styles. During the Komnenos dynasty (1081–1180), the Byzantine style, which had been rigid and highly formalized up to that point, began to move towards realism and emotional expression in the figures and in their settings.

The artists who created the wall paintings during the Paleologos dynasty continued to display similar attention to the emotional and aesthetic qualities of their art.

Paintings inside the church illustrate scenes from the New Testament. Among the earliest paintings here are the *Entry to Jerusalem*, and the warrior saints George and Theodore brandishing their panoply of arms. The ceiling of the main vault depicts the **Transfiguration of the Lord** on Mount Tabor and the **Raising of Lazarus** from

Interior of Timios Stavros church

◀ Mountain village in Troodos

the dead, conveying the startling impression the events made on the disciples of Jesus and the relatives of Lazarus.

The **Crucifixion** in the north transept shows the Sun and Moon personified weeping over the fate of the dying Jesus. A painting of the **Resurrection**, depicts the women coming to visit the grave and being informed of Christ's resurrection by an angel at the empty tomb. The painting dates from the Lusignan period.

The **Nativity** in the south transept vault shows the Virgin Mary breastfeeding the Christ Child. Painted around it is an idyllic scene with pipe-playing shepherds and animals. Adjacent is a shocking 12th-century painting of the 40 **Martyrs of Sebaste** – Roman soldiers who adopted Christianity and were killed for it – being pushed by soldiers into the freezing waters of an Anatolian lake. In the dome vault is an image of **Christ Pantocrator**.

A picturesque narrow street in old Kakopetria

⍟ Kakopetria

Road Map B3. 80 km (50 miles) from Nicosia.

This old village in the Solea region, in the valley of the Kargotis river, displays interesting stone architecture. At an elevation of 600 m (1,968 ft), its climate is mild enough to allow the cultivation of grapes. Besides wine, Kakopetria was once renowned for its production of silk. Now it is a weekend retreat for Nicosia residents. The village derives its

Agios Nikolaos tis Stegis, featuring magnificent wall paintings

name "Accursed Rocks" from the rocks which, during an earthquake, once killed a great number of people.

The surrounding district has several intriguing churches and chapels, including the **Archangelos** church which dates from 1514, covered with a ridge roof. It is decorated with paintings depicting the life of Jesus. The paintings in the **Agios Georgios** church are influenced by folk tradition.

⍟ Panagia tis Podithou

Road Map B3. Panagia tis Podithou: Galata. **Open** collect key from café on the village square. **Tel** 22 922 394. Donations welcome.

Dating from 1502, this church is also known as Panagia Elousa (Our Lady of Mercy). Originally, it was a monastery church dedicated to St Eleanor. Later, it belonged to the Venetian family of Coro. The wall paintings that decorate the church date from the Venetian period. Created by Simeon Axenti, their style betrays both Byzantine and Italian influences. They are an example of the strong influence that Western art exerted at that time on Cypriot decorative art. The poignant **Crucifixion** is particularly interesting, painted within a triangle and revealing Italian influences. Mary

Magdalene can be seen at the foot of the cross, her hair loose, alongside a Roman soldier and the two crucified thieves. The **Communion of the Apostles** in the apse is flanked by the figures of two kings: Solomon and David. The painting in the narthex depicts **Our Lady the Queen of Heaven**; painted below it is the image of the church's founder – Dimitrios Coro – with his wife.

It is worth spending some time visiting the early 16th-century church **Agios Sozomenos**, with its cycle of folk-style wall paintings created in 1513, also by Simeon Axenti. Take a closer look at the painting depicting St George fighting the dragon, whose tail is entwined around the hind legs of the knight's horse, as well as the image of St Mamas riding a lion while carrying a lamb in his arms. The nearby church of **Agia Paraskevi** features the remains of some 1514 wall paintings, probably created by a disciple of Axenti.

The charming church of Panagia tis Podithou

For hotels and restaurants in this region see p164 and pp173–4

Fresco in Panagia Forviotissa church

㉒ Panagia Forviotissa (Panagia tis Asinou)

Road Map B3. 5 km (3 miles) southwest of Nikitari village. **Tel** 99 830 329. **Open** 9:30am–1pm, 2–4pm Mon–Sat, 10am–4pm Sun & public hols. Donations welcome.

Beyond the village of Nikitari, the road climbing towards the Troodos mountains leads through a dark forest and into a valley overgrown with pine trees. Here, on a wooded hillside, stands the small 12th-century church of Panagia Forviotissa, also known as Panagia tis Asinou. With its red tiled roof, this church dedicated to Our Lady of the Meadows is listed as a UNESCO World Cultural Heritage Site.

The church was founded in 1206 by Nikiforos Maistros, a high-ranking Byzantine official, portrayed in the paintings inside. At first glance the building, with its rough stone walls and simple ridge roof, does not resemble a church. However, this humble one-room structure hides a number of genuine treasures. There are frescoes dating from the 12th to the 16th centuries, which were restored in the 1960s and 1970s.

The wall and ceiling decorations are among the finest examples of Byzantine frescoes, starting with the Christ Pantocrator (Ruler of the World) on the vault of the narthex. There are also figures of the apostles, saints, prophets and martyrs. The following frescoes date from 1105: the *Baptism in the Jordan River*, the *Raising of Lazarus*, the *Last Supper*, the

Crucifixion and the *Resurrection*. They were painted by artists from Constantinople who represented the Komnenos style.

Altogether there are over 100 frescoes here, illustrating various religious themes. It is worth taking a closer look at the extraordinarily realistic painting covering the westernmost recess of the vault – the *Forty Martyrs of Sebaste*. Next to this are the *Pentecost* and the *Raising of Lazarus*.

The cycle of paintings in the nave illustrates the life of Jesus, from the Nativity to the Crucifixion and Resurrection. Seen in the apse is the *Communion of the Apostles*; Jesus offers the Eucharist to his disciples, with Judas standing aside.

The best paintings include the *Dormition of the Virgin*, above the west entrance, and the terrifying vision of the *Last Judgment*. Above the south entrance is a portrait of the founder, Nikiforos Maistros, presenting a model of the church to Christ.

The narthex offers further surprises. The moufflon and two hunting dogs on the arch of the door herald the arrival of the Renaissance; Byzantine iconography did not employ animals. Here, too, is another image of the church founders, praying to the Virgin and Child, with Christ Pantocrator surrounded by the Apostles. Between 1965 and 1976, the frescoes underwent a process

of meticulous cleaning and restoration, under the supervision of Harvard University Byzantine art experts.

Environs

The village of **Vyzakia**, some 6 km (4 miles) down the valley from Panagia Forviotissa, is worth visiting to see the small, wooden-roofed Byzantine **Church of the Archangel Michael** with its frescoes depicting the life and the martyrdom of Jesus. Dating from the early 16th century, these wall paintings reveal a strong Venetian influence.

The little 12th-century church of Panagia Forviotissa

㉓ Panagia tou Araka

Road Map C3. Lagoudera. **Tel** 99 557 369. **Open** 9am–noon, 2–5pm daily. Donations welcome. 📷 Feast of the Birth of the Virgin (6–7 Sep).

The 12th-century church of Panagia tou Araka stands between the villages of Lagoudera and Saranti. Its interior is decorated with some of the island's most beautiful frescoes, painted in 1192 by Leon Authentou, who arrived from Constantinople and worked in

Panagia tou Araka Church, surrounded by mountains

Christ Pantocrator fresco in the
Church of Panagia tou Araka

the aristocratic Komnenos style.
This church contains some of
the most interesting examples
of pure Byzantine art in Cyprus.

The most magnificent of the
paintings depicts Christ
Pantocrator in a blue
robe, surrounded by
images of angels and
prophets. In the apse
are images of 12 early
Christian saints,
including St Barnabas,
the patron saint of
Cyprus. Above them
is the Virgin Mary
enthroned, with the
Child Jesus on her
knees, flanked by the
Archangels Gabriel and Michael.

Another interesting fresco is
the *Birth*, showing the Infant
Jesus being bathed, watched by
angels, shepherds, a flock of
sheep and a white donkey.

The small, richly carved and
gilded iconostasis contains
only four icons. On the right
is a larger-than-life painting of
the Madonna of the Passion
(*Panagia Arakiotissa*), to whom
the church is dedicated.

Environs

The mountain hamlet of **Spilia**
has a splendidly preserved oil
press housed in a stone building.
In the central square are
monuments commemorating
the EOKA combatants who
fought the British, blowing
themselves up in a nearby
hideout used to produce
bombs. Some 2 km (1.2 miles) to
the north of Spilia, in the village
of **Kourdali**, is a three-aisle
basilica, **Koimisis tis Panagias**,

Relief from Panagia
tou Araka

which once belonged to a
former monastery. Inside, the
Italian-Byzantine wall paintings
depict figures dressed in
Venetian clothes. The Virgin,
fainting at the foot of the
cross, wears a dress with
exposed shoulders. Other
interesting paintings here
include: *Doubting Thomas*, the
Praying Virgin (Virgin Orans) and
the *Dormition of the Blessed Virgin*.
The best times to visit are 14–15
August, which are local feast days.

Another site worth visiting is
the diminutive **Church of
Timiou Stavrou** in **Agia Eirini**,
which contains more paintings
depicting the life and death of
Jesus. It also has a deisis – an
image of the Mother of God
and John the Baptist sitting
on both sides of Christ, who
holds in his hand
the prophecy
pronouncing him
the Messiah and
adjudicator on the Day
of the Last Judgment.
An attractive local
walk leads along the
Madhari ridge to the
top of **Mount Adhelfi**,
at 1,612 m (5,288 ft).
From here there is a
stunning panoramic view over
the Troodos mountain region.

㉔ Stavros tou Agiasmati

Road map C3. 6 km (3½ miles) north
of Platanistasa. **Open** times vary; collect
key from custodian in the coffee shop.
Donations welcome. 🎨 13 & 14 Sep.

A rough road leads to this small
church, in an isolated setting on
the mountainside of Madhari.
Originally built as the chapel for
an older monastery, its low

main door was designed to
prevent Arab and Turkish
invaders from entering on
horseback, a common way
of desecrating churches.

Inside Stavros tou Agiasmati
is the island's most complete
cycle of paintings illustrating
the Gospel. Some parts refer
to the Old Testament. Another
cycle of paintings illustrates
the story of the Holy Cross.
Together they form a fine
assemblage of 15th-
century frescoes.

The church's interior is
divided into two horizontal
zones of paintings: the lower
zone displays life-size figures
of the saints while the upper
zone has 24 scenes from the
New Testament.

Behind the iconostasis, the
apse features a magnificent
image of the Virgin uniting
Heaven and Earth. Some of the
paintings depict scenes not
known anywhere else, like the
fresco of the *Last Supper* in
which only Christ is present; or
the *Raising of Lazarus* in which a
group of Jews is clearly
offended by the smell of the
resurrected Lazarus. The fresco
of *Peter's Denial* includes a
shockingly large image of a
rooster. One of the niches in the
north wall features a series of
ten paintings that illustrate the
discovery of the Holy Cross by
St Helena, the mother of the
Emperor Constantine. The
frescoes are partly the work of
Philip Goul, a Lebanese artist
who is characterized by his
spare yet profound style.

Standing in the north wall
niche is a magnificently
decorated cross, which gives
Stavros tou Agiasmati (Church
of the Holy Cross) its name.

Stavros tou Agiasmati church, in its remote mountainside location

CENTRAL CYPRUS

With the exception of the divided city of Nicosia, the heartland of Cyprus remains surprisingly unexplored by visitors. The plains are covered with colourful carpets of cultivated fields, crisscrossed by roads that link the small villages. They descend radially towards Nicosia *(see pp116–35)*, whose suburbs sprawl across the Pentadaktylos range. The eastern part of the Troodos mountains – the Pitsillia area is – incorporated in this region.

The vast plain on Mesaoria (meaning "the land between mountains") is a gently undulating area dotted with small towns and old-fashioned villages. The watchtowers and fences occasionally seen from the road are reminders of the "Green Line" – the buffer zone border. The defunct airport to the west of Nicosia once provided international service.

Central Cyprus is the island's least developed region from a tourist's point of view. It is almost devoid of hotels and restaurants, although here and there you can find a small agrotourism farm or a *kafeneion* – a local café. Tourists usually visit this region on their way to the beautiful Troodos mountains, or to the bustling seaside resorts in the south.

The most interesting historical sites of central Cyprus are the ruins of ancient Tamassos and Idalion. Tamassos, which was established around 4000 BC, grew rich thanks to the copper ore deposits discovered nearby. Today, items made of this metal are among the most popular souvenirs from this region.

Also of interest are the convent of Agios Irakleidios, the unusual subterranean Church of Panagia Chrysospiliotissa and Machairas monastery on the northeastern slopes of the Troodos mountains, in the Pitsillia area. Nearby are the mountain villages of Fikardou, Lazanias and Gourri, and further south the town of Agros, which is famous for its roses.

Roadside vineyard in central Cyprus

◄ Panagia tou Machaira monastery and church, Troodos

Exploring Central Cyprus

Central Cyprus, stretching south of Nicosia and covering the Pitsillia area of the eastern Troodos mountains, has limited facilities for visitors. Nevertheless, when travelling to the Troodos mountains or Nicosia it is worth exploring this region, especially the ruins of ancient Tamassos, the centre of the copper-producing area since the Bronze Age. Peristerona, home to one of the most beautiful Byzantine churches in Cyprus, as well as a fine mosque, is well worth a visit. Life proceeds slowly in the picturesque villages, with their bougainvillea-clad houses.

The lively Dali municipality, near ancient Idalion

Getting There

Central Cyprus is easily accessible. From Larnaka airport the A2 motorway runs inland towards Nicosia. From the main port in Limassol, a motorway follows the coastline and branches off as the A1 road towards Nicosia. The route from Pafos airport leads through the mountains. The road is good, and you can combine the journey with a tour of the Troodos mountains.

For hotels and restaurants in this region see p164 and pp174–5

Peristerona Mosque, one of the oldest and finest mosques in Cyprus

The gleaming Royal Doors in Archangelos Michael church

Sights at a Glance

1 Peristerona
2 Archangelos Michael
3 Panagia Chrysospiliotissa
4 Agios Irakleidios Monastery
5 Tamassos
6 Perachorio
7 Idalion
8 Potamia
9 Machairas
10 Palaichori
11 Agros
12 Louvaras

Key

═══ Motorway
▬▬▬ Major road
▬▬ Secondary road
······ Minor road
▬▬ Scenic route
– – Track
▬▬ Regional border
■ ■ Green Line

For additional map symbols *see back flap*

❻ Pera Chorio

Road Map C3. 17 km (10½ miles) south of Nicosia.

The small village of Pera Chorio is the setting of the hilltop **Church of the Holy Apostles** (Agioi Apostoloi). This domed, single-aisle building has several side chapels.

The church, in a scenic setting, conceals fragments of beautiful 12th-century frescoes, in a style similar to those in the church of Panagia Forviotissa *(see p104)*. Experts regard these as the best examples of the Komnenos style anywhere on the island. The most interesting are the images of angels in the dome, below the damaged painting depicting Christ Pantocrator. Another interesting painting shows two shepherds conversing casually, their shoulder bags hanging from a tree, while the infant Jesus is bathed. The apse features a picture of the Virgin, flanked by St Peter and St Paul. Also depicted are saints, martyrs, emperors and demons.

Nearby is the 16th-century church of Agios Dimitrios.

The ancient Church of the Holy Apostles in Pera Chorio

❼ Idalion

Road Map D3. 20 km (12 miles) south of Nicosia. 🎭 Adonis Festival (spring).

The ancient Idalion, whose remains can be seen in the present-day municipality of Dali, was one of the oldest city-states on the island. According to legend, it was founded by King Chalcanor, a Trojan War hero.

The town is built on top of two hills; only a small portion of its ruins has so far been unearthed, including tombs along the road to Larnaka. Idalion existed from the Bronze Age up to about 1400 BC. The town had 14 temples, including those dedicated to Aphrodite, Apollo and Athena. Archaeological excavations are still under way. The best artifacts can be seen in the Cyprus Museum in Nicosia.

The remains of Idalion had already sparked interest in the 19th century. The American consul, Luigi Palma di Cesnola, plundered thousands of tombs in this area, robbing them of all their valuable items. Local farmers also found large numbers of votive figurines of Aphrodite while working in the fields, which indicates that this was a major site of the cult of Aphrodite, the most important Cypriot goddess.

Legend tells of Aphrodite's love for Adonis, son of Zeus and Hera. Ares, the jealous god of war, turned himself into a wild boar and killed Adonis in a nearby forest. Each spring, millions of red poppies and anemones cover the area, said to spring from his blood.

Ruins of the ancient city-state of Idalion, near present-day Dali

A stone church in the Potamia area

❽ Potamia

Road Map D3.

Situated close to the Green Line, the little village of Potamia is one of the few places in the south with a small Turkish community. The village has a history of coexistence and today elects both a Greek- and a Turkish-Cypriot mayor.

Not far from the village are the ruins of the Lusignan kings' summer palace, and several Gothic churches.

Environs

The surrounding area is not of great interest, due to the many factories and industrial estates built in the immediate vicinity of Nicosia. To the southwest of the derelict village of **Agios Sozomenos** are the ruins of **Agios Mamas** church, built in the Franco-Byzantine style. This is one of the best Gothic historic sites on the island. Construction began in the early 15th century, in the Gothic style which was prevalent on the island at that time. However, it was never completed. Today visitors can see the walls of the three-apsed aisles, separated by intricate arcades, and the monumental portico.

The village of Agios Sozomenos was abandoned early in 1964, when Greek Cypriot police attacked the village inhabited by Turkish Cypriots in retaliation for the killing of two Greeks. Both sides suffered severe losses. The stone wall surrounding the village is a reminder of these events.

Cypriot Church Frescoes

The shady, forested valleys of the Troodos mountains hide small Byzantine churches; ten of these have been named UNESCO World Cultural Heritage Sites. Along with a few other churches and chapels throughout the island, they conceal frescoes representing some of the most magnificent masterpieces of Byzantine art. In keeping with Orthodox canons, the interiors are divided according to theological order. The dome symbolizes Heaven, presided over by Christ Pantocrator, the Ruler of the World, usually surrounded by archangels and prophets. Below are the main scenes from the New Testament, including the saints and fathers of the Church. The apse behind the altar features an image of the Virgin with Child. The portico usually contains the Last Judgment, painted above the exit.

Christ Pantocrator
Often painted within the dome, the Omnipotent King of the World looks down from heaven. His right hand is raised in a gesture of benediction; his left hand holds a book as a symbol of the Law.

The Life of Jesus and Mary
The life of the Holy Family has been depicted in many frescoes, as illustrations of the New Testament.

Agios Mamas
Mamas is one of the most celebrated and popular of all Cypriot saints. His name has been given to many churches throughout the island.

The Praying Virgin (Virgin Orans)
Mary raises her hands towards heaven in a pleading gesture. Her eyes are turned towards the people, urging them to trust in Christ.

The 40 Martyrs of Sebaste
In the early days of Christianity, many followers suffered death for their faith. These men, despite being subjected to freezing temperatures and then fire, held to their faith and were martyred.

The Way of the Cross
The images of the way of the cross and the Lord's Passion are among the most dramatic subjects for fresco painters.

❾ Machairas Monastery

Road Map C3. 41 km (25 miles) southwest of Nicosia. **Tel** 22 359 334 **Open** 8:30am–5:30pm daily (groups only 9am–noon Mon, Tue & Thu).

On the northern slopes of the Troodos mountains, in the area known as Pitsillia, stands one of Cyprus' most famous monasteries – Machairas (Panagia tou Machaira). The monastery rises like a fortress from the mountainside of Kionia, almost 800 m (2,625 ft) above sea level. Its name originates from the word *mahera*, which means "knife" and probably derives from the knife found next to an icon hidden in a cave. Two hermits from Palestine found the icon in the cave, and then built a church dedicated to the Virgin Mary in 1148. In 1187, Emperor Manuel Komnenos provided the funds to build a bigger church; he also exempted it from the jurisdiction of the local bishop.

The monastery buildings in their present form date from the early 20th century. The beautiful church, surrounded by cloisters, contains numerous beautiful and well-preserved icons and cult objects. A Gospel printed in Venice in 1588, is held in the treasury. The monks are extremely pious; their vows are as severe as those taken by the brothers from Mount Athos in Greece.

For Cypriots, this place is associated with EOKA commander Grigorios Afxentiou, who hid here disguised as a monk. British soldiers ambushed him in a nearby bunker. His comrades surrendered, but Afxentiou chose to fight and resisted the attacks of 60 British soldiers for several hours. Only flame-throwers could put an end to this heroic battle. On the spot where Afxentiou fell now stands a larger-than-life statue depicting the hero.

View of Palaichori village

Environs
Beyond the village of Lythrodontas, where the paved road ends, is a small monastery dedicated to the Prophet Elijah (Prophitis Elias), hidden in the Machairas Forest.

❿ Palaichori

Road Map C3.

The village of Palaichori lies in a deep valley, near the source of the Peristerona river. The village and the surrounding area feature several churches and chapels, but the most interesting of these is the **Metamorfosis tou Sotiros chapel**. Erected in the early 16th century, this small church is decorated with frescoes. On the south wall is the scene that gives the chapel its name. It shows a luminous figure of Christ, with prophets and disciples, atop Tabor Mountain at the time of the Transfiguration.

Lions are the predominant motif of the remaining paintings: in the den with Daniel, preparing to bury the body of St Mary the Beatified of Egypt and, finally, St Mamas riding a particularly elongated predator *(see p115)*.

Environs
The three picturesque villages of **Fikardou**, **Gourri** and **Lazanias** at the eastern end of the Pitsillia area form a legally protected conservation zone, due to their unique traditional architecture. The largest number of typical folk buildings have survived in Fikardou, which now looks more like an open-air museum than a village. The village was declared a monument of national culture by Europa Nostra in 1987, for being the best example of rural architecture from the past few centuries. It has narrow alleys paved with stone, and neat little timber houses, two-storeys high, with wooden balconies. The old houses of Katsinioros

Courtyard of the Machairas monastery

and Achilleas Dimitri, which are some of the loveliest in the village, have been turned into a **Rural Museum** with a collection of tools and period furnishings. They include a loom, distillery equipment and an olive press.

🏛 Rural Museum
Fikardou. **Tel** 22 634 731.
Open Apr–Oct: 9am–5pm daily ; Nov–Mar: 8am–4pm daily. 🖼

⓫ Agros

Road Map C3. 🚌 66 from Limassol.

Agros is a large village lying at an altitude about 1,000 m (3,280 ft) above sea level, in the picturesque Pitsillia area. The village is famous for its delicious cold meats, particularly its sausages and hams, as well as its fruit preserves and products made of rose petals. The locally cultivated Damask rose is said to have been brought here by the father of Chris Tsolakis, in 1948. Chris now owns a small factory of rose products, making rose water, liqueur, rose wine, rose-petal jam and rose-scented candles. Rose petals are harvested in the summer months.

The charms of Agros and its environs are promoted enthusiastically by Lefkos Christodoulu, who runs the largest local hotel – Rodon.

His efforts have resulted in the creation of numerous walking trails. The neighbourhood is home to several Byzantine churches decorated with frescoes. Agros itself has no historic sights. The old monastery, which stood here until 1894, was pulled down by the villagers in a dispute with the local bishop. Agros boasts an excellent climate, reputedly good for a long lifespan.

Interior of the Chapel of St Mamas, Louvaras, with frescoes of Jesus' life

⓬ Louvaras

Road Map C4. 25 km (15½ miles) north of Limassol.

Louvaras is a small village situated among the hills. The local attraction is the **Chapel of St Mamas**, decorated with exquisite late-15th-century frescoes depicting scenes from the life of Jesus. They include

Detail of a colourful fresco from St Mamas chapel

the *Teaching in the Temple*, *Meeting with the Samaritan Woman at the Well*, and the *Resurrection*, in which the guards wear medieval suits of armour. The figures above the door, dressed in Lusignan clothes, are likely to represent the original donors.

St Mamas is one of the most popular Cypriot saints. He is portrayed on the north wall riding a lion while cradling a lamb in his arms. The scene is associated with an interesting legend. Mamas, a hermit, was ordered to pay taxes by the local governor. He refused to do so, claiming to live solely from alms. The governor lost patience and ordered Mamas to be thrown in jail. As the guards led Mamas away, a lion leapt from the bushes and attacked a lamb grazing peacefully nearby. The saint commanded the lion to stop, took the lamb into his arms and continued his journey on the back of the chastened lion. Seeing this miracle, the governor freed St Mamas, who became the patron saint of tax-evaders.

The village of Agros, scenically located among the hills

SOUTH NICOSIA

Near the centre of the island, Nicosia (Lefkosia in Greek) is Europe's only divided capital city. The numerous historic sights and traditional atmosphere of South Nicosia have been carefully preserved. The Old Town lies within imposing defence walls erected by the Venetians in the 16th century. In the evenings, the narrow streets fill with strolling crowds of Cypriots and tourists alike, who come to dine and socialize in the buzzing streets and neighbourhoods of the Old Town.

Nicosia is the business and financial centre of the Republic of Cyprus, as well as its seat of government, home to the president. It is composed of three districts: the Old Town, the modern city, and the sprawling suburbs where most families live, extending beyond the city far into the Mesaoria valley.

The charming Old Town, with its narrow streets, is surrounded by Venetian walls stretching for 4.5 km (3 miles). The walls are punctuated by 11 bastions and three gates. The Porta Giuliana (Famagusta Gate) houses a Cultural Centre. Visitors heading for the border foot-crossing to Turkish-controlled North Nicosia (near the Ledra Palace Hotel) are greeted by the grim Pafos Gate, near the

demarcation line. Crossing the border is much easier these days thanks to the partial lifting of restrictions.

The Laiki Geitonia district, east of Eleftheria Square (Plateia Eleftherias), has narrow, winding alleys filled with restaurants, art galleries and boutiques set between traditional houses, typical of Cypriot urban architecture. Ledra and Onasagorou streets are prestigious pedestrian precincts with smart boutiques, restaurants and bars. One of the crossings to North Cyprus is located here. At the heart of Nicosia stands the Archbishop's Palace.

South Nicosia has a wide range of museums that are worth a visit, including the wonderful Cyprus Museum.

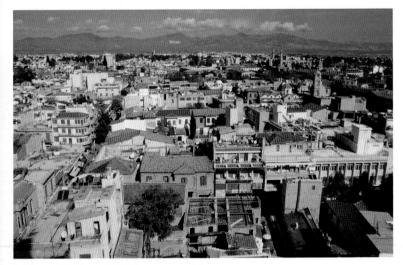

Rooftop view of the tightly packed Nicosia area

◀ Laiki Geitonia in the Old Town area

Exploring South Nicosia

The majority of historical sights in Nicosia are found within the mighty town walls. The main attractions, not to be missed, are the Cyprus Museum, the Archbishop's Palace and St John's Cathedral. The latter contains pristine 18th-century frescoes on Biblical themes. The Cyprus Museum holds the island's largest collection of archaeological artifacts, gathered from many sites. The bustling Ledra and Onasagorou streets and the surrounding neighbourhood provide a wide choice of food and drink options with numerous cafés, restaurants, bars and tavernas. The Cyprus Tourism Organization also offers free tours of the capital *(see p125).*

5th-century BC figurine from the Cyprus Museum

Key

▬▬ City wall

▦▦ Pedestrianized street

Church in South Nicosia

Getting There

You can reach South Nicosia via the A2 motorway from Larnaka international airport, or the A1 motorway from Limassol port. The town stands against the backdrop of the Pentadaktylos mountain range, situated on the Turkish side of the border. A good, wide road leads through the suburbs almost to the centre of Nicosia. You can cross the border to North Nicosia at the Ledra Palace Hotel and Ledra Street.

A decorated shutter from the Ethnological Museum, Hadjigeorgakis Kornesios House

Sights at a Glance

1. The National Struggle Museum
2. Folk Art Museum
3. Archbishop Makarios Cultural Centre
4. Cathedral of St John the Theologian
5. Hadjigeorgakis Kornesios House
6. Omar Mosque
7. Panagia Chrysaliniotissa
8. Centre of Visual Arts and Research
9. Famagusta Gate
10. Constanza Bastion
11. Town Hall
12. Laiki Geitonia
13. Leventis Museum
14. Tripiotis Church
15. Bank of Cyprus Cultural Foundation
16. Araplar Mosque
17. Cyprus Museum
18. A. G. Leventis Gallery
19. State Gallery of Contemporary Art

For additional map symbols see back flap

0 metres   200
0 yards   200

Street-by-Street: South Nicosia

South Nicosia is surrounded by Venetian defence walls and bastions, and has served as the capital since the 11th century. During the Lusignan era, this was a magnificent city, home of the Royal Palace and scores of churches. Today, the area within the old walls is full of museums, sacred buildings and historical buildings, which help to recreate the atmosphere of bygone centuries. It is enjoyable to stroll along the streets of old Nicosia, stopping for coffee, or taking a shopping trip to the rebuilt district of Laiki Geitonia.

❸ Archbishop Makarios Cultural Centre
The island's largest, most precious collection of magnificent icons and mosaics is housed here.

Richly decorated
19th-century houses are the pride of the southern part of the Old Town.

← Laiki Geitonia

The Archbishop's Palace
was built in 1956-60 in Neo-Byzantine style.

❻ Omar Mosque
A former Augustinian church was converted into a mosque in 1571, following the capture of the city by Ottomans. It is the largest mosque in southern Cyprus.

❺ Hadjigeorgakis Kornesios House
This historic 18th-century building, a former home of the Cypriot dragoman, was awarded the Europa Nostra Prize following its restoration. Now it houses a small Ethnological Museum.

❷ Folk Art Museum
The highlight here is the collection of 19th- and early-20th-century Cypriot folk art. The textiles, ceramics, wooden artifacts and folk costumes are housed in the Old Archbishop's Palace.

Locator Map
See pp118–19

❶ The National Struggle Museum
Here are documents, photographs and weapons associated with the struggle for independence from 1955 to 1959.

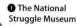

Liberty Monument
on the Podocataro Bastion symbolizes the liberation of the Cypriot nation.

❹ Cathedral of St John the Theologian
Erected by Archbishop Nikiforos, this small church contains beautiful 18th-century frescoes.

Key

— Suggested route

❶ The National Struggle Museum

Plateia Archiepiskopou Kyprianou.
Tel 22 305 878. **Open** 8:30am–2:30pm
Mon–Fri.

Housed in a building just behind the Old Archbishop's Palace is The National Struggle Museum. Its collection of photographs, documents, weapons and other objects chronicles the bloody struggle of the EOKA organization against the colonial British army from 1955 to 1959. The exhibits illustrate the fights carried out by EOKA against the British.

The collection also includes materials documenting British reprisals, including arrests, interrogations and torture. The museum is primarily intended for Cypriots and school groups.

Façade of The National Struggle Museum

The Folk Art Museum, housed in the Old Archbishop's Palace

❷ Folk Art Museum

Plateia Achiepiskopou Kyprianou.
Tel 22 432 578. **Open** 9:30am–4pm
Mon–Fri, 9am–1pm Sat.

Behind the cathedral is the Old Archbishop's Palace, which now houses the Folk Art Museum. On display here is a diverse array of exhibits illustrating the culture of Cyprus. Outside, the main museum attractions are the wooden water wheel, olive presses and carriages. Inside are folk costumes dating from the 19th and 20th centuries, household furnishings and other domestic implements, ceramics, textiles, Lefkara laces and silver jewellery.

❸ Archbishop Makarios Cultural Centre

Plateia Achiepiskopou Kyprianou.
Byzantine Museum: **Tel** 22 430 008.
Open 9am–4pm Mon–Fri, 9am–
1pm Sat. **Closed** Sat pm in Aug.
w makariosfoundation.org.cy

This cultural centre, adjacent to the New Archbishop's Palace, houses several libraries, the School of Ecclesiastical Music and the Byzantine Museum, which first opened in 1982.

Also known as the Icon Museum, the Byzantine Museum contains the largest and most valuable collection of icons in Cyprus. Around 230 icons span the 8th to the 19th centuries. Through the exhibition you can follow the changing trends in the art of icon "writing", and see the idiosyncratic images of Jesus, the Virgin Mary, the saints and the apostles. The best exhibits include the 13th-century icon by the main door, portraying the Prophet Elijah being fed by a raven, and the image of the Virgin holding the dead body of Christ – the equivalent of the Roman Catholic *Pietà*.

The reconstructed apse was rescued from the church of Agios Nikolaos tis Stegis in the Troodos mountains.

Crown exhibit from the Byzantine Museum

For several years the museum has displayed 6th-century Byzantine mosaics stolen during the 1970s from Panagia Kanakaria church in Lythrangomi in the Turkish-occupied Karpasia peninsula. Following a lengthy court battle, the Cypriot government recovered the mosaics. They depict various religious figures, including the Virgin Mary, the archangels Michael and Gabriel, and several apostles. The figure of Jesus, depicted in one of the mosaics clutching a scroll of parchment, has the appearance of a Hellenic god. All of the figures have un-naturally large eyes, a characteristic trait of early-Christian art.

In addition to mosaics and icons, the museum's collection includes ecclesiastical garments and books.

The New Archbishop's Palace was erected in 1956–60 in the Neo-Byzantine style to a design by Greek architect George Nomikos. Usually closed to visitors, it does open occasionally, when you can visit the bedroom of Archbishop Makarios, where his heart is kept.

Located near the Makarios Cultural Centre, and housed in a former power plant, is the **Municipal Arts Centre**, which serves as a venue for major art exhibitions.

❹ Cathedral of St John the Theologian

Plateia Achiepiskopou Kyprianou. **Tel** 22 432 578. **Open** 8am–noon, 2–4pm Mon–Fri, 8am–noon Sat.

The small Cathedral of St John (Agios Ioannis) dates from 1662. Built of yellow stone and covered with a barrel vault, it stands on the ruins of a medieval Benedictine monastery. Its interior is decorated with magnificent paintings depicting Biblical scenes from the life of Jesus, from birth to crucifixion, including a striking **Last Judgment** above the entrance.

The four paintings on the right wall, next to the Archbishop's throne, show the discovery of the relics of the apostle Barnabas, founder of the Cypriot church. They also show the privileges granted by Byzantine emperor Zeno to the Cypriot Church, including *autokefalia* (independence from the Patriarch of Constantinople) and the right of the Archbishop to wear purple garments during ceremonies, to use the sceptre instead of the crosier, and to sign letters with red ink. The paintings tightly covering the walls and ceiling are by the 18th-century artist Filaretos.

To the right, by the door leading to the courtyard, stands a small marble bust of Archbishop Kyprianos, who was hanged by the Turks in 1821 in retaliation for the outbreak of

Ornately decorated interior of the Hadjigeorgakis Kornesios House

Greek national insurgence. Kyprianos founded the first secondary school in Cyprus. The Pancyprian Gymnasium, regarded as the most prestigious high school in the Greek part of the island, exists to this day. Its Neo-Greek building is on the opposite side of the street.

❺ Hadjigeorgakis Kornesios House

Ethnological Museum: Patriarchou Grigoriou 20. **Tel** 22 305 316. **Open** 8:30am–3:30pm Tue–Fri, 9:30am–3:30pm Sat. 🖼

One of the town's most interesting buildings is the House of Hadjigeorgakis Kornesios, a well-preserved building from the late 18th century. Kornesios, a highly educated Greek Cypriot businessman and philanthropist, served from 1779 as a dragoman – a liaison between the Ottoman government and

the Greek Cypriot population. Despite serving the Turks for a number of years, he was arrested and executed by them.

The opulent house is decorated with Anatolian-style columns and lattice-work. The bedroom and Turkish-style drawing room lined with carpets occupy the first floor. The ground floor contains servants' quarters and a *hammam* – a Turkish bath. Part of the house holds a small ethnological exhibition.

❻ Omar Mosque (Ömeriye Cami)

Trikoupi and Plateia Tyllirias. **Open** daily, except during services. Donations welcome.

This mosque takes its name from Caliph Omar, who supposedly reached Nicosia in the course of the 7th-century Arab raids on Cyprus.

The site now occupied by this mosque was once home to a 14th-century church, which served the local Augustine monastery. The Church of St Mary drew pilgrims in great numbers from Cyprus and throughout Europe to visit the tomb of the Cypriot saint John de Montfort, a member of the Knights Templar.

Minaret of the Omar Mosque

The church was converted into a mosque after the town was captured by the Ottomans, led by Lala Mustapha Pasha, in the 16th century. On the floor of the mosque are Gothic tombstones, used by the Turks as building material.

The mosque is used by resident Muslims from Arab countries. It is open to visitors; please remove your shoes before entering. It is also possible to climb to the top of the minaret, from where there are lovely views of Nicosia.

The small, yellow-stone Cathedral of St John the Theologian

Chrysaliniotissa church, renowned for its collection of icons

❼ Panagia Chrysaliniotissa

Chrysaliniotissas.

The Chrysaliniotissa church, the capital's oldest house of worship, is dedicated to Our Lady of the Golden Flax. It stands at the centre of the district bearing the same name, right on the Green Line. It was built in c.1450 by Helen, the Greek-born wife of the Frankish king John II. The church takes its name from a miraculous icon found in a field of flax.

This L-shape building, with two domes and a slender belfry, is famous for its collection of rare icons of the Byzantine era.

Located nearby at Dimonaktos 2 is the small **Chrysaliniotissa Crafts Centre**. Various types of Cypriot art and handicrafts can be seen and purchased in this small crafts centre, which is modelled on a traditional inn.

Prior to the division of Nicosia, the opposite side of Ermou Street, called Tahtakale Cami after the mosque that stood here, was home to many Turkish Cypriots. Based on the Nicosia Master Plan, the old houses are being renovated and new occupants are moving in. Thanks to the founding of the Municipal Cultural Centre in Famagusta Gate, the district is becoming popular, with boutiques, restaurants, bars and tavernas springing up.

❽ Centre of Visual Arts and Research

Ermou Street 285. **Tel** 22 300 999. **Open** summer: 9:30am–4:30pm Tue–Thu, Sat & Sun; winter: 10am–6pm Mon–Sat. 🔲 cvar.severis.org

Located opposite Famagusta Gate, the Centre of Visual Arts and Research offers visitors a peek into the history and culture of Cyprus and its neighbours through paintings, antique costumes and other exhibits. The Travelling Artists Collection has more than 1,000 artworks created by artists who visited the island during 18th–20th centuries. The Costumes Collection, featuring clothes, bed linen and embroidery, showcases the influence of other cultures on the development of Cypriot attire. There are also smaller collections of books, many of them rare and old, photographs and colonial memorabilia.

Chrysaliniotissa church detail

❾ Famagusta Gate

Leoforos Athinon. **Tel** 22 797 660. **Open** 10am–1pm, 4–8pm Mon–Fri.

One of three city gates, Famagusta Gate is situated in the

Caraffa bastion of the Venetian defence walls. Low-built and comprising a log tunnel ending at a wooden gate, it resembles the Venetian gate from Iraklion, in Crete. The side facing town is decorated with six Venetian coats-of-arms.

The structure was thoroughly renovated in the 1980s. Now it houses the **Municipal Cultural Centre**. The main room is used for exhibitions, concerts and theatrical performances. The smaller side room is devoted to art exhibitions.

Environs
The medieval Venetian defence walls are the most distinctive element of old Nicosia. They were erected during 1567–70 to a design by Italian architect Giulio Savorgnano. The present-day Famagusta Gate was originally called the Porta Giuliana, in honour of the architect.

The 5-km- (3-mile-) long Venetian walls contain 11 artillery bastions and three gates – the other two are called the Pafos and Kyrenia Gates, after the towns they face.

The defence walls fit in well with Nicosia's overall appearance. The bastions and the areas between them have been converted into car parks and market squares. The d'Avila bastion, near the Plateia Elefteria (Eleftheria Square), is the site of the town hall and the municipal library. The Podocataro bastion features the Liberty Monument, which depicts the goddess of Liberty clad in ancient robes, while two EOKA soldiers at her feet open prison bars from which a group of Cypriots emerges.

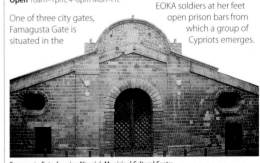

Famagusta Gate, housing Nicosia's Municipal Cultural Centre

Entrance to the town hall building, resting on Ionian columns

The project to rebuild and restore the Laiki Geitonia district was honoured with the prestigious Golden Apple ("Pomme d'Or") Award, granted by the World Federation of Journalists and Travel Writers in 1988.

Guided tours around South Nicosia start from outside the Cyprus Tourist Organization office located at 35 Odos Aristokyprou, in the Laiki Geitonia district. It is worth joining one of these tours, as they take visitors to many interesting sites that are normally closed to tourists.

❿ Constanza Bastion

Leoforos Konstantinou Palaiologou.
🚪 Wed. Bayraktar Mosque: closed to visitors.

One 11 bastions protruding from the Venetian walls of the old quarter of Nicosia, Constanza Bastion is the site of the Bayraktar Mosque, erected to commemorate a Turkish soldier killed during the siege of Nicosia. Every Wednesday and Saturday, the area in front of the mosque turns into a colourful fruit and vegetable market.

⓫ Town Hall

Plateia Eleftheria (Eleftheria Square).

Built in the Classical Greek style, the single-storey town hall stands on the d'Avila bastion, next to the municipal library. An ornamental semicircular stairway leads to the portal, which rests on Ionian columns. **Plateia Eleftheria** (Eleftheria Square), opposite the town hall, has undergone a multi-million-euro renovation based on a design by renowned architect Zaha Hadid.

Eleftheria Square is the starting point for the two main shopping streets of old Nicosia: **Onasagorou** and **Ledra**. Both are lined with dozens of shops, tavernas, *kafenia* (coffee shops), restaurants and bars.

At the end of Ledra Street, whose name evokes the ancient town that once stood on the site of present-day Nicosia, is a checkpoint and crossing to North Nicosia, with a monument to those Greek Cypriots who went missing during the Turkish invasion. There is a small museum here.

⓬ Laiki Geitonia

The pedestrianized Laiki Geitonia (Popular Neighbourhood) is a restored section of Old Nicosia near the brooding Venetian defence walls, the town hall and Onasagorou Street. Clustered within a small area of narrow, winding alleys in prettily restored houses are numerous restaurants, shady cafés, handicraft workshops and souvenir shops aimed primarily at tourists. Here you will also find tourist information offices, offering free maps and brochures.

Figurine, Leventis Museum

⓭ Leventis Museum

Ippokratous 15–17, Laiki Geitonia.
Tel 22 661 475. **Open** 10am–4:30pm Tue–Sun.
🌐 leventismuseum.org.cy

The fascinating Leventis Museum houses a collection devoted to the history of Nicosia, from ancient times until today. Its creators have succeeded in putting together an intriguing exhibition showing the everyday life of Nicosia's residents. Of particular interest to visitors are the exhibits relating to the times of the Franks and the Venetians, including medieval manuscripts and the opulent clothes of the city's rulers. Also of note are the documents and photographs dating from the colonial era.

British-period costumes on display at Leventis Museum

⓮ Tripiotis Church

Solonos Street. **Open** 9am–5pm daily.

Dedicated to the Archangel Gabriel, Tripiotis church is the loveliest of the surviving Gothic churches in south Nicosia. This three-aisled, square edifice topped with a small dome was built in 1695 by Archbishop Germanos. Designed in the Franco-Byzantine style, it has a rich and interesting interior with Gothic windows, while the exterior has a medieval stone relief depicting lions, mermaids and sea monsters. The pride of the church is its intricately carved iconostasis, which contains several old icons covered with silver revetments. The church takes its name from the district of Nicosia in which it stands.

⓯ Bank of Cyprus Cultural Foundation

Phaneromeni 86–90. **Tel** 22 128 157. **Open** 10am–7pm Mon–Sun.
Ⓦ boccf.org

One of Cyprus' most prominent private art collections, the George and Nefeli Giabra Pierides collection, is housed here. The Cultural Foundation is an institution that sponsors scientific research and conducts educational and cultural activities. The magnificent exhibits represent works from the early Bronze Age (2500 BC) to the end of the Middle Ages. The exhibits, numbering over 600 items, include ancient bronze and gold jewellery and Mycenaean amphorae and goblets. Also on display are terracotta figurines, anthropomorphic red-polished vases and realistic limestone Hellenic statues depicting, among others, Apollo and Hercules. Glazed ceramics dating from the Middle Ages can also be seen.

Close to the Bank of Cyprus Cultural Foundation stands the **Agia Faneromeni** church, the largest church within the city

View of the three-aisled Tripiotis church

walls, built in 1872 on the site of a former Greek Orthodox monastery. *Faneromeni* in Greek means "found through revelation". Inside is a beautiful iconostas and a marble mausoleum containing the remains of the bishops and Greek priests who were murdered by the Turks in 1821.

Adjacent to the church is the imposing Neo-Classical building of the **Faneromeni High School**.

⓰ Araplar Mosque

Odos Lefkonos.

Standing close to the Agia Faneromeni church, the Araplar Mosque (Stavros tou Missirikou) was founded in the converted 16th-century Stavros tou Missirikou church, which had been designed in the Gothic-Byzantine style.

Although the mosque is usually closed, it is sometimes possible to peek inside and see its imposing interior with the octagonal-drummed dome supported on columned arches.

⓱ Cyprus Museum

Leoforos Mouseiou 1. **Tel** 22 865 864. **Open** 8am–6pm Tue–Fri, 9am–5pm Sat, 10am–1pm Sun.
Ⓦ cyprusmuseum.org

Jug, Bank of Cyprus Cultural Foundation

The island's largest and best archaeological museum occupies a late-19th-century Neo-Classical building. It houses a range of exhibits illustrating the history of Cyprus, from the Neolithic era (7000 BC) to the end of Roman rule (AD 395).

The museum is arranged in chronological order. **Room 1** displays the oldest traces of mankind's presence on the island. This area exhibits objects from Khirokitia, stone bowls, primitive human and animal figures carved in andesite, limestone idols, and jewellery made of shells and cornelian (which would have been imported to Cyprus). There are also early ceramics, both without decoration and with simple geometric patterns, Bronze Age amulets and cross-shaped figurines carved in soft, grey steatite.

Room 2 contains clay bowls and vessels decorated with figurines of animals. Here you will find a miniature model of a temple and a collection of ceramic vessels and figurines. **Room 3** houses a collection of ceramics up to Roman times, including Mycenaean vases and craters dating from the 15th century BC. There is also a collection of several thousand terracotta figurines depicting smiling gods.

Room 4 holds a collection of terracotta votive figurines found in the Agis Eirini sanctuary near the Kormakitis peninsula, in the north of the island. In the sculpture gallery in **Room 5** is a statue of Zeus hurling a lightning-bolt. There is a stone head of Aphrodite, the famous marble statue of Aphrodite of

Soloi dating from the 1st century AD, and an exquisite Sleeping Eros.

Room 6 features a larger-than-life bronze statue of the Emperor Septimius Severus (c.193-211), a masterpiece of Roman sculpture. The adjoining rooms contain a bronze statue of a Horned God from Engomi at the eastern end of the island and interesting collections of coins, jewellery, seals and other small artifacts. There are also sarcophagi, inscriptions, alabaster vases and the mosaic of Leda with the Swan found in Palea Pafos (**Room 7a**).

Further rooms contain reconstructed ancient tombs, as well as items found during excavations in the Salamis area, including a marble statue of Apollo with a lyre. **Room 11** contains a reconstructed royal tomb from Salamis with the famous bronze cauldron decorated with griffons and the heads of sphinxes. **Room 12** has items found in the Royal Tombs, such as a throne decorated with ivory and a silver-encrusted sword. Other exhibits include a collection of silver and gold Byzantine vessels – part of the Lambousa Treasure.

The **Municipal Garden**, on the opposite side of the street, is a green oasis set in the town centre, providing welcome shade on hot days. Named Victoria Gardens in honour of Queen Victoria, construction of the garden started in 1901. A short distance away, in Leoforos Nechrou, stands the **Cyprus Parliament** building. Adjacent to the nearby Pafos Gate, stands the Roman Catholic **Church of the Holy Cross** and the **Apostolic Nunciature**. Nearby is a UN-controlled border crossing, linking the two parts of the city. The **Ledra Palace Hotel** is the headquarters of the UN Peacekeeping Forces in Cyprus.

⓲ A. G. Leventis Gallery

A. G. Leventis Street 5. **Tel** 22 668 838.
Open 10am–5pm Mon & Thu–Sun, 10am–10pm Wed. 🅿
🆆 **leventisgallery.org**

The latest addition to Nicosia's cultural scene, the A. G. Leventis Gallery opened in 2014. It houses more than 800 works of art by Cypriot, Greek and international artists, collected by Cypriot businessman Anastasios George Leventis. Among the prominent displays is the Paris Collection showcasing paintings by Monet, Renoir, Pissarro, Chagall and other renowned painters. The collection contains French antique furniture dating from the reigns of Louis XV and Louis XVI, Chinese porcelain and an impressive selection of historic objects. The Greek Collection has significant artworks by 19th- and 20th-century Greek artists such as Parthenis, Papaloukas, Tsarouchis and Moralis. The gallery also hosts works by prominent Cypriot artists, including Adamantios Diamantis' monumental piece, *The World of Cyprus*.

⓳ State Gallery of Contemporary Art

Corner of Leoforos Stasinou and Kritis.
Tel 22 458 228. **Open** 10am–4:45pm Mon–Fri, 10am–12:45pm Sat.

This gallery occupies a splendid building situated beyond the walls, level with the Constanza Bastion. It displays a representative collection of the best works by Cypriot artists dating from 1930 to 1980. When entering Nicosia from the south you will come across the **Cyprus Handicraft Centre**, situated in Athalassa Avenue, adjacent to St Barnabas church. Traditional Cypriot handicrafts are produced here, including embroidery, lace, woodcarvings, ceramics, metalwork, mosaics, leather and textile goods, and traditional costumes. The centre was established in order to cultivate the tradition of artistic handicrafts in Cyprus, and give employment to refugees from the North.

Bronze statue of Septimius Severus, the Cyprus Museum

Environs

In the suburban district of Strovolos, 2½ km (1½ miles) southwest of the Old Town, stands the **Presidential Palace**. It is located in an extensive park, with only its dome visible from the street. Built by the British, the palace was destroyed by fire during the riot of 1931. Rebuilt by the British governor Sir Ronald Storrs, it became his official residence. The first president of the independent Republic of Cyprus, Archbishop Makarios, had his office here and lived in the Archbishop's Palace in Old Nicosia.

Paintings on display at A. G. Leventis Gallery

NORTH CYPRUS

Inhabited and governed by the Turks, and isolated from the southern Greek side of the island since the Turkish invasion in 1974, North Cyprus has some of the most beautiful spots on the entire island. The sandy beaches along Famagusta Bay and the wild Karpasia (Karpas) peninsula attract thousands of tourists, although there are still far fewer here than in southern Cyprus. The heart of the region is North Nicosia, home to over one third of the population of North Cyprus.

Most hotels and facilities can be found on the northern side of the Pentadaktylos mountains, whose rugged peaks contrast with the azure of the sea. Kyrenia (Girne) has a charming yacht harbour, one of the most attractive in the Mediterranean, with a vast, old castle recalling the time the island was under Byzantine rule. Nearby, on the northern slopes of the Pentadaktylos range (Beşparmak), lies the most beautiful village in Cyprus – Bellapais, with the romantic ruins of a Gothic abbey. Nearby St Hilarion Castle is one of three fortresses in North Cyprus, alongside the castles of Buffavento and Kantara.

The western plains, in the vicinity of Morfou (Güzelyurt), are planted with citrus orchards. Wedged between the mountains and the blue sea are the archaeological excavation sites of Soloi and ruins of the Persian palace, located on top of Vouni Hill.

Numerous fascinating relics from the Lusignan, Venetian and Ottoman eras are enclosed by the Venetian walls of North Nicosia. Old Famagusta, full of Gothic remains, is equally interesting, with its Othello's Tower and several fascinating historic sights close by – including ancient Salamis (the island's first capital), as well as Engomi and St Barnabas monastery.

Nature lovers will be enchanted by the Karpasia peninsula, inhabited by tortoises and feral donkeys and boasting nearly 60 species of orchid.

A fruit and vegetable stall in Belediye Bazaar, in North Nicosia

◀ The walls of the historic Kantara Castle, affording impressive views of Famagusta Bay

Exploring North Cyprus

Previously, this region was fairly inaccessible, but is now visited by increasing numbers of tourists. The largest choice of hotels can be found in the regions of Kyrenia and Famagusta. The area has good main roads, and is best explored by car. Nicosia, Europe's only divided capital, is full of medieval churches, caravansarais and museums. Famagusta is equally rich in historic sights. It's old town, enclosed by a ring of Venetian walls, has a unique atmosphere. Nature lovers will be drawn to the wild Karpasia peninsula, while those interested in architecture should travel to the Kyrenia mountains, with its medieval castles and Bellapais abbey.

Window from the Church of St Mary of Carmel Mountain, in Famagusta

Apostolos Varnavas monastery, built near the tomb of St Barnabas

Key

━━━ Motorway

� Major road

━━ Secondary road

···· Minor road

━━ Scenic route

– – Track

━━ Green Line

For hotels and restaurants in this region see p165 and pp176–7

Getting There

There are no direct flights to Ercan (Tymvou) airport from anywhere but Turkey, and ferries sail only from Turkish ports. These include a twice-daily service from Tasucu, a three-times-a-week sailing from Mersin and a catamaran ferry from Alanya (summer only). EU passport holders may cross from the south of the island to the north via the pedestrian-only Ledra Palace and the end of Ledra Street crossing points, or via one of five vehicle crossing points (at Agios Dometios, Pergamos, Zodia, Kato Pyrgos and Strovilia). North Cyprus is best explored by car but you will need to take out inexpensive special insurance if using a car rented in the South.

The picturesque harbour of Kyrenia

The view from St Hilarion Castle

Sights at a Glance

For additional map symbols *see back flap*

❶ North Nicosia (Lefkoşa)

Following the invasion by Turkish troops in 1974, the northern part of Nicosia became the capital of the Turkish part of the island. It is home to over half the population of North Cyprus, as well as the seat of government. It is also the administrative, business, banking and commercial centre of North Cyprus. The majority of local historic sights are found within the old Venetian walls – Gothic churches turned into mosques, bazaars, Ottoman fountains, baths and caravansarais stand among the often ugly residential buildings.

Exploring North Nicosia

The Old Town is best explored on foot. At the bus station you can board a free bus that will take you to the centre of old Lefkoşa. Do not take photographs in the vicinity of the "Green Line" that divides the city, guarded by UN and Turkish troops.

The roof terrace of the Saray Hotel in Atatürk Square (Atatürk Meydanı) provides a great view. The best place for coffee and a rest is the former caravanserai, Büyük Han.

🕌 Büyük Han

Asma Altı Sokağı. **Open** 8:30am–3:30pm daily.

The Big Inn, a former caravanserai, is one of the most interesting Ottoman buildings in Cyprus. The Turks built it shortly after the capture of Nicosia in 1572, as an inn for visiting merchants. Its architectural style is redolent of other inns of that period seen in Anatolia. Under British administration, it became Nicosia's main prison. Following its restoration, the 68 former rooms spread around the inner courtyard now house souvenir shops, art galleries, cafés and a wine bar. The courtyard

Colourful fruit and vegetable stalls in Belediye Ekpazarı bazaar

itself features a small octagonal Muslim shrine and prayer hall (mescit) with an ablution fountain. Büyük Han is frequently used for theatrical performances, concerts and exhibitions.

The nearby Ottoman "Gamblers' Inn" (Kumarcılar Han), in Asma Altı Square, was built in the late 17th century. Its entrance hall features two Gothic arches, since the inn was built on the ruins of a former monastery. Now it houses the North Cyprus centre for the conservation of historic sites.

Büyük Han, a former caravanserai with a Muslim shrine in the courtyard

🛒 Belediye Ekpazarı

Open 7am–5pm Mon–Fri, 7am–2pm Sat.

This covered bazaar, situated between the Bedesten and the "Green Line" that bisects old Nicosia, was the main shopping area in Ottoman times. It remains a market, where you can buy fresh meat and vegetables, as well as Turkish sweets and souvenirs. Hanging by the exit from the bazaar, on the wall of one of the houses, a plaque marks the centre of the Old Town.

🕌 Bedesten

By the Selimiye Mosque. **Closed** for restoration.

The 12th-century Byzantine Church of St George was remodelled in the 1300s in the Gothic style by the Lusignan kings. After the 16th-century occupation of Nicosia by the Turks, it was used as a warehouse, and later as a market for selling jewellery and precious metal objects. The word bedesten means "lockable bazaar". The north wall has an original Gothic portal, a variety of carved stonework elements and the escutcheons of the Venetian nobility.

Selimiye Camii, the former Gothic Cathedral Church of St Sophia

🕌 Selimiye Camii (Aya Sofya Cathedral)

At the centre of the Old Town, in Arasta Sokağı. **Open** 24 hours daily.

The former Cathedral Church of St Sophia (the Divine Wisdom), erected by the Lusignan kings from 1208 to 1326, is the oldest and finest example of Gothic architecture in Cyprus. Once regarded as one of the most magnificent Christian buildings in the Middle East, its unique features include the entrance portal, stone-carved window and huge columns that support the criss-cross vaulting. It was here that the Frankish rulers were crowned kings of Cyprus. This ceremony preceded a second, nominal coronation as Kings of Jerusalem, performed in St Nicholas Cathedral, in Famagusta.

The cathedral was destroyed, in turn, by the Genoese, the Mamelukes and several earthquakes. Following the capture of Nicosia by the Turks in 1570, the cathedral was transformed into Hagia Sophia mosque, which, in 1954, was renamed Selimiye Camii (Aya Sofya Cathedral). All images have been removed and the Gothic stone sculptures in the main portal have been chipped away. The interior has been stripped of all ornamentation and painted white. Two 50-m-(164-ft-) tall minarets, entirely out of keeping with the rest of the building, have been added on the sides of the main façade.

Other adaptations made to the interior include the addition of three *mihrabs* indicating the direction of Mecca, and carpets.

🕌 Sultan Mahmut II Library
Kirilzade Sokağı. **Open** 8am–3:30pm daily. 🖼

Shield above entrance to Lapidary Museum

This small domed, stone building is a classic example of Ottoman architecture. The library was erected in 1829 by Turkish governor, Al Ruchi. It holds a collection of 1,700 books and manuscripts, including a handwritten Koran and exquisite works by Turkish and Persian calligraphers.

🏛 Lapidary Museum
Kirilzade Sokagi.
Open 8am–3:30pm daily.
The 15th-century Venetian building at the rear of the Selimiye Mosque, near the Sultan Mahmut II Library, houses a collection of stone sculptures removed from Gothic tombs, old houses and churches.

The garden includes a Lusignan royal sarcophagus, fragments of columns, stone rosettes and Venetian winged Lions of St Mark.

🅒 Haydarpaşa Mosque
Haydarpasa Sokağı. **Open** 8am–1pm, 2:30–5pm Mon–Fri, 8am–1pm Sat.
Originally St Catherine's Church, erected by the Lusignans in the 14th century. Their coats of arms can be seen on the south portal in carved stone.

VISITORS' CHECKLIST

Practical Information
Road map C3. 🔼 50,000.
ℹ️ Kyrenia Gate, 0392 822 21 45.

Transport
🚌 Kemal Aşik (next to Atatürk Cad). ✈️ Ercan, 20 km (12 miles) southeast of North Nicosia. The border crossing to South Nicosia is by the Ledra Palace Hotel or via Ledra Street.

Following the occupation of Nicosia, the Turks converted the church into Haydarpaşa Camii (Haydarpaşa Mosque), adding a disproportionate minaret. Today it houses a modern art gallery.

Haydarpaşa Mosque, originally the Gothic Church of St Catherine

---

North Nicosia City Centre

① Büyük Han
② Belediye Ekpazarı (bazaar)
③ Selimiye Camii
   (Aya Sofya Cathedral)
④ Sultan Mahmut II Library
⑤ Lapidary Museum
⑥ Haydarpaşa Mosque
⑦ Kyrenia Gate
⑧ Mevlevi Tekke
⑨ Atatürk Square
⑩ Dervish Pasha Mansion
⑪ Arabahmet Mosque
   (Arabahmet Camii)

0 metres 400
0 yards 400

Key
▪▪ Green Line

Ercan
20 km (12 miles)

Barbaro (Musalla) Bastion
Quirini (Cephane) Bastion
Kyrenia Gate ⑦
Loredano (Cevizli) Bastion
Mevlevi Tekke ⑧
Mula (Zahra) Bastion
ATATÜRK MEYDANI
Haydarpaşa Mosque ⑥
Flatro (Sibeli) Bastion
Arabahmet Mosque ⑪ ⑩
Dervish Pasha Mansion
Büyük Hamam
Büyük Han ①
Selimiye Camii
Lapidary Museum ⑤
④ Sultan Mahmut II Library
② Belediye Ekpazarı
Roccas (Kaytazağa) Bastion
Pafos Gate

❷ Lysi (Akdoğan)

Road Map D3. 23 km (14.3 miles) southeast of Tymvou (Kirklar).

A small farming village in the southeastern part of the Mesaoria plain, Lysi lies close to the "Green Line". Its most interesting historic site is the unfinished Byzantine-style church decorated with Neo-Gothic architectural elements.

Environs

Along the road to Ercan airport are the remains of Ottoman aqueducts. The surrounding area is home to several neglected Orthodox churches, including Agios Themonianos, Agios Synesios, Agios Andronikos and Moni Agiou Spyridona monastery in Tremetousha (Erdemli). The latter is guarded, and visitors should not approach it.

The unfinished Neo-Byzantine church in Lysi

❸ Engomi-Alasia

Road Map E3. **Open** summer: 8am–7pm daily; winter: 8am–3:30pm daily. 🖼

Remains of a Bronze Age town have been found near the village of Engomi-Alasia. Archaeologists estimate that Alasia was founded in the 18th century BC. The town grew rich on trading in copper, which was excavated on the island and exported to Anatolia, Syria and Egypt.

Alasia was the capital of Cyprus and its main town – its name synonymous with the entire island. In the 12th century BC, when the Mycenaeans arrived here, the town's

Ruins near the village of Engomi, a few kilometres west of Salamis

population numbered an impressive 15,000. Following an earthquake in the 11th century BC, the town was deserted and its inhabitants moved to Salamis.

Excavation works conducted since 1896 have unearthed the ruins of a Late Bronze Age settlement, with low houses lining narrow streets.

The Alasia ruins yielded a tablet with Cypriot-Minoan writing, not yet deciphered, and the famous bronze statue of the Horned God, dating from the 12th century BC, which is now kept in the Cyprus Museum in Nicosia. Strolling around the excavation site you will come across the Horned God's sanctuary and the "House of Bronzes", where many bronze objects were discovered.

Environs

Along the road to Famagusta is the village of Engomi (Tuzla). Next to the shop is a white platform, known as the **cenotaph of Nikokreon**. It contains the remains of Nikokreon – the last king of Salamis. Refusing to surrender to the Hellenic king of Egypt, Ptolemy I, Nikokreon committed suicide by setting

fire to the royal palace. He perished, along with his entire family, in the flames that day.

❹ Royal Tombs

Road Map E3. **Open** summer: 8am–7pm daily; winter: 8am–3:30pm daily. 🖼

The royal necropolis by the side of the road leading to St Barnabas monastery has over 100 tombs from the 7th and 8th centuries BC. Some have been given names, and others designated numbers. Almost all of the tombs are open to the east. Each one was approached by a slanting corridor known as a *dromos*, on which the most interesting artifacts were found.

Most of the tombs were looted in antiquity, but some, in particular numbers 47 and 49, contained a multitude of objects that could be useful to the royals in the next world. The most famous finds include an ivory inlaid royal bed and throne, showing clear Phoenician and Egyptian influences. The kings of Salamis were buried here with their servants and horses.

Tomb number 50, the so-called "St Catherine's prison", was built during Roman times on top of older tombs. According to legend, the Alexandrian saint, a native of Salamis, was imprisoned by her father, the Roman governor, for refusing to marry the man chosen by him. The tomb's walls bear the remnants of Christian decorations.

The site also features a small museum with plans and photographs of the tombs, and a reconstructed chariot used to carry the kings of Salamis on their final journey.

Royal Tombs from the 7th and 8th centuries BC, west of Salamis

St Barnabas monastery, built near the tomb of the apostle Barnabas

❺ St Barnabas Monastery

Road Map E3. **Open** summer: 8am–7pm daily; winter: 8am–3:30pm daily. 🖼

The monastery of St Barnabas was erected in 477 on the western end of the Constantia (Salamis) necropolis, near the spot where the apostle's grave was discovered. The construction was financed by the Byzantine emperor Zeno himself.

Two centuries later, it was demolished in one of the devastating Arab raids on Cyprus. All that remains of the original Byzantine edifice are the foundations. The present church and monastery were constructed in 1756 on the orders of Archbishop Philotheos, during Ottoman rule. The three-aisled church is covered with two flat domes resting on high drums. It now houses an **Icon Museum**.

Much more interesting, however, is the small **Archaeological Museum** occupying former monks' cells around the courtyard of the monastery. Displayed in a series of rooms are Neolithic tools and stone vessels, as well as a large number of ceramic items such as amphorae, jugs, vases and cups. Among the more curious items are a polished bronze mirror, swords, hatchets and spearheads, made of the same metal. There are also terracotta figurines of people and animals, including an unusual horse with wheels instead of hooves, and clay baby rattles shaped like boars.

Other interesting exhibits are the black-glazed ceramics imported from Attica. These are decorated with intricate motifs of animal and human figures, including lions, wild boars and hares. There is also gold jewellery, a collection of Roman glass, and a stone figure of a woman holding a poppy – probably the goddess Demeter. The Classical period is further represented by sphinxes, showing the Egyptian influence, and carved lions. A short distance

A terracotta figurine, Archaeological Museum

east of the monastery stands a small **Byzantine-style church**. This rectangular, domed chapel was erected over the tomb of the apostle Barnabas. A stone staircase leads down to two chambers hewn into the rock where, according to legend, St Barnabas was buried. The saint was killed near Salamis for preaching Christianity, and his body was cast into the sea. His disciples fished the body out, and he was buried with St Matthew's gospel on his chest, under a lonely breadfruit tree to the west of Salamis.

From 1971 until the Turkish occupation of 1974, the St Barnabas monastery was inhabited by the last three monks, the brothers Barnabas, Chariton and Stephen, who made a humble living by selling honey and painting icons.

St Barnabas

Born in Salamis, Barnabas accompanied St Paul on his missionary travels around Cyprus and Asia Minor. After parting from his master, Barnabas continued to promote Christianity on the island, for which he was killed in the year AD 57. St Mark buried the body in secret.

St Barnabas acquired fame following a miracle that occurred after his death, when he revealed the site of his burial to Anthemios, the Bishop of Salamis. The discovery of the saint's relics, and the prestige they brought, helped preserve the autonomy of the Cypriot Church.

The tomb of St Barnabas

⊙ Salamis

The former Roman Salamis, which later became Byzantine Constantia, was the island's main port and capital for a thousand years. Destroyed by the Arabs in 648, Salamis is still the largest and the most interesting archaeological excavation site on Cyprus. The unearthed relics date from the Roman and Byzantine periods. Allow a full day for a visit, including a relaxing break on the nearby beach.

Caldarium
The hot bath chamber, fitted with a central heating system, had walls decorated with abstract mosaics.

Sudatorium
The Greek-Roman baths complex included a steam bath, which was also decorated with mosaics. An underfloor heating system is in evidence.

Latrines
This semicircular colonnaded structure contained a latrine which could be used by 44 people simultaneously.

Gymnasium
A colonnade surrounded the rectangular *palaestra* of the gymnasium, which was devoted to the training of athletes.

KEY

① **Two pools** with cold water were located beyond the east portico.

② **The backstage area** housed dressing rooms for the actors.

Map of Salamis

Trikomo

Roman Baths

Amphitheatre

Gymnasium
Turkish Baths
Theatre

Roman Villa

Granite Forum

Basilica
Agios Epifanios

Byzantine Cistern

Roman Agora

Zeus's Temple

Kambanopetra Basilica

MEDITERRANEAN SEA

Aqueduct Ruins

Royal Tombs

St Barnabas Monastery

Enkom

Famagusta

0 metres 400
0 yards 400

Key

▢ Building

▢ Road

▢ Footpath

VISITORS' CHECKLIST

Practical Information
Road map E3. 8 km (5 miles) north of Famagusta. 🚌 *i*
0392 366 28 64. Archaeological site: **Open** summer: 8am–7pm daily; winter: 8am–5pm daily. 📷
Necropolis: 1 km (0.6 mile) west of Salamis. **Tel** 0392 378 83 31. **Open** summer: 9am–7pm; winter: 9am–1pm & 2–4:45pm. 📷

Aqueduct
To the east of the gymnasium are the stone cisterns and other remains of an aqueduct that used to supply the baths and the pools with water.

★ Roman Theatre
Built 2,000 years ago, during the reign of Emperor Augustus, this auditorium could hold 15,000 spectators. Today the restored theatre serves as a venue for summer performances.

Amphitheatre
Built by the Romans in the early years of the modern era, it was destroyed by an earthquake in the 6th century.

❼ Famagusta (Ammochostos/ Gazimağusa)

Once the world's wealthiest city, present-day Famagusta (Ammochostos in Greek and Gazimağusa in Turkish) presents a depressing sight. Yet within the mighty fortifications that kept out the Turkish army for nearly a year, and amid the many derelict buildings, are true gems of Gothic architecture. Former magnificent churches have been destroyed or turned into mosques. South of Famagusta, within the Venetian walls, lies the deserted Old Town of Varosha, once Cyprus' biggest resort.

Namik Kemal Square, once the site of the Venetian Palace

Exploring Famagusta

Virtually all of Famagusta's major historic sights are within the Old Town, surrounded by the Venetian fortifications. The best way to enter the city is through the Land Gate, leaving your car behind. The tourist information office is located by the gate. It is possible to explore the city by foot.

🇨 Lala Mustafa Pasha Mosque

Namik Kemal Meydanı.
Open 24 hours daily. 🎟

This former cathedral was built between 1298 and 1312 to a Gothic design modelled on Reims Cathedral in France. It was here that Lusignan royalty, after their coronation in Nicosia, received the symbolic title of "King of Jerusalem".

Following the capture of the city in 1571, the victorious Turks converted the cathedral into a mosque and named it after the

Gothic portal of Lala Mustafa Pasha Mosque

commander of the besieging army – Lala Mustafa Pasha. They also added a minaret to the left tower. The building is still a functioning mosque; visitors are admitted only outside the hours of prayer.

The white interior has 12 columns to support the Gothic vaulting. There is a modest *minbar* (pulpit) in the right aisle. The façade with its unusual window and enormous rosette, basking in the light of the setting sun, is one of the most beautiful sights in Cyprus.

🏛 Agia Zoni and Agios Nikolaos

Hisar Yolu Sokağı.
Open 24 hours daily.

This small Byzantine-style church, decorated with wall paintings, dates from about the 15th century. It stands in an empty square, surrounded by a handful of palm trees. Close by is the larger Church of St Nicholas, which is partly demolished.

🏛 Fountain and Jafar Pasha Baths

Naim Effendi Sokağı.

Located northwest of Namik Kemal Square, the fountain and baths were built in 1601 in Ottoman style by the Commander of the Sultan's Navy and the Ottoman Governor of Cyprus.

Jafar Pasha ordered the building of the aqueduct in order to supply the city with water. Both the aqueduct and the original town fountain have been destroyed. The current fountain was reconstructed using fragments of the original.

🇨 Sinan Pasha Mosque

Abdullah Paşa Sokağı.
Closed to visitors.

The former church of saints Peter and Paul was turned into a mosque after the capture of the city by the Turks. This beautiful Gothic edifice, built of yellow stone and maintained in excellent condition, now houses the municipal library collection.

A former church turned into the Sinan Pasha Mosque

🏛 Venetian Palace

Namik Kemal Meydanı
Open 24 hours daily.

Not much remains of the former palace of the Lusignan kings and Venetian governors, built during Lusignan times. The area marked by its jutting stone walls is now a car park.

On the side of Namik Kemal Square stands a triple-arched façade supported by four granite columns from Salamis. Above the central arch is the coat of arms of Giovanni Renier – the Venetian military commander of Cyprus. Between 1873 and 1876, the left section of the building was used as a prison in which Turkish poet and playwright Namik Kemal was locked up on the Sultan's order. Now it houses a museum.

Remains of the Venetian Palace

Nestorian Church

Somuncuoğlu Sokağı.
Closed to the public.

Syrian merchant Francis Lakhas built this church in 1338 for Famagusta's Syrian community. The façade is adorned with a lovely rose window. Inscrip-tions inside are in Syrian, the language of the Nestorian liturgy.

Later, the church was taken over by Greek Cypriots and renamed Agios Georgios Exorinos. The word *exorinos* means "exiler". Greeks believe that dust taken from the church floor and sprinkled in the house of an enemy will make him die or leave the island within a year.

Churches of the Knights Templar and Knights Hospitaller

Kişla Sokağı.

These two adjacent medieval churches are known as the twins. On the north façade, above the entrance, you can still see the carved stone coats of arms of the Knights Hospitaller. In the early 14th century, following the dissolution of the Knights Templar order, their monastery

Romantic ruins of the Gothic Church of St John (Latin)

and the Chapel of St Anthony were handed over to the order of St John of Jerusalem (the Knights Hospitaller). The Hospitallers' chapel, featuring a lovely rose window in the façade, now houses a theatre and an art gallery.

Church of St John (Latin)

Cafer Paşa Sokağı.
Open 8am–3:30pm daily.

Built in the late 13th century, during the reign of the French king Louis IX, the Church of St John was one of Famagusta's ealiest churches, and a splendid example of Gothic architecture. Now largely in ruins, the original north wall with the presbytery and tall Gothic windows remains standing. The capital of the surviving column is decorated with floral motifs and winged dragons.

VISITORS' CHECKLIST

Practical Information
Road map E3. 42,000.
Land Gate, 0392 366 28 64.
Famagusta International
Festival (Jun–Jul).

Transport
Gazi Mustafa Kemak Blvd.
east of the Sea Gate (for tickets, call 0392 366 45 57).

Famagusta City Centre

1. Lala Mustafa Pasha Mosque
2. Agia Zoni & Agios Nikolaos
3. Fountain & Jafar Pasha Baths
4. Sinan Pasha Mosque
5. Venetian Palace
6. Nestorian Church
7. Churches of the Knights Templar & Knights Hospitaller
8. Church of St John (Latin)

0 metres 300
0 yards 300

For keys to map symbols *see back flap*

❽ Trikomo (İskele)

Road Map E2.

This small town lies close to the base of the Karpas peninsula. At its centre, right by the roundabout, stands the tiny Dominican **Church of St James** (Agios Iakovos). Intricately carved in stone, it resembles an encrusted jewellery box. At the western end of the town stands the two-aisled, single domed **Panagia Thetokos** church, which was erected in the 12th century. The church was restored in 1804, when it was also given its marble-panelled belfry. Inside you can still see the original wall paintings dating from the 12th century.

The **Icon Museum**, opened here in 1991, houses a collection of icons removed from local Greek churches. The images are modern and of little artistic merit, yet the museum is worth visiting for its lovely interior frescoes.

🏛 Icon Museum
Panagia Theotokos Church.
Open 8am–3:30pm daily. 🖼

A mosque in Trikomo, a town at the base of the Karpas peninsula

❾ Bogazi (Boğaz)

Road Map E2. On the road leading to the Karpas peninsula.

At this little fishing port on Famagusta Bay you can watch the fishermen returning with their catch, and also buy fresh fish each morning. Fishing trips are available for visitors, as are lessons in scuba diving. There are beautiful long, sandy

The imposing walls of Kantara Castle, overlooking Famagusta Bay

beaches in this area. A half-dozen local restaurants specialize in fish and seafood. European cuisine is also on offer at some places.

❿ Kantara Castle

Road Map E2. **Open** summer: 8am–5pm daily; winter: 8am–3.30pm daily. 🖼

Kantara Castle is the easternmost medieval fortress of North Cyprus. It lies 630 m (2,068 ft) above sea level, at the base of the Karpasia peninsula, on a spot affording views of both Famagusta Bay and the shores of Asia Minor. This was already the site of a castle in Byzantine times. It was here that the English king Richard the Lionheart finally caught up with his adversary, Byzantine governor Isaac Komnenos, in 1191 and forced him to capitulate.

The castle rooms were mostly torn down by the Venetians, but the mighty walls survive in excellent condition. The route to the castle leads through a barbican with two towers; the vast southeastern tower has a water cistern at its base, also used as a dungeon. The two adjacent former army barracks are in good condition. The southwestern wing of the castle features a secret passage that

enabled the defenders to sneak out and launch a surprise attack on the besiegers. The north towers and the bastions afford magnificent views of the surrounding area.

Environs
A dozen or so kilometres (7½ miles) west of the castle, close to the sea, is the lonely Late Byzantine **Panagia Pergaminiotissa** church.

⓫ Karpasia Peninsula

Road Map E2, F1–2.
ℹ Yialoussa, 0392 374 49 84.

This long, rocky spit is the least developed part of the island, with sandy beaches on its north and south coasts, and a scattering of historic Christian churches, including the monastery of Apostolos Andreas, which is awaiting restoration, to be funded by the UN and the EU. Known as Karpaz Yarımadası (sometimes Karpas) to the Turks, this quiet

Picturesque Panagia Pergaminiotissa

peninsula has rolling hills, where wild donkeys roam, fringed by empty beaches which provide nesting grounds for sea turtles. The eastern part of the peninsula is a nature reserve, home to birds and donkeys.

The best starting point for exploring the peninsula is the fishing village of **Bogazi**. A few kilometres to the left of the main road, near the village of **Komi** (Büyükkonuk), stands a small Byzantine church with beautiful 6th-century mosaics. The church is surrounded by the ruins of a Roman town. Only the apse remains of the 5th-century Church of Panagia Kanakaria, on the edge of **Lythrangkomi** (Boltaşlı), east of **Leonarisso** (Ziyamet); the mosaics that used to decorate it can be seen in the Byzantine Museum, in Nicosia. The rest of the church dates from the 11th century, except the tamboured dome which was added in the 18th century. The church is now closed.

The last petrol station is in **Yialousa** (Yenierenköy). Further south is the village of **Sipahi** (Agia Trias) with a three-aisled early Christian basilica. Dating from the 5th century, it was discovered by archaeologists in 1957, and is noted for its handsome floor mosaics. The marble-encrusted, cruciform font in the baptistry is the biggest in the island.

Beyond the small village of **Agios Thyrsos** stands Hotel Theresa, with the best accommodation on the peninsula.

Rizokarpaso (Dipkarpaz) is the peninsula's biggest, if somewhat neglected, village. It has a population of 3,000, comprised mainly of immigrants from Anatolia. Some 3 km (2 miles) to the north are the ruins of the 5th-century church of **Agios Philon**, standing amid the ruins of the Phoenician town of Karpatia. The 10th-century basilica was later replaced by a chapel; just the south wall and the apse remain.

North of Agios Philon stands an ancient stone breakwater. A narrow road running along the coast leads to **Aphendrika**, with the ruins of an ancient harbour, a Hellenic necropolis and a fortress erected on bare rock. It also has three ruined churches: the Agios Georgios dating from the Byzantine period; the 12th-century Romanesque Panagia Chrysiotissa; and Panagia Assomatos, the best preserved of all three. On the opposite side of the peninsula is the beautiful **Nangomi Beach**.

Apostolos Andreas – the monastery of St Andrew

⑫ Apostolos Andreas

Road map F1. **Open** 24 hours daily.

Near the tip of the Karpasia peninsula stands the monastery of St Andrew (Apostolos Andreas), an irregular edifice of yellow stone with a white bell tower. According to legend, it was here that the saint's invocation caused a miraculous spring to appear, whose water cures epilepsy and ailments of the eyes, and grants pilgrims their wishes. During the Byzantine period, a fortified monastery occupied the site; some historians believe that it was here, rather than in Kantara, that Richard the Lionheart caught up with Isaac Komnenos.

In the early 20th century the monastery gained a reputation for its miracles, and became the target of mass pilgrimages. After 1974, the site was taken over by the Turkish army. Today it is once again open to visitors.

The 19th-century church has been stripped of its icons, but on the Feast of the Assumption (15 August) and St Andrew's Day (30 November), services are held for the pilgrims arriving from southern Cyprus.

In the crypt beneath the church the holy well, famed for its healing properties, still gushes the "miraculous" water. The site is regarded as holy by Greeks and Turks alike.

Environs

Less than 5 km (3 miles) from Apostolos Andreas monastery is **Zafer Burnu**, the furthest point of the Karpasia peninsula. This cave-riddled cape was a Neolithic settlement known as **Kastros**, one of the earliest places of known human habitation in Cyprus. In ancient times it was the site of a temple to the goddess aphrodite.

The offshore **Klidhes islets** (the "Keys" islets) are a haven for a variety of sea birds.

Nangomi (Golden) Beach on the Karpasia peninsula

⑰ Kyrenia (Girne)

Enjoying a picturesque location flanked by a range of craggy hills and the sea, Kyrenia is built around a charming harbour – the most beautiful in Cyprus – guarded by a mighty medieval castle. Its compact Old Town is full of bars, tavernas and restaurants, yet remains a tranquil place. The nearby seashore is lined with the best hotels in North Cyprus. Home to a sizeable expatriate community until 1974, there is still a small number of expats living here today.

Town hall building with its forecourt fountain

View of the Lusignan Tower in the castle *(see pp152–3)*

Exploring Kyrenia

Once you arrive in Kyrenia, it is best to leave your car at the car park near the town hall, and then continue exploring on foot. Most of Kyrenia's historic sights are clustered around the old harbour. The tourist information office is housed in the former customs house. The town's main attractions – the harbour, castle and small museums – can be explored in a day.

🏛 Byzantine Tower

Ziya Rizki Caddesi and Atilla Sokağı. **Open** summer: 9am–5pm daily; winter: 9am–3:30pm daily.

This massive stone defence structure, with walls several metres thick, once formed part of the town's defence walls. It now houses an art gallery selling local handicrafts, including rugs, paintings and other souvenirs. Strolling down Atilla Sokağı you will come

across a similar, but more derelict tower; also a number of Greek and Roman tombs.

🏛 Market

Canbulat Sokağı. **Open** 8am–7pm. The covered town bazaar was once a food market, but funding from the UN has allowed it to be renovated into a revitalised area with trendy restaurants and a handicraft centre. The market stands along Canbulat Street leading towards the shore.

🏛 Folk Art Museum

The old harbour. **Open** 8am–3:30pm daily.

Set in a centuries-old Venetian house midway along the harbour, the Folk Art Museum houses a small collection of traditional village costumes, household implements, furniture and tools. Also on display is a giant olive press made of olive wood.

Art gallery inside the Byzantine Tower

🏛 Town Hall

This modern building stands on a small square, just a stone's throw from the Old Town. Standing in the forecourt is a unique fountain featuring three huge birds carved in white stone.

The nearby Muslim cemetery is full of the distinctive tombs – *baldaken türbe*.

☪ Djafer Pasha Mosque (Cafer Paşa Camii)

In the Old Town, close to the castle and the harbour. **Open** 24 hours daily.

This small mosque with a stocky minaret was erected in 1589 by Djafer Pasha, commander of the Sultan's army and navy, and three times the Turkish governor of Cyprus. The founder's body rests in the small stone tomb to the right of the entrance. The simple prayer hall is lined with carpets.

About a dozen metres (40 ft) west of the mosque is the small, abandoned Chysospiliotissa church which was erected by the Lusignans in the early 14th century.

⚓ Harbour

Kyrenia's once-important harbour was heavily fortified and the safest haven along the north coast of Cyprus. In ancient times the Romans built a defence castle here; later on the Lusignans and the Venetians rebuilt it, creating a vast fortress. In the Middle Ages the harbour entrance was protected by a strong iron chain. Evidence of its former importance are the medieval stone lugs that were used to fasten the mooring lines of large ships.

Now the old harbour is devoted exclusively to yachts

and pleasure boats, ready to take visitors on cruises along the coast. It is lined with an array of dining spots, particularly fish restaurants, with tables set close to the water's edge. The harbour looks particularly enchanting at night, when the calm waters reflect myriad sparkling lights.

🏛 Archangelos Church and Icon Museum

Near the harbour. **Open** 8am–3:30pm daily. 📷

The former church of the Archangel Michael, standing on top of a hill close to the old harbour, now houses the Icon Museum.

This white edifice with its slender belfry was built in 1860. Some of its original furnishings remain, including the exquisite

The distinctive white silhouette and belfry of the Archangelos church

carved wooden iconostasis and pulpit. The walls are now hung with over 50 icons, dating from the 18th–20th centuries, that were removed from local churches. One of the oldest was painted in 1714. Other objects

Kyrenia's natural horseshoe harbour, the most beautiful in Cyprus

VISITORS' CHECKLIST

Practical Information
Road Map C2. 🏛 14,000. 🛈 Kordon Boyu Cad, by the entrance to the old harbour, 0392 822 21 45.

Transport
🚌 Fergün, 0392 822 23 44.

on display are sacral books and a carved crosier. Outside are marble sarcophagi, dating from the Byzantine period.

During summer, Catholic Mass is celebrated in the late-Gothic **Chapel of Terra Santa**, situated further west, in Ersin Aydın Sokağı. The only other Christian place of worship in Kyrenia is the Anglican **Church of St Andrew**, which was built in 1913 close to the castle and the Muslim cemetery.

🏛 Fine Arts Museum

Open 8am–3:30pm daily. 📷

This fine arts museum is housed in a somewhat ostentatious villa that was built in 1938 in the western part of Kyrenia. Its eclectic collection of artwork comprises a variety of unrelated exhibits, ranging from anonymous paintings (both oil and watercolour) to European porcelain, to Oriental jewellery.

Kyrenia Town Map

① Byzantine Tower
② Market
③ Folk Art Museum
④ Town Hall
⑤ Djafer Pasha Mosque (Cafer Paşa Camii)
⑥ Harbour
⑦ Archangelos Church and Icon Museum

For keys to symbols see back flap

Kyrenia Castle and Shipwreck Museum

Kyrenia Castle was built by the Byzantines on the site of a Roman fort and later extended by the Lusignans. The Venetians turned it into a vast fortress occupied by the Turks in 1570. The castle was never taken by force.

Today it houses a Tomb-Finds Gallery and a Shipwreck Museum, with the wreck of an ancient vessel dating from the time of Alexander the Great. The magnificent view from the city walls encompasses the harbour and St Hilarion Castle.

Shipwreck Museum
On display here is what remains of a merchant vessel that sank in a storm some 2,300 years ago.

Amphorae
Nearly 400 clay amphorae for storing wine were found in the wreck of a sailing vessel, probably bound for Anatolia from the Greek islands.

The Lusignan Tower
Arranged in the vaulted rooms of the two-storey tower are figures of medieval soldiers standing by the guns.

The Courtyard
Surrounded by stone walls, the courtyard has a number of stone balls lying around and a quern (millstone) of volcanic rock.

KEY

① **The Tomb-Finds Gallery** comprises a reconstructed late-Neolithic dwelling and tombs from both Kirini and Akdeniz (Agia Irini).

② **Square Tower**

③ **West Wall**

The Venetian Tower
The southeast section of Kyrenia Castle includes the Venetian Tower. Arranged in its gloomy casemates are figures of resting soldiers and Venetian gunners in action.

VISITORS' CHECKLIST

Practical Information
Road Map C2. Kyrenia Castle and Shipwreck Museum:
Open summer: 9am–7pm daily; winter: 9am–5pm daily. 🔁 The visitors' entrance is located in the eastern part of the old harbour.

Defence Walls
Once powerful castle fortifications are now severely dilapidated.

Coat of Arms
A medieval knight's stone-carved coat of arms is preserved in the castle walls.

Entrance
The castle is reached via a narrow bridge spanning a moat, once filled with sea water.

㉓ Morfou (Güzelyurt)

Road Map B3. 🎨 Orange Festival (May).

The Turkish name Güzelyurt means "beautiful place". And, indeed, the local citrus groves and picturesque bay add to the lovely scenery here.

It was close to the town that archaeologists discovered the earliest traces of human habitation in Cyprus, dating from the Neolithic and Early Bronze eras when copper was produced and exported.

The best historic site in Güzelyurt is the **church and monastery of Agios Mamas**, built during the Byzantine period on the site of a former pagan temple. In the 15th century it acquired Gothic embellishments, and in the 18th century a dome.

The interior features the throne of St Mamas, a Gothic window carved in stone, an iconostasis and a marble sarcophagus of the saint.

Until 1974 swarms of pilgrims streamed to Agios Mamas from all over Cyprus, but after the Turkish invasion it was shut and used to store icons brought here from nearby Orthodox churches. It is now an **Icon Museum**.

Other than Agios Mamas, the town has few tourist attractions. Next to the church is the **Archaeology and Natural History Museum**. Besides several exhibits of stuffed animals

Monastery buildings of Agios Mamas in Morfou

Atatürk's statue in Léfka

and birds, and a collection of ancient ceramics, the museum also houses an exhibition of Late Bronze Age objects found in the course of excavations conducted in Töumba and Skourou.

🏛 **Icon Museum & Archaeology and Natural History Museum**

Agios Mamas. **Open** summer: 9am–6pm daily; winter: 9am–3:30pm daily. 🎨

㉔ Léfka (Lefke)

Road Map B3.

Inhabited for over 400 years by Turks, Lefke is a major centre of Islam on the island. The central square sports a huge equestrian statue of Atatürk. A few hundred metres further on stands the early 19th-century mosque of **Piri Osman Pasha**, built in the Cypriot style. The garden surrounding the mosque contains the tomb of Vizier Osman Pasha, who was supposedly killed by poison – a victim of a palace intrigue. His marble sarcophagus is one of the loveliest surviving works of its kind from the Ottoman period.

Lefke European University, one of five universities in North Cyprus, trains students from many countries of the Middle East and Central Asia. Along the coastline, there are a number of restaurants serving local cuisine and fresh seafood. Lefke was once the seat of Kibrisi

Logo of the university in Léfka

Şeyh Nazim, the *murshid* or spiritual leader of the Naqshbandi order of Sufism, who decides on all spiritual aspects of life of the faithful.

Environs
In the nearby coastal town of Karavostasi (Gemikonaği) is the excellent **Mardinli** restaurant, standing on a beach surrounded by a garden and orchard that provide its kitchen with fruit and vegetables. On the other side of town, between the road and the sea, stands an imposing monument to a Turkish pilot killed during the 1974 invasion.

㉕ Soloi (Soli Harabeleri)

Road Map B3. 20 km (12½ miles) west of Morfou. **Open** summer: 9am–6pm daily; winter: 9am–3:30pm daily. 🎨

Soloi, a one-time city-state of Cyprus, was supposedly founded at the suggestion of the Athenian law-giver Solon, who persuaded King Philocyprus of Aepea to build a new capital close to the river Ksero. In his honour, the town was named Soloi. The reality, however, was probably quite different. As long ago as Assyrian times (c.700 BC) a town called Sillu stood on this site. It was a stronghold of Greek culture, and was the last town to fall to the Persians.

The town gave its name to the entire region of Solea, on the northern slopes of the Troodos mountains, where Cypriot copper was mined near the present-day town of Skouriotissa. The extraction and export of this metal spurred the growth of Soloi, particularly during Roman times. There was a good harbour, needed for the export of copper, and abundant water.

It was in Soloi that St Mark converted a Roman named

Auxibius to Christianity; he later became bishop of Soloi. Stones taken from the ruins of the ancient town were used by the British and the French in the building of the Suez Canal and the coastal town of Port Said. It was only in the late 1920s that Swedish archaeologists unearthed a theatre, and in 1964 a Canadian team uncovered the basilica and part of the agora (market place).

The Roman theatre was built for an audience of 4,000 people, and has been restored. During the summer it is used as a venue for shows and concerts.

Above the theatre the archaeologists uncovered remains of palaces and a temple to Athena. The famous 1st-century marble statuette of Aphrodite found nearby can now be seen in the Cyprus Museum in Nicosia *(see pp126-7)*. Lower down are the ruins of a 5th-century Byzantine basilica, destroyed in the course of the 632 Arab raid.

Displayed under a makeshift roof are some fairly well-preserved mosaics from the temple floor, featuring geometric and animal motifs. The most interesting mosaics depict water birds surrounded by dolphins. Another small medallion features a swan.

Unearthed to the north of the ruined basilica is a poorly preserved agora.

Soloi is surrounded by vast burial grounds, dating from various periods of antiquity.

Ruins of the ancient palace in Vouni

㉖ Vouni (Vuni Sarayı)

Road Map B3. 27 km (17 miles) west of Morfou. **Open** summer: 9am–6pm daily; winter: 9am–3:30pm daily. 🚫

This magnificent, somewhat mysterious palace stands atop a coastal hill, 250 m (820 ft) above sea level. The site is extraordinarily beautiful, with panoramic views over the North Cyprus coast and the Troodos mountains to the south.

Mosaic from Soloi

The palace was likely built by a pro-Persian king of Marion (a city near present-day Polis), as evidenced by its Oriental architectural details.

Occupying a strategic spot, the residence was probably intended to intimidate the nearby pro-Athenian town of Soloi. Following an anti-Persian insurrection, Vouni (which means "mountain" in Greek) was taken over by the supporters of Greece.

Having occupied the palace, they rebuilt it, adding a temple to Athena, among other things. When the reversal of military fortunes resulted in the Persians returning to power, the palace was burned down in 380 BC.

Today the ruins are reached via a new, narrow and winding road. Above the car park are the scant remains of a temple to Athena, dating from the late 5th century BC. The stairs on the opposite side lead to the palace courtyard, which features a guitar-shape stone stele with a hole in it and an unfinished face of a woman, probably a goddess. The adjacent cistern was used to supply water to the luxurious baths in the northwestern portion of the palace, which reputedly had 137 rooms.

Environs

The small rocky island off the west coast, visible from Vouni palace, is **Petra tou Limniti**. This is the oldest inhabited part of Cyprus, colonized as early as the Neolithic era.

Remains of the ancient agora in Soloi

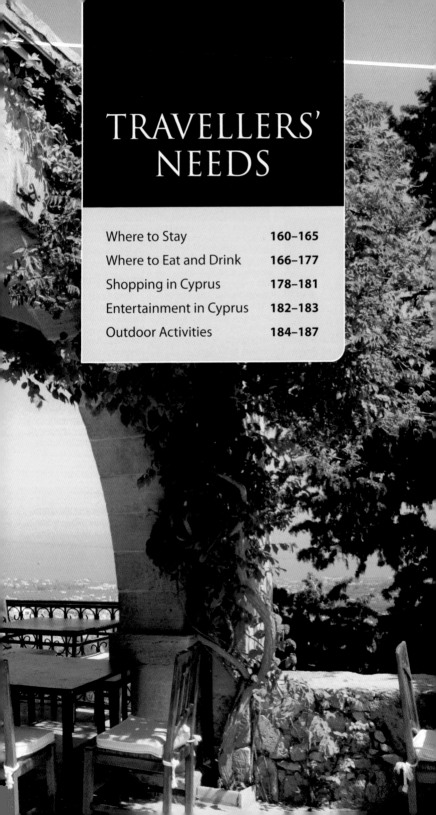

TRAVELLERS' NEEDS

The Flavours of Cyprus

Cypriot food is a mixture of Greek, Turkish and Middle Eastern cooking, and features all the rich flavours typical of Mediterranean produce. Fruit such as oranges, lemons, cherries and figs are all grown locally, and the island's grapes are made into delicious wines. Vegetables, herbs and olives (to eat and for oil) grow in abundance. Meat is predominently lamb, pork and chicken, and fresh fish and seafood is plentiful along the coast. A good way to try a selection of local food is with a platter of *mezédhes* (*mezze* for short), which may comprise of up to 20 dishes.

Oregano and thyme

Cypriot fisherman preparing his catch for sale

Southern Cyprus

The cuisine of the south is inspired by the flavours of the Mediterranean area. Popular ingredients include olives and fresh herbs from the rich soils of the foothills of the Troodos mountains, and lemons from the groves found largely in the western region near Pafos. Locally made cheeses such as

anari and *halloumi* give a distinctive taste to many dishes. Most meals start with a selection of dips made using recipes that have been handed down from generation to generation for centuries. These recipes have their roots in Greek cuisine, and are generally served with a freshly baked "village" loaf. Bread plays an important part in the diet of southern Cypriots. A flattish-

domed loaf, village bread, is usually plain white but may also be flavoured with *halloumi* or olives. Main courses tend to be meat-based rather than fish. Chickens, pigs and goats are reared in most rural areas and provide meat that is usually cooked on the grill, either plain or marinated with herbs and served with the famous Cyprus potatoes grown in the red soil found in the Larnaka area. A

Pita breads   Grilled *halloumi*   *Kupepia*

Roasted red peppers   Taramasalata

                                    Olives   Tzatziki

Selection of typical Cypriot *mezédhes*

Regional Dishes and Specialities

Dishes of the south include *afelia* (pork simmered in red wine with coriander) and *kleftiko*. Moussaka and *kupepia* (stuffed vine leaves) are among the dishes drawn from Greek cuisine. Dips include *taramosalata* (puréed salted mullet roe) and *tzatziki* (yoghurt, cucumber, garlic and mint). The cuisine of northern Cyprus includes dishes such as *imam bayıldı* (tomato-and onion-stuffed aubergines), *böörek* (cheese-filled pastries) and *bamya basti* (tomato and okra stew). Meat dishes include *döner* kebabs of sliced, spiced roast lamb, *iskender* or *bursa* (kebabs in a thick, spicy tomato sauce) and *adana*, a length of minced lamb bound together with red pepper flakes and cooked on a skewer.

Sweet pastries

Souvlakia are small chunks of pork, marinated in lemon juice, herbs (usually oregano) and olive oil, grilled on skewers.

Local grocer offering a wide range of fresh and dried produce

"village salad" (*choriatiki salata*), made of lettuce, cabbage, tomatoes, cucumber, onions, pepper, olives and feta cheese is a typical accompaniment to the main course. Bananas, oranges and cherries are among the many fruits grown in this part of the island and, along with sweet cakes, generally complete a meal.

Northern Cyprus

Cuisine in North Cyprus takes its influences from the island itself and the Turkish mainland, where many of the staple dishes were inspired by Middle-Eastern and Central Asian cooking. Spices such as saffron and paprika, along with garlic, chillies and peppers, are used extensively; these ingredients give a colourful hue and a spicy kick to traditional northern dishes. Most meals are based around meat, usually chicken or lamb, and vegetables grown on the flat plains south of the Pentadaktylos mountain range and along the coast. Many recipes come from the days of the Ottoman Empire and are characterized by their spicy

Cypriot coffee, served strong and black with pastries

tomato-, yoghurt- and cream-based sauces. Meze-style meals, usually for large groups of friends or family, are a staple on the menu too, but differ slightly from those found in the south in that they are more often inspired by Turkish cuisine. Main courses are generally served with rice, boiled potatoes and salad accompaniments, and are usually followed by sweet pastries, such as *baklava*, or milk puddings and fresh fruit, especially citrus fruits, which grow prolifically in the north of the island.

What to Drink

Cyprus offers the ideal climate and geography for growing grapes for wine-making, and production can be traced back to around 2000 BC. Of the over 40 varieties, the most famous is Commandaria, a sweet wine dating from the time of Richard the Lionheart. Maratheftiko, Xinisteri, Spourtiko, Lefkada are some of the island's indigenous grape varieties producing excellent wines. *Zivania* is a popular drink, while Brandy Sour is Cyprus' signature cocktail. Freshly squeezed fruit juices are also very good, and inexpensive. Cyprus, however, is above all the land of the coffee shop and villagers, mostly men, will spend hours over a strong Cypriot coffee, which is always served with a glass of cold water.

Scharas means "from the grill". Here, swordfish has first been marinated in lemon juice, olive oil and herbs.

Kleftiko is usually goat meat wrapped in paper and slow-cooked in a plinth oven so that the flavours are sealed in.

Giaourti kai meli (yoghurt with honey) is a popular dessert that is found everywhere, from cafés and tavernas to fancy restaurants.

**LOFOU: Lofou Traditional
Tavern** €
Cypriot **Map** B4
Tsindouri, Lofou village, 4716
Tel *25 470 202*
For a real Cypriot experience
this lovely tavern housed in an
old stone cottage serves home-
made local dishes and fine wines.
Listen to the jovial owner Costas
playing traditional folk music in
the background.

**MONIATIS: Paraskeuas
Restaurant** €
Cypriot **Map** B3
Moniatis village, 4747
Tel *25 433 626*
Serves a good variety of grilled
dishes such as pork ribs,
souvlakia, sheftalia and chicken
kebabs. Eat inside or alfresco on
its vine-covered terrace.

OMODOS: Stou Kir Yianni €
Greek/Cypriot **Map** B4
Linou 15, 4760
Tel *25 422 100*
Housed in a restored village
house, this eatery serves an
interesting array of Greek, Cypriot
and Middle Eastern dishes. Live
folk music on weekends.

DK Choice

**PANAGIA: Vouni
Panagias** €
Cypriot **Map** A3
*Archiepiskopou Markariou
III 60, 8640*
Tel *26 722 770*
Enjoy gorgeous panoramic
views while dining at the
restaurant and outdoor
terrace of this winery. Classic
Cypriot dishes with an
emphasis on fresh organic
produce are accompanied by
the winery's own labels. The
menu changes regularly to
feature seasonal vegetables.

Scenic views from the alfresco dining terrace at Vouni Panagias, Panagia

PEDOULAS: Platanos €
Cypriot **Map** B3
V. Hadjioannou, 2850
Tel *99 438 820*
Visit this coffee shop to sample
traditional delicacies such as
mezédhes, souvlakia, home-made
sausages, *sheftalia, halloumi* and
"village salad". End your meal with
Cypriot coffee and spoon sweets.

PELENDRI: Symposio €
Cypriot **Map** B3
Prodromou 61, 4878
Tel *99 404 348*
A lovely tavern serving *mezédhes,
souvla* and *kleftiko* along with
home-made bread. The
ingredients are sourced from
the owner's garden.

PLATRES: Psilo Dendro €
Cypriot **Map** B3
13 Aidonion, 4820
Tel *25 813 131*
Busy restaurant with a great
location near the waterfalls.
Try the legendary freshly caught
trout cooked with herbs and
lemon, sourced from the owner's
own trout farm.

**STATOS-AGIOS FOTIOS: Kolios
Restaurant** €
Cypriot **Map** A3
Kolios Winery, 2651
Tel *26 724 090*
This large, modern restaurant
is part of the Kolios Winery
complex. After a tour of the
winery, sit back and enjoy local
delicacies such as *mezédhes.*
Reservation recommended.

**TROODOS: Fereos Park
Restaurant** €
Cypriot **Map** B3
Troodos village, 1504
Tel *25 420 114*
Fereos Park is an attractive local
eatery that serves local dishes. Try
the excellent *souvlakia* and
barbecued *sheftalia.*

VASA: Ariadne Restaurant €€
Cypriot **Map** B4
Vasa village, 4505
Tel *25 944 064*
Sample from an extensive
selection of *mezédhes* dishes,
including *tahini* and *skordalia*
dips, grilled *halloumi* and herb
sausages with fresh bread. Lovely
courtyard seating.

VOUNI: Orea Ellas €€
Greek **Map** B4
Ellados 3, 4772
Tel *25 944 328*
Housed in a beautiful building,
Orea Ellas dishes up sumptuous
dishes such as *saganaki* (a Greek
appetizer), oven-baked pies, cour-
gette balls and Greek sausage.

Central Cyprus

DK Choice

AGROS: Kelada €
Cypriot **Map** C3
Agros Ave, 4860
Tel *25 521 303*
Located on the central square
of Agros, Kelada offers a taste of
the authentic cuisine of Cyprus.
Souvla (pork, lamb or chicken),
*koupepia, makaronia tou
fournou* (pasta with béchamel
sauce and minced pork) are
some of its specialities. Dine at
the outdoor patio in summer.

**AGROS: Rodon Hotel
Restaurant** €
International **Map** C3
Rodon Hotel, Rodou 1, 4860
Tel *25 521 201*
Cypriot and international cuisine
are served in this bright and
spacious fine-dining restaurant
located in a renovated country
house. Imaginative home-
made desserts.

**AGROS: To Mpakaliko
toy Hapsi** €
Cypriot **Map** C3
114 Agros Ave, 4860
Tel *99 409 108*
Enjoy lovely views over Agros
while sipping coffee or tea at this
traditional *kafenia.* When hungry,
order the platter of charcuterie
and local cheese, accompanied
by Greek or Cypriot wines.

DALI: Daliou Mills €
Cypriot **Map** D3
Archbishop Makarios III 41, 2540
Tel *22 521 308*
One of Dali's few eateries, and
believed to be its oldest taverna,

in mainlan
also buy tr
sausages,
and a varie
sweets. Sa
colourful s
the stalls.
Every no
also find a
reasonable

Food

One of the
foods is h
traditiona
is exceller
delicious
Another t

The charming, homely dining room at Archontiko Papadopoulou, Kornos

soujoukka
filling cov
grape juic
The bes
Cyprus is
sun" – the
Comman
rich, warn
bouquet.
beverage
produced
classified
the popu
the ones
Other go
include o
and rose
fruit jellie
Cypriot v
delight. T
produced
Geroskip
village pi
version c
highland
herb-sce
popular
are oreg
of the M
and spic

the Daliou Mills is best known for
its *mezédhes* platters and scrump-
tious *kleftiko*. Call ahead.

FIKARDOU: O Yiannakos €
Cypriot **Map** C3
Fikardou village, 2623
Tel *22 633 311*
Popular restaurant housed in
a renovated centuries-old stone
house. Good Cypriot menu with
koupepia and *sheftalia* highly
recommended. Call ahead for
opening times.

**KORNOS: Archontiko
Papadopoulou** €€
Cypriot **Map** C3
Archbishop Makarios III 67, 7640
Tel *22 531 000*
Set in a beautifully restored
village house, this restaurant
dishes up local cuisine with a
creative twist. Try their *mezédhes*
named *Ta Pilina*, as the food is
served in little clay pots *(pilos)*.
Good wine list.

LAKATAMIA: Mageirisses €
Cypriot **Map** C3
Archbishop Makarios III 110, 2323
Tel *22 381 822*
True to its name, which means
two women cooks, this modern
tavern is run by two sisters.
Offers *souvlakia, sheftalia, ttavas*
(a casserole dish) and other
Cypriot dishes.

LAZANIA: Estiatorio Mageia €
Cypriot **Map** C3
Lazania village, 2618
Tel *22 781 083*
Estiatorio Mageia is one of a
handful of small eateries in this
traditional cobbled village.
Known for its delicious *kleftiko*,
which is cooked in its outside
domed oven, and *souvlakia* that
sizzles on the barbecue.

South Nicosia

Café La Mode €
International **Map** C3
Archbishop Makarios III 12A, 1065
Tel *22 510 788*
One of five branches in the city,
this lovely café serves everything
from salads and light lunches to
steaks, along with delicious
coffees and desserts.

**Fanous Lebanese
Restaurant** €
Lebanese **Map** C3
Solonos 7C, 1011
Tel *22 666 663*
Choose from a menu of
traditional and contemporary
Lebanese and Palestinian
dishes. There is belly dancing
on Saturdays.

Il Forno €
Italian **Map** C3
Ledras 216–218, 1011
Located on the busiest pedestrian
street of the capital. The menu is
simple and consists of thin-crust
pizzas baked in a wood-fired
oven, savoury pastas and *antipasti*.

Zanettos €
Cypriot **Map** C3
Trikoupi 65, 1016
Tel *22 765 501*
One of the best places in South
Nicosia to taste *mezédhes*. Choose
from an extensive selection of
dishes – "village salad", *koupepia,
souvlakia*, dips, village pasta and
lots more. First-rate wine list.

Aigaio €€
Cypriot/Greek **Map** C3
Ektoros 40, 1016
Tel *22 433 297*
Favoured by loyal diners for
over 25 years, Aigaio dishes

up the best of classic Cypriot
and Greek cuisines. Superb
selection of wines. Reservations
are advised.

Akakiko €€
Asian **Map** C3
Achaion 1, 2413
Tel *77 778 022*
Relish flavourful Japanese, Thai
and Korean dishes at this
modern Asian restaurant located
adjacent to Hilton Park Hotel.
There is a wide range of sushi
on offer. Advance booking
is recommended.

DK Choice

**Brasserie Au Bon
Plaisir** €€
French **Map** C3
97 Larnakos Ave, 1046
Tel *96 755 111*
The only French restaurant
in Nicosia, this fine-dining
establishment serves
delectable dishes such as
foie gras in a Madeira sauce,
oysters, mussels, beef
bourguignon, *Charolaise*
steak and veal with a Béarnaise
sauce. Guests can choose
from a good list of French
and Cypriot wines. Cosy,
welcoming interior.

D.O.T €€
International **Map** C3
6A Athinas Ave, 1016
Tel *22 101 228*
Enjoy Mediterranean-inspired
cuisine in a lovely industrial-chic
setting. From tasty burgers and
artfully prepared salads and
pastas, the seasonally changing
menu offers good choices to
diners. Brunch is served
throughout the week.

Beautifully

For more information on types of restaurants *see pp166–7*

SH

Cyprus is
the intric
fabrics c
food and
well as s
Commar
A variety
and perf

Where

Souvenir
anywhere
boutique
found in
larger tow
promena
resorts. Ir
small fam
commod
foodstuff
marmalac
honeys, c
from thei
shops or
locations
  Near ev
you will f
typical lo
and hanc
common
amphora
traditiona
  Supern
shops, wl
late, have
stuffs, bu
drinks an
or from c
found ev
hotels ha

Openir

The peak
to mid-S

A typical Cy

crossings) and noise – Agia Napa, especially, is geared to younger visitors.

Photography

Be aware that taking photographs of military bases or facilities, and the border between Southern Cyprus and the North is strictly prohibited. United Nations soldiers guarding the Green Line are used to groups of tourists, but taking photographs at any point is strictly forbidden.

Archaeological sites can be photographed and filmed free of charge; however, the state museums generally charge a fee for taking photographs.

In places of worship, ask in advance whether photography is permitted. Most churches will not allow you to use flash photography.

Electrical Equipment

The mains supply on the island is 220/240V, with standard

British triple rectangular-pin plugs. Anyone travelling from outside of the EU should ensure they have a suitable adaptor but if needed most hotel reception desks will provide you with the correct type for your devices. Some hotel rooms are equipped with hair dryers, and irons are usually available to borrow.

Time

Cyprus lies within the Eastern-European time zone, and local time is 2 hours ahead of GMT. Like the UK, Cyprus puts its clocks forward by 1 hour from late March to late October. "Morning" in South Cyprus is *proi*; "afternoon" – *mesiméri*; "evening" – *vrádhi*; and "night" – *níchta*.

Weddings

Cyprus is one of the world's most popular wedding destinations and some hotels have their own wedding chapel as well as wedding planners to

SURVIVAL GUIDE

DIRECTORY

Embassies & Consulates

Australia
Pindarou 27, Nicosia.
Tel 22 753 001.
w cyprus.highcommission.gov.au

Germany
Nikitaras 10, Nicosia.
Tel 22 451 145.
w nikosia.diplo.de

Ireland
Aiantos 7, 1082 Nicosia.
Tel 22 818 183.
w embassyofireland.com.cy

Representation of the European Commission
Byron 30, 1096 Nicosia.
Tel 22 817 770.
w ec.europa.eu/cyprus

Russia
Arch. Makarios III, 2406 Engomi, Nicosia.
Tel 222 774 622.
w cyprus.mid.ru

UK
Alexandrou Palli 1, 1106 Nicosia.
Tel 22 861 100.
w ukincyprus.fco.gov.uk/en

USA
Ploutarchou, Nicosia.
Tel 22 393 939.
w american embassy.org.cy

Tourist Organizations

Association of Independent Tour Operators
w aito.co.uk

Cyprus Hotel Association
Andreas Araouzos 12, 1303 Nicosia.
Tel 22 452 820.
w cyprushotel association.org

Cyprus Tourism Organization (CTO)
Leoforos Lemesou 19, Nicosia.
Tel 22 691 100.
w visitcyprus.com

Cyprus Tourist Guide Association
Spyrou Kyprianou 14, 1, Nicosia. **Tel** 22 765 755.
w cytouristguides. co

North Cyprus Tourism Centre
w welcometonorthcyprus.co.uk

Turkish Republic of Northern Cyprus Ministry of Economy & Tourism
Tel 0392 228 96 29.

Weddings

Union of Cyprus Municipalities
Rigenis 78, Nicosia.
Tel 22 445 170.
w ucm.org.cy

Religion

The Cypriot Orthodox Church, which is dominant in the south of the island, is independent of the Greek Orthodox Church. It is also the oldest national church in Christendom, its history tracing back to the time of St Paul.

In the towns, you often encounter Orthodox priests dressed in long black robes. The main Orthodox services, lasting 2 to 3 hours, are held on Saturday evenings and Sunday mornings.

Monasteries have served as Cypriot pilgrimage sites for centuries. Today, they are visited by tourists in such vast numbers that access to some of them has been restricted.

In the North, the dominant religion is Islam, though, like Turkey, the North is a secular state. All larger towns and cities have mosques, from which the muezzin's voice calls the faithful to prayer five times a day. Services are held on Friday afternoons.

Façade of a Cypriot mosque with an imposing minaret

Travelling with Children

Major brands of baby food, medicines and toiletries, including nappies (diapers), are sold in all supermarkets and pharmacies. Both parts of the island are family-friendly, with children welcomed everywhere and plenty of kids' facilities. However, risks for smaller children include sunburn, occasional rough waters and pests such as jellyfish, sea urchins and stinging insects.

Worshipper inside an Orthodox church, southern Cyprus

Young Visitors

Cyprus is an ideal holiday destination for young people. Its sunny beaches, clean water, watersports facilities, and rich and varied nightlife attract young people in thousands. Hundreds of nightclubs, discos, pubs and bars await the revellers.

Holders of ISIC or Euro<26 cards qualify for discounts on public transport and reduced admission to museums and some other tourist sights.

Women Travellers

Women travelling alone or together should exercise normal caution. However, Cyprus is generally safe for women.

Disabled Visitors

Facilities for the disabled have improved considerably in the last few years. However, many museums are housed in older buildings without the provision of lifts. Access to archaeological sites is also difficult. Pavements in towns and villages are often uneven. A leaflet with information on facilities for wheelchair users is available from the CTO.

ΑΠΑΓΟΡΕΥΕΤΑΙ Η ΛΗΨΗ ΦΩΤΟΓΡΑΦΙΩΝ PHOTOGRAPHS ARE PROHIBITED

Sign in Greek prohibiting photography

Banking and Local Currency

Banks in Cyprus operate efficiently. There is a wide bank network on the island, and many foreign banks also have branches here. Cash machines can be found along the main streets and in hotel lobbies, making debit and credit cards a convenient way to withdraw cash. Most larger shops and boutiques, as well as hotels and restaurants, accept credit and debit cards.

Tourists drawing money from a cash machine

Banks and Cash Machines

Bank opening hours are from 8:15am to 1:30pm (Monday to Friday) in summer (8:30am–1:30pm, 3:15–4:45pm in winter); closed Saturday and Sunday. Some banks in the tourist resorts are open every afternoon, from 3 to 5pm. The bank desks in Larnaka and Pafos airports remain open until the last plane of the day lands.

Cash machines operate around the clock. They are typically installed outside banks and in some hotels, as well as in larger towns and holiday resorts. You can withdraw cash using all major credit cards. VISA, MasterCard and American Express are widely accepted.

Money Exchange

Bureaux de change are found in the centres of larger towns and at the airports. They are open 24 hours a day; currency exchange counters in the banks are open during normal banking hours. Money exchange transactions are always subject to a commission fee; look around to get the best deal – the rates are clearly posted for you to see.

Hotels also offer exchange facilities, but their rates of exchange tend to be less favourable than either banks or bureaux de change, and they usually charge a higher commission, too.

Both foreign currency and travellers' cheques are accepted, in exchange for euro or Turkish lira. Travellers' cheques are also honoured by many hotels, shops and restaurants.

Many shops in both the Republic of Cyprus and in North Cyprus accept common foreign currencies, including US dollars and British pound sterling.

Cash machine in one of Nicosia's streets

Banks and Currency Exchange in North Cyprus

In North Cyprus, the bank networks are less extensive than in the south. Banks are open from 8am until noon. Travellers' cheques are widely accepted in shops, hotels and restaurants. They can also be exchanged for Turkish lira in banks and bureaux de change. When exchanging money, use only reputable dealers. In light of the high rate of inflation, it is worth changing smaller amounts of money more frequently, rather than a large amount.

Entrance to a Turkish bank in North Cyprus

Traveller's Cheques and Credit Cards

Banks, bureaux de change and other exchange facilities will cash your traveller's cheques into either euros or Turkish lira.

Credit cards are accepted by most larger shops, restaurants and hotels, although in markets and small shops only cash is accepted. Many debit cards are accepted, but check with your bank that your card is valid internationally. It may be difficult to find a cash machine in provincial towns and villages, so it is advisable to bring enough cash with you. Banks and credit card providers will charge foreign transaction fees on charges made while you are abroad so check the rates before you travel to avoid an unnecessarily large bill.

Currency

The Republic of Cyprus joined the Eurozone on 1 January 2008. Following a changeover period of one month, during which time both the Cyprus pound and the euro were in circulation, the Cyprus pound ceased to be legal tender.

The currency used in North Cyprus is the Turkish lira (TL or, more officially, TRY). This currency is not readily available abroad, so you need to change money on arrival in the island. North Cyprus also accepts payments in euros.

crossings) and noise – Agia Napa, especially, is geared to younger visitors.

Photography

Be aware that taking photographs of military bases or facilities, and the border between Southern Cyprus and the North is strictly prohibited. United Nations soldiers guarding the Green Line are used to groups of tourists, but taking photographs at any point is strictly forbidden.

Archaeological sites can be photographed and filmed free of charge; however, the state museums generally charge a fee for taking photographs.

In places of worship, ask in advance whether photography is permitted. Most churches will not allow you to use flash photography.

Electrical Equipment

The mains supply on the island is 220/240V, with standard British triple rectangular-pin plugs. Anyone travelling from outside of the EU should ensure they have a suitable adaptor but if needed most hotel reception desks will provide you with the correct type for your devices. Some hotel rooms are equipped with hair dryers, and irons are usually available to borrow.

Time

Cyprus lies within the Eastern-European time zone, and local time is 2 hours ahead of GMT. Like the UK, Cyprus puts its clocks forward by 1 hour from late March to late October. "Morning" in South Cyprus is *proí*; "afternoon" – *mesiméri*; "evening" – *vrádhi*; and "night" – *níchta*.

Weddings

Cyprus is one of the world's most popular wedding destinations and some hotels have their own wedding chapel as well as wedding planners to assist with the preparation for the big day. The bride and groom are required to have all the correct documentation.

Discussing Politics

The events of 1974, when the island was divided between the Turkish and the Greek Cypriots, are still remembered with bitterness. In both the South and the North, local people vehemently argue the justice of their cause. Politics and recent history are therefore subjects that are best avoided for open discussion.

Military Zones

Britain's sovereign bases in the south, at Akrotiri (Episkopi) and Dhekelia, are also used by US forces and are likely to be on heightened alert in these security-conscious times. Do not intrude on military installations. The same applies to Turkish Army personnel, equipment and installations in the occupied North.

DIRECTORY

Embassies & Consulates

Australia
Pindarou 27, Nicosia.
Tel 22 753 001.
w cyprus.
highcommission.gov.au

Germany
Nikitaras 10, Nicosia.
Tel 22 451 145.
w nikosia.diplo.de

Ireland
Aiantos 7, 1082 Nicosia.
Tel 22 818 183.
w embassyofireland.
com.cy

Representation of the European Commission
Byron 30, 1096 Nicosia.
Tel 22 817 770.
w ec.europa.eu/cyprus

Russia
Arch. Makarios III, 2406 Engomi, Nicosia.
Tel 222 774 622.
w cyprus.mid.ru

UK
Alexandrou Palli 1, 1106 Nicosia.
Tel 22 861 100.
w ukincyprus.fco.
gov.uk/en

USA
Ploutarchou, Nicosia.
Tel 22 393 939.
w american embassy.
org.cy

Tourist Organizations

Association of Independent Tour Operators
w aito.co.uk

Cyprus Hotel Association
Andreas Araouzos 12, 1303 Nicosia.
Tel 22 452 820.
w cyprushotel
association.org

Cyprus Tourism Organization (CTO)
Leoforos Lemesou 19, Nicosia.
Tel 22 691 100.
w visitcyprus.com

Cyprus Tourist Guides Association
Spyrou Kyprianou 14, 1640 Nicosia. **Tel** 22 765 755.
w cytouristguides. com

North Cyprus Tourism Centre
w
welcometonorthcyprus.
co.uk

Turkish Republic of Northern Cyprus Ministry of Economy & Tourism
Tel 0392 228 96 29.

Weddings

Union of Cyprus Municipalities
Rigenis 78, Nicosia.
Tel 22 445 170.
w ucm.org.cy

Useful Websites in the Republic of Cyprus

w cyprus-mail.com
w visitcyprus.com
w kypros.org
w pio.gov.cy
w windowon
cyprus.com
w in-cyprus.com

Useful Websites in North Cyprus

w cypnet.com
w northcyprus.net

Personal Security and Health

Cyprus has a low crime rate, but even here crimes do occur; chances can be minimized by taking simple precautions. The risk of theft is greatest in crowded places. Take extra care on crowded promenades or streets and in markets to protect your belongings. Keep documents, money and credit cards hidden from view, and leave what you don't need in the hotel safe. Never leave anything visible in your car when you park it. When in need, you can always ask a policeman for help. Basic medical advice is available at pharmacies. All medical treatment must be paid for; insurance is strongly advised.

Entrance to a police station in the North

Any case of theft should be reported immediately to the police. Passport theft should also be reported to your embassy in Nicosia.

Personal Belongings

Before travelling abroad, it is wise to ensure that you have adequate insurance to protect yourself financially from the loss or theft of your property. Even so, it is advisable to take precautions against loss or theft in the first place. Be vigilant when you are out and about but especially in crowded places, where the risk of theft is greatest.

Make photocopies of your important documents and keep these with you, leaving the originals behind in the hotel safe (where you can also deposit money and jewellery).

Make a note of your credit card numbers and the phone number of the issuing bank, in the event of loss or theft.

Cameras and camcorders should be carried on a strap or inside the case. Your car should always be locked, with any valuables kept well out of sight.

Cyprus Police

The police in Cyprus are friendly towards tourists and ready to offer advice. The majority of them also speak English. But in the event that you are caught breaking the law, they can be stern and unwilling to accept excuses.

Heavy fines are levied for failing to wear a seat belt and for using a mobile telephone when driving a vehicle.

Personal Security in the North

In terms of personal safety, North Cyprus is no different from the south. Special care should be taken when visiting the buffer zone and when passing by military facilities, of which there is no shortage. In particular, resist the temptation to photograph any military installations, vehicles or soldiers. The latter are visible in great

Typical southern Cyprus police car

numbers, but if you follow the rules of normal behaviour, they will not interfere with your visit.

Roads in North Cyprus are comfortable, wide and of very high quality, including the mountain roads.

Manned lifeguard post at one of the beaches

Beaches

During the holiday season, most beaches employ lifeguards. The areas allocated for swimming are marked with coloured buoys. While swimming outside the marked areas is not prohibited, it is inadvisable, particularly for weaker swimmers. Some beaches have first-aid stations, with lifeguards trained to help casualties.

Beach facilities, such as showers, are standard almost everywhere. Hotels with direct access to the sea have stretches of beach allocated to them.

Smaller beaches have no lifeguards; they are generally found in coves sheltered from the open sea, so their waters are calm and safe. The most beautiful beaches are found in the regions of Agia Napa in the South, and Famagusta in North Cyprus. The south coast beaches are generally rocky and pebbly.

In summer, Cyprus has some of the highest temperatures in Europe, and it's easy to get sunburned anytime from early April to late October. Young children are especially vulnerable to the hot sun. Avoid being directly in the sun during the middle of the day, when the rays are strongest. Sunhats, sunglasses, a high factor sunscreen and sunblock are vital to protect your skin. During the day, carry bottled water with you, and drink lots of it, to avoid dehydration.

Medical Care

Cyprus is free from most dangerous infectious diseases (although AIDS is present), and no immunizations are required. Drinking tap water is safe. However, all medical treatment must be paid for, and comprehensive insurance to cover hospital and medical charges, as well as emergency repatriation, is advisable. Before travelling to the North, double check that your insurance policy will cover you there.

Some medical procedures (such as dental treatment) are not covered by insurance.

Emergency medical care in the Republic of Cyprus is free for all European Union citizens. The European Health Insurance Card (EHIC), available from the UK Department of Health or from a main post office, provides access to healthcare at a reduced cost or sometimes for free. The card comes with a booklet that contains general health advice and information about how to claim medical treatment when travelling abroad. You may find that you have to pay and reclaim the money later.

Hotels can usually recommend a local doctor or dentist, many of whom speak English. All bills must be settled at the time of treatment, but these practitioners will provide a receipt for you to

ΦΑΡΜΑΚΕΙΟ

ΠΑΝΑΓΙΩΤΑ ΚΑΛΑΪΤΖΗ

Pharmacy sign with the easily recognizable green cross

claim a refund from your insurance company.

Visitors on package holidays to Cyprus should check with their tour operator if medical insurance is included.

Pharmacies

Most pharmacies keep normal shop opening hours (see p178). They display the green cross sign and the word *farmakeio* or *eczane*. A list of pharmacies that open at night and on holidays can be found in the English-language *Cyprus Mail* and *Cyprus Weekly*. In an emergency, an all-night pharmacy can offer medical help and advice.

In tourist resorts and large cities pharmacists speak English. They can usually advise on remedies for minor ailments and injuries, but if you need specialist prescription drugs it is best to bring an adequate supply.

A uniformed fireman

Fire Service

Winters are dry and mild, and summers are hot, creating prime conditions for fires, which can spread with alarming speed and present a particular danger to forests. Mountain fires, especially, are difficult to put out.

Cyprus has two types of fire brigade; one that responds to general emergency calls, the other specifically dedicated to forest fires.

During excursions to the island's drier inland areas, or when camping, you must take particular care not to start a fire, or keep one under control. Be especially careful to extinguish cigarettes thoroughly and dispose of them safely. When leaving a picnic area or campsite, ensure that any bonfires are completely extinguished when you are leaving, and take all glass bottles with you to prevent accidental fires.

DIRECTORY

Emergency Services

Police
Tel 112 (South), 155 (North).

Fire Brigade
Tel 112 (South), 199 (North).

Forest Fire Teams
Tel 1407 (South), 177 (North).

Ambulance
Tel 112.

Hospitals

General Hospitals
Agia Napa/Paralimni.
Tel 23 200 000.
Famagusta.
Tel 0392 366 28 76.
Kyrenia.
Tel 815 2266.
Larnaka.
Tel 24 800 500.
Limassol.
Tel 25 801 100.
Nicosia.
Tel 22 603 000.
North Nicosia.
Tel 228 5441.
Pafos.
Tel 26 803 100.

Pharmacies

Information in English
Famagusta.
Tel 90 901 413.
Larnaka.
Tel 90 901 414.
Limassol.
Tel 90 901 415.
Nicosia.
Tel 90 901 412.
Pafos.
Tel 90 901 416.

Standard fire engine of the Cyprus Fire Brigade

Communications

The quality of telecommunications services in Cyprus is very good, especially in the south. Public telephone booths are widespread. In larger towns and cities, you will have no trouble finding an Internet café, if your hotel doesn't have access. Postal services are efficient. A good selection of newspapers and magazines is available, and there's no shortage of TV or radio stations.

Telephone and discount card

Using the Telephone

Cyprus has a well-developed telephone network. Public phones accept coins, as well as phonecards, which can be purchased from newsagent kiosks, post offices and banks in various denominations. Instructions for using the phone are provided in both Greek and English. Calls to the police, fire brigade or ambulance service are free.

Hotel rooms are equipped with telephones, but calls made from them are usually very expensive; make sure you check the rates before using them. The country code for Cyprus is 357 except for North Cyprus, where it is 90 (for Turkey) followed by (0)392. Local area codes in Cyprus include: Nicosia 22; Limassol 25; Larnaka 24; Pafos and Polis 26; Agia Napa and Protaras 23.

When making an international call from Cyprus, first dial 00,

Public phone booths

followed by the country code, and then the area code (omitting the zero that precedes some area codes). Useful country codes are: UK (44), USA and Canada (1), Ireland (353), Australia (61), New Zealand (64) and South Africa (27). All public telephones in the South can be used to make international calls. Calls are cheaper at night (after 6pm) and at weekends.

Every hotel and many public buildings have Yellow Pages directories where, in addition to local phone numbers, you can find information on hotels, restaurants, and many outfits offering activities and entertainment.

Telephones in North Cyprus

There are fewer public telephones in the North than in the South and the quality of connections can be poor. In the North, phones don't accept coins; instead you insert a pre-paid phone card (*telekart*). These are available from *Telekomünikasyon* offices, post offices and newsagents. There are also metred counter phones (*kontürlü telefon*) where you speak first and pay after completing the call. These calls are more expensive than card-operated phones. Metered phones can be found in *Telekomunikasyon* branches.

Hotel room telephones are the most expensive. To avoid unpleasant surprises, check the rates first.

The area codes for Northern Cyprus are as follows:
228 for Nicosia (Lefkoşa);
822 for Kyrenia (Girne);
366 for Famagusta (Gazimağuza);
723 for Morfou (Güzelyurt);

and 660 for Lefke. The remaining area codes are the same as for Southern Cyprus.

Mobile Phones

The Cyprus mobile telephone (cellphone) network covers most of the island, although reception may be patchy, especially in the mountainous regions. Mobile phone usage is widespread in Cyprus, and international visitors who bring their own mobile phone are likely to experience few problems, although individual calls will invariably cost more than at home.

Making and receiving calls requires an active roaming facility on the phone. While abroad, mobile telephone users are charged for both outgoing and incoming calls, as well as text messages. Information on the cost of calls, travel bundles and packages and how to activate international roaming can be obtained from individual network providers.

A cheaper alternative may be to buy a prepaid SIM card upon arrival in Cyprus to use with your mobile. Handsets must be GSM-compatible, and users will need to check with their local service provider that the handset is unlocked to allow for a new SIM card.

Prepaid SIM cards and top-up vouchers are available from newspaper stands, petrol stations and convenience stores. The SIM card gives the user a local mobile number, allowing for standard local rates, very reasonable international rates and free incoming calls. Prepaid data packages are also available for smartphones.

Useful Numbers

- Directory enquiries 11892 (South), 192 (North)
- International directory enquiries 11894 (South), 192 (North)
- International calls via the operator 80000198
- Speaking clock 1895
- Infoline 132
- International access code 00

Internet

The Internet is a great way to research your trip before heading off. Hotels will have their own websites where you can view the facilities available, make reservations and plan your trip. The same is true of car hire companies and various organized activities. A particularly informative site is the CTO's own website www.visitcyprus.com.

Once you're in Cyprus, the Internet is a valuable resource to stay in touch with people back home, and to learn more about Cyprus. Internet cafés can be found in all the island's major towns, and most hotels provide Internet access. Visitors can enjoy access to free Wi-Fi in almost all cafés, bars and restaurants in towns and cities.

Postal Services

Most post offices in the South are open from 7:30am to 5:30pm in towns and from 8am to 3pm in rural areas (except in July and August, when they close daily at noon). They are closed from noon on Wednesdays. Letters and postcards sent to European

Postage stamp vending machine

countries arrive quite quickly, taking about four days to reach their destination.

In the North, post offices are open from 8am until 5pm on weekdays, with a lunch break from 1 to 2pm; and on Saturdays from 9am until noon.

Post offices accept letters and parcels and postage stamps can be bought at post offices and almost any shop that sells postcards. You can also post your letter at the reception desk in most hotels.

Beware posting mail in the North – it will invariably take longer to reach its destination. This is due to the international non-recognition of North Cyprus, all mail sent from here has to travel via Turkey to reach its destination.

Radio and Television

Cyprus has an extraordinary number of TV channels for a country of its size.

In the South there are five free-to-air island-wide channels plus several local stations in each town. Many Cypriots also subscribe to one or more Pay-TV channels. Greek national TV is relayed to the South and Turkish TV to the North. Most

large hotels have satellite TV tuned to CNN, BBC World and other foreign-language channels.

The most popular of the English-language radio stations in Cyprus is BFBS (www.bfbs. com), which is primarily aimed at the British Forces stationed on Cyprus, but is listened to by English-speakers throughout the island. Its two channels resemble BBC Radio 1 and BBC Radio 2, though the latter also transmits programmes from BBC Radio 4 and Radio 5 Live.

Cyprus' has its own national broadcaster, CyBC (www.cybc. com.cy), which provides a limited English-language TV service on Channel 2, and there are also several independent English-language stations to tune in to, including Radio Napa (106.3 FM broadcast in Agia Napa) and Coast FM (91.4 FM broadcast in Limassol).

Range of English-language newspapers available at Larnaka airport

Press

English-language newspapers published in southern Cyprus include the daily *Cyprus Mail* and the weekly *Cyprus Weekly*, as well as the *Cyprus Lion* – the British Forces newspaper. In the North, you can find the English-language *Cyprus Times*. Many popular British newspapers (*Daily Mail*, *Daily Express* and *Mirror*) are on sale on the day of publication.

These newspapers are sold at newsagent kiosks, airports and hotels. There are also a dozen or so local papers published in Cyprus. The cultural bulletins, published in several languages, contain information on current events and activities, and may be useful to visitors interested in what's happening on the island.

Post office in Pafos, with the bright-yellow letter box outside

Banking and Local Currency

Banks in Cyprus operate efficiently. There is a wide bank network on the island, and many foreign banks also have branches here. Cash machines can be found along the main streets and in hotel lobbies, making debit and credit cards a convenient way to withdraw cash. Most larger shops and boutiques, as well as hotels and restaurants, accept credit and debit cards.

Tourists drawing money from a cash machine

Banks and Cash Machines

Bank opening hours are from 8:15am to 1:30pm (Monday to Friday) in summer (8:30am–1:30pm, 3:15–4:45pm in winter); closed Saturday and Sunday. Some banks in the tourist resorts are open every afternoon, from 3 to 5pm. The bank desks in Larnaka and Pafos airports remain open until the last plane of the day lands.

Cash machines operate around the clock. They are typically installed outside banks and in some hotels, as well as in larger towns and holiday resorts. You can withdraw cash using all major credit cards. VISA, MasterCard and American Express are widely accepted.

Money Exchange

Bureaux de change are found in the centres of larger towns and at the airports. They are open 24 hours a day; currency exchange counters in the banks are open during normal banking hours. Money exchange transactions are always subject to a commission fee; look around to get the best deal – the rates are clearly posted for you to see.

Hotels also offer exchange facilities, but their rates of exchange tend to be less favourable than either banks or bureaux de change, and they usually charge a higher commission, too.

Both foreign currency and travellers' cheques are accepted, in exchange for euro or Turkish lira. Travellers' cheques are also honoured by many hotels, shops and restaurants.

Many shops in both the Republic of Cyprus and in North Cyprus accept common foreign currencies, including US dollars and British pound sterling.

Cash machine in one of Nicosia's streets

Banks and Currency Exchange in North Cyprus

In North Cyprus, the bank networks are less extensive than in the south. Banks are open from 8am until noon. Travellers' cheques are widely accepted in shops, hotels and restaurants. They can also be exchanged for Turkish lira in banks and bureaux de change. When exchanging money, use only reputable dealers. In light of the high rate of inflation, it is worth changing smaller amounts of money more frequently, rather than a large amount.

Entrance to a Turkish bank in North Cyprus

Traveller's Cheques and Credit Cards

Banks, bureaux de change and other exchange facilities will cash your traveller's cheques into either euros or Turkish lira.

Credit cards are accepted by most larger shops, restaurants and hotels, although in markets and small shops only cash is accepted. Many debit cards are accepted, but check with your bank that your card is valid internationally. It may be difficult to find a cash machine in provincial towns and villages, so it is advisable to bring enough cash with you. Banks and credit card providers will charge foreign transaction fees on charges made while you are abroad so check the rates before you travel to avoid an unnecessarily large bill.

Currency

The Republic of Cyprus joined the Eurozone on 1 January 2008. Following a changeover period of one month, during which time both the Cyprus pound and the euro were in circulation, the Cyprus pound ceased to be legal tender.

The currency used in North Cyprus is the Turkish lira (TL or, more officially, TRY). This currency is not readily available abroad, so you need to change money on arrival in the island. North Cyprus also accepts payments in euros.

Republic of Cyprus

Banknotes

Euro banknotes have seven denominations. The 5 note (grey in colour) is the smallest, followed by the 10 note (pink), 20 note (blue), 50 note (orange), 100 note (green), 200 note (yellow) and 500 note (purple). All notes show the 12 stars of the European Union.

5 euros

10 euros

20 euros

50 euros

Coins

The euro has eight coin denominations: 2 and 1; 50 cents, 20 cents, 10 cents, 5 cents, 2 cents and 1 cent. The 1 and 2 coins are both silver and gold in colour. The 50-, 20- and 10-cent coins are gold. The 5-, 2- and 1-cent coins are bronze.

100 euros

200 euros

500 euros

North Cyprus

Banknotes

North Cyprus does not have its own currency; it uses the Turkish lira (abbreviated to TL). The banknotes, in six denominations from 5 to 200 TL, come in a range of colours, and bear Turkish national symbols and major historical figures. The euro is also accepted in the North.

5 lira

10 lira

20 lira

Coins

There are six coins in circulation, ranging in value from 1 kuruş, 5 kuruş, 10 kuruş, 25 kuruş and 50 kuruş to 1 TL – equal to (100 kuru).

50 lira

100 lira

200 lira

TRAVEL INFORMATION

Most visitors travel to Cyprus on a package holiday combining flights, accommodation, transport to and from the airport, and often car hire. International airports are located in Larnaka and Pafos and handle both scheduled flights and charters. Fares and schedules can be obtained from travel agents, airline offices and via the Internet. It is difficult to reach Cyprus by boat as passenger services no longer operate from Greece. The only ferry routes now available link Turkey to Kyrenia and Famagusta in North Cyprus. Cruises between Greece and Cyprus are also an option.

Road networks are good, with clearly marked signs. Cars drive on the left side of the road. A decent bus service operates between main towns and big resorts.

Air Travel

The international airports in Pafos and Larnaka, both in the Republic of Cyprus, handle flights by the majority of European airlines, serving many European capital cities and regional hubs. Budget airlines, such as easyJet and Ryanair, also fly to Cyprus. During summer, the airports become crowded due to the large number of charter flights. Scheduled flight tickets are generally more expensive than charters, but offer more flexibility and greater comfort.

Charter flights are at their busiest from April through October, with weekly departures. Most seats on charter flights are bought in blocks by tour operators, as part of their holiday packages, but "flight-only" charters are also available. These can be an affordable and convenient option for holiday-makers who prefer independent arrangements. Information on ticket availability can be obtained from travel agents

Pafos international airport

and from airline representatives. The airports have duty-free shops, cafés and restaurants, but the food and beverages on offer are over-priced.

Bus services from the airports to the main towns are frequent but it is worth checking the schedule to your destination in advance. The tourist information centres should be able to help you with this.

The best way of getting to town is by taxi or hired car. Taxi ranks are situated immediately next to the exit from the arrivals hall. For short distances, taxis are a comfortable and affordable mode of transport. Many of the larger car hire companies have offices at the airports, as well as in major towns on the island.

Visitors travelling to Larnaka airport with a tour operator should turn left, towards the coach parking, after leaving the terminal building. Visitors hiring a car should take care to follow the signs after leaving the terminal building.

At Larnaka, as well as at Pafos airport, services, amenities and transport links are clearly signposted at the terminal.

Ferries

Travel by ferry is often cheaper than flying, but currently there are few options to travel to Cyprus by sea. There are no passenger ferries to South Cyprus at the present time. The only regular ferry services available for tourist travellers sail from Turkey to North Cyprus.

Determined budget travellers can sail into Limassol from ports such as Piraeus (the port of Athens) and from some of the Greek islands, such as Patmos or Rhodes, but often this will be aboard a cargo ship. Journey times can be long: a direct sailing from Piraeus to Cyprus can take around 40 hours.

Cruise ships provide regular links between Cyprus and Haifa (Israel), Beirut (Lebanon) and

Interior of Larnaka international airport

Port Said (Egypt). These services begin in spring, at the start of the tourist season. Between May and October, the ferries sailing to the Middle East are used mainly by people on holiday in Cyprus. From the South there are a number of popular trips, including the journeys to Israel, Egypt, Lebanon and the Greek islands.

Some travel operators offer organized three-day trips to Egypt and the Holy Land, which include visits to Jerusalem and Bethlehem. These excursion vessels depart from Limassol Port.

There are a number of luxury cruiseliners that travel the Mediterranean and Middle East, with Cyprus being a popular stopping-off point.

North Cyprus

The quickest way to reach North Cyprus is by plane. All flights to Ercan airport originate in Turkey – from Alanya, Dalaman, Istanbul and Izmir. It is not possible to fly direct to North Cyprus from any other country. Flights are operated by Turkish Airlines. In order to reach Ercan airport you have to travel to Turkey from one of the European airports and then change for the flight to North Cyprus.

Convenient package holidays offer the same combination of flights, accommodation, airport transfers and, generally, car hire as those to the South, making this the easiest way to visit. You can also reach the North by ferry, which is a cheaper

Ferry harbour in Kyrenia, North Cyprus

option, recommended for those who wish to bring their own car to the island. Ferry journeys which set sail from southern Turkey take much longer than flying. The journey from Taşucu to Kyrenia lasts 6 hours while from Mersin to Famagusta, it can take up to 10 hours.

Travelling to North Cyprus can test your patience, as it usually involves long hours of waiting at Turkish airports for connecting flights – an important consideration when travelling with children or the elderly. These delays are due to the timetables not being very well coordinated.

Since the Republic of Cyprus joined the European Union in 2004, all citizens from the South are allowed to cross the border into North Cyprus without any hindrance, at least in theory, and stay as long as they wish. Visitors to the South who want to see North Cyprus can also cross the border to the North at the official checkpoints. Crossing anywhere other than an official checkpoint may result in arrest.

Airport terminal building at Ercan, North Cyprus

DIRECTORY

Cyprus Tourism Organization (CTO)

W visitcyprus.com
Larnaka.
Tel 24 654 322.
Limassol.
Tel 25 362 756.
Nicosia.
Tel 22 674 264.
Pafos.
Tel 26 932 841.
Troodos.
Tel 25 421 316.

International Airports

Ercan.
Tel 0392 600 5000.
W ercanhavalimani.com
Larnaka.
Tel 77 778 833.
W hermesairports.com
Pafos.
Tel 77 778 833.
W hermesairports.com

Ports

Cyprus Ports Authority (covers ports in Famagusta, Larnaka, Limassol and Pafos).
Tel 22 817 200.
W cpa.gov.cy

Airport Transfer

Kapnos Airport Shuttle
Nicosia to Pafos and Larnaka.
Tel 77 771 477.
W kapnosairportshuttle.com

Limassol Airport Express
Limassol to Pafos and Larnaka.
Tel 77 777 075.
W limassolairportexpress.eu

Getting Around Cyprus

Most visitors to Cyprus explore the island by bus or hire car. Buses provide good links between the towns, while for shorter distances taxis are a good option – both comfortable and affordable. In Cyprus, vehicles are right-hand drive. The roads throughout the island are in good condition, and signposting is clear.

North Cyprus sign indicating cars should drive in the left lane

Car Hire

It is expensive to hire a car on the island, especially in the main tourist season from April through October. You may find more attractive prices during low season. The price usually includes full insurance, a certain mileage allowance and VAT (value-added tax). Drivers under the age of 25 require additional insurance. Cypriot authorities honour international diving licences, as well as foreign licences. Both manual and automatic cars are available for hire, as are motorcycles and scooters.

You only need a four-wheel-drive vehicle if you are planning to tour the mountain regions in winter using some of the rough tracks, or go off-road in the Akamas peninsula. Major international car hire companies – Hertz, Avis and Europcar – have offices at the airports and in large cities, including Nicosia, Larnaka, Limassol and Pafos. Driving a hire car across the border to North Cyprus is not prohibited, but you will have to take out extra insurance on the Turkish side.

Rules of the Road

Driving is the easiest way to get around Cyprus. Roads are good, with motorways connecting Nicosia with Larnaka, Limassol, Pafos and Agia Napa. Distances are short – it is less than 160 km (100 miles) from Pafos to Nicosia.

Cypriots drive on the left side of the road, and drivers should give way to vehicles approaching from the right. Road signs are provided in both Greek and English in the South.

Road sign in the South: sharp bend

Distances and speed limits are in kilometres – 100 km/h (60 mph) on motorways, 80 km/h (50 mph) on most other roads, and 50 km/h (30 mph) in built-up areas. There are on-the-spot fines for speeding and for failing to wear a seat belt. Driving under the influence of alcohol is a criminal offence with serious consequences, as is using a mobile phone while driving.

Roads

The condition of the roads in Cyprus is very good. Since the 1980s, many stretches of road have been built, and others modernized. Roundabouts (traffic islands) have also appeared at intersections; the right of way goes to drivers approaching from the right.

Finding your way to the major historic sites is not difficult, as road signs show the way. Difficulties may arise, however, in the narrow streets of small towns, where signs are usually absent.

Pedestrians, especially those who may not be used to left-hand traffic, should exercise caution when crossing the road, and warn children to be particularly careful when stepping into the road.

Maps

When hiring a car, you will usually be given a very basic road map of the island. It is certainly worth purchasing a more detailed map of Cyprus or the part of the island you'll be exploring; these are available in many book stores and petrol stations. It may be easier to purchase a map from home and bring it with you, so that you'll be prepared from the outset. Bear in mind that many mountain roads are accessible only by four-wheel drive vehicle or motorcycle (or scooter).

Remember, too, that place names in the North may be different from those on a map purchased in the South, so you may have to cross-reference maps.

Driving in Nicosia

The capital of Cyprus is the biggest and most congested city on the island. Traffic jams occur during rush hour and tourists may have difficulty negotiating the traffic at these times, especially in the narrow streets of parts of the city. The worst congestion

A well-maintained road in the Troodos mountains

can be expected on the trunk roads leading into and out of the city and – particularly in high season – on roads to the main historical sites. Outside of rush hour, driving in Nicosia is relatively easy and comfortable.

Street names throughout the city are clearly visible, and major tourist attractions are well signposted.

Buses

Bus services between the large towns are efficient and comfortable, and tickets are inexpensive. There are at least six services daily between the four main southern towns. Transport links to major seaside resorts are also good.

Local buses also connect outlying communities with the nearest main town, but they are geared to the needs of school children and villagers, so departures are only early morning and mid-afternoon. Travellers will find it hard to get to and from the smaller towns and villages by bus.

Before travelling, check the timetable to see when the last return bus departs, to ensure that you will be able to get back. At weekends, there are reduced services.

Taxis

Metered taxis operate in all the main towns in Cyprus. Unmetered rural taxis serve most larger villages, charging 31–49 cents per kilometre.

Traffic moving along one of Kyrenia's busy streets

There are also shared "service taxis" or minibuses, which take passengers door to door so you can choose the most convenient point for getting on or off. Service taxis operate between all the major towns half-hourly between 6am and 6pm (to 7pm in summer) Monday to Friday, and 7am to 5pm at weekends.

A taxi sign in North Cyprus

Taxi fares are reasonable – particularly when you take a larger car and share the cost between several people – and provide a very convenient way of getting around.

Hitchhiking

Hitchhiking is not illegal in Cyprus but it is better avoided altogether in the larger towns, where a decent public transport system and affordable taxis provide safer alternatives. In more remote areas, the locals readily give lifts to people standing by the road.

It can be difficult to hitch a lift during the peak holiday season, and temperatures soar, making the wait uncomfortable. Be sure to carry a bottle of water with you and wear a sunhat. Women who hitchhike should take special care.

DIRECTORY

Buses

Intercity
Intercity Buses. **Tel** 80 00 77 89.
W intercity-buses.com

Larnaka
Zinonas Buses. **Tel** 80 00 77 44.
W zinonasbuses.com

Nicosia
OSEL. **Tel** 77 77 77 55.
W osel.com.cy

Pafos
Osypa Limited. **Tel** 80 00 55 88.
W pafosbuses.com

Taxis

Acropolis Vassos Taxi
Akamia Centre, Larnaka.
Tel 24 622 000.

Cyprus Taxi
W cyprustaxi.com

Euro Taxi
Ifigenias 24, Nicosia.
Tel 22 513 000.

Golden Taxi
Lysis Fasis 33, Limassol.
Tel 70 000 882.

Mayfair Taxi
Agapinoros 46, Pafos.
Tel 26 954 200.

Car Hire

Avis
Tel 22 713 333.
W avis.com.cy

Europcar
Tel 25 880 222.
W europcar.com.cy

Hertz
Tel 22 208 888.
W hertz.com.cy

A local Cypriot bus

General Index

Acknowledgments

Dorling Kindersley and Wiedza i Życie would like to thank the following people and institutions, whose contributions and assistance have made the preparation of this guide possible.

Publishing Manager
Kate Poole

Managing Editors
Vivien Antwi, Vicki Ingle

Publisher
Douglas Amrine

Senior Cartographic Editor
Casper Morris

Senior DTP Designer
Jason Little

Additional Picture Research
Rachel Barber, Rhiannon Furbear, Ellen Root

Revisions Editor
Anna Freiberger

Revisions Designer
Maite Lantaron

Revisions Team
Beverley Ager, Emma Anacoootee, Uma Bhattacharya, Emma Brady, Emer FitzGerald, Carole French, Swati Handoo, Vinod Harish, Mohammad Hassan, Shobhna Iyer, Jasneet Kaur, Juliet Kenny, Sumita Khatwani, Vincent Kurien, Laura Jones, Jude Ledger, Maria Massoura, Deepak Mittal, Alison McGill, Sonal Modha, Catherine Palmi, Helen Peters, Andrea Pinnington, Rada Radojicic, Erin Richards, Lokamata Sahoo, Sands Publishing Solutions, Avijit Sengupta, Ankita Sharma, Azeem Siddiqui, Rituraj Singh, Christine Stroyan, Roseen Teare, Priyansha Tuli, Dora Whitaker, Sophie Wright

Production Co-ordinator
Wendy Penn

Jacket Design
Tessa Bindloss

Consultant
Robin Gauldie

Factchecker
John Vickers

Proofreader
Stewart Wild

Index
Hilary Bird

Additional Photography
Wojciech Franus, Carole French, Robin Gauldie, Konrad Kalbarczyk, Grzegorz Micuła, Bernard Musyck, Ian O'Leary, Ronald Sayegh, Jon Spaull, Andrzej Zygmuntowicz

Special Assistance
Dr. Fotos Fotiou, Aleksander Nikolaou, Irfan Kiliç, Suleyman Yalin, Latif Ince, Artur Mościcki, Joanna Egert-Romanowska, Maria Betlejewska, Małgorzata Merkel-Massé.Latif Ince, Artur Mościcki, Joanna Egert-Romanowska, Maria Betlejewska, Małgorzata Merkel-Massé.

The publishers would also like to thank all the people and institutions who allowed us to use photographs from their archives:

Bernard Musyck, Ronald Sayegh (www.CyprusDestinations.com, skiing and agrotourism site)

Picture Credits
a = above; b = below/bottom; c = centre; f = far; l = left; r = right; t = top.

7 St. Georges Tavern: 170br; A. G. Leventis Gallery, Nicosia, Cyprus: 127bl; Almyra Hotel: 160cla; Alamy Images: Ros Drinkwater 158-9; Greg Balfour Evans 45b, 116; Peter Horree 169tl; Hemis 11tc; Doug Houghton40 203bl; Iconotec 17b; imagebroker/ Maria Breuer 190cra; imagebroker/Siepmann 169cr; iWebbtravel 106; LOOK Die Bildagentur der Fotografen GmbH 13tr; Victor Lucas 186–7; nagelstock.com 2–3; David Newham 10tr; Piamen Peev 55bl; Stuwdamdorp 197cr; Peter Titmuss 200c; Rawdon Wyatt 203tc; StockFood GmbH 5cr; Zoonar GmbH 1c. Archontiko Papadopoulou: 175t; Bellapais Gardens Hotel & Restaurant: 176br; The Trustees of the British Museum 97bc; Cleopatra Lebanese Restaurant: 172t; Corbis Bettmann 30, 38clb, 75br; Jonathan Blair 28c, 29cra, 38tr; Tom Brakefield 155cr; James Davis/ Eye Ubiquitous 20clb, 95crb, 152cla; John Heseltine 168cl; Jo Lillini 26bc, 185bl; Chris Lisle 28bl; Hans Georg Roth 6–7; Cyprus Police 194bl; Cyprus Tourism Organisation: 13bc, 56tr; Y.Vroullou 10bl; 123tc, Y. Vroullou 112clb; Domus Lounge Bar & Restaurant: 167tr; Dreamstime.com: Rostislav Ageev 12tr; Senai Aksoy 12br; Ruzanna Arutyunyan 128, 182cra; Debu55y 9tr, 9cr; Evgeniy Fesenko 85br; Gillian Hardy 8br; Bensliman Hassan 100–1; Kirill Makarov 18t, 19br, 40-1; Noamfein 200bl; Nushahru 8cl; Otk1986 182br; Michalakis Ppalis 11b, 185tr; Tupungato 64; Tetiana Zbrodko 16; Episkopiana Hotel: 160br; Carole French 196bl; Getty Images: Esen Tunar Photography 44; Nejdetduzan 146-7; Hill View: 163tr; Hilton Cyprus: 161bc, 165br; Jashan's: 177tl; Karatello Tavern, member of Carob Mill Restaurants Ltd.: 172bc; KEO Beer: 181tc; The Leventis Municipal Museum of Nicosia: 125br; Maria Massoura: 22tr; George Mitletton: 52bl; Grzegorz Micuła 21ca/bl, 23br, 56cb, 53c, 71cr, 96tr, 186br, 187tl, 196cla; George Mitletton: 52bl; Bernard Musyck: 29bl; New Helvetia Hotel: 164tc; Oliveto Stonegrill Dining: 167bl; Onar Holiday Village: 161tl; Ta Piatakia: 173br; Superstock: imagebroker.net 88; TAGO Konrad Kalbarczyk 17b, 182t; Thanos Hotels - Anassa: 162bl; Vouni Panayia Winery: 174bl; Zambartas Wineries: 181tl.

Front Endpaper

Alamy Images: Greg Balfour Evans Rcra; iWebbtravel Lbl; Dreamstime.com: Ruzanna Arutyunyan Rbr; Tupungato Rbc; Getty Images: Esen Tunar Photography Ltl; Superstock: imagebroker.net Ltr.

Jacket
Front and Spine – 4Corners: Johanna Huber / SIME.

All other images © Dorling Kindersley

For further information see www.dkimages.com

English–Greek Phrase Book

There are no clear-cut rules for transliterating modern
Greek into the Latin alphabet.
The system employed in this guide follows the rules generally
applied in Greece, adjusted to fit in with English pronunciation.
On the following pages, the English is given in the left-hand
column, the right-hand column provides a literal system of
pronunciation and indicates the stressed syllable in bold.
It is also worth remembering that both the Cypriot Greek and
Cypriot Turkish alphabets differ slightly from those used on the
mainland, and their accents are distinctive, too.

In Emergency

Help!	**Voítheia**	vo-**ee**-theea
Stop!	**Stamatíste**	sta-ma-tee-steh
Call a doctor!	**Fonáxte éna yatró**	fo-nak-steh **e**-na ya-tro
Call an ambulance!	**Kaléste to asthenofóro**	ka-le-steh to as-the-no-**fo**-ro
Call the police!	**Kaléste tin astynomía**	ka-le-steh teen a-sti-no-**mía**
Call the fire brigade!	**Kaléste tin pyrosvestikí**	ka-le-steh teen pee-ro-zve-stee-**kee**
Where is the nearest telephone?	**Poú eínai to plisiéstero tiléfono?**	poo ee ne to plee-see-**e**-ste-ro tee-**le**-pho-no?
Where is the nearest hospital?	**Poú eínai to plisiéstero nosokomeío?**	poo ee-ne to plee-see-**e**-ste-ro no-so-ko-**mee**-o?
Where is the nearest pharmacy?	**Poú eínai to plisiéstero farmakeío?**	poo ee-ne to plee-see-**e**-ste-ro far-ma-ke**e**-o?

Communication Essentials

Yes	**Nai**	neh
No	**Ochi**	**o**-chee
Please	**Parakaló**	pa-ra-ka-**lo**
Thank you	**Efcharistó**	ef-cha-ree-**sto**
Excuse me	**Me synchoreíte**	me seen cho-ree-teh
Goodbye	**Antío**	an-**dee**-o
Good morning	**Kaliméra**	ka-lee-**me**-ra
Good evening	**Kalinychta**	ka-lee-**neech**-ta
Morning	**Proí**	pro-**ee**
Afternoon	**Apógevma**	a-**po**-yev-ma
Evening	**Vrádi**	**vrath**-i
Yesterday	**Chthés**	chthes
Today	**Símera**	**see**-me-ra
Tomorrow	**Avrio**	**av**-ree-o
Here	**Edó**	ed-**o**
There	**Ekeí**	e-**kee**
What?	**Tí?**	tee?
Why?	**Giatí?**	ya-**tee**?
Where?	**Poú?**	poo?
How?	**Pós?**	pos?

Useful Phrases

How are you?	**Tí káneis?**	tee **ka**-nees
Very well, thank you	**Poly kalá, efcharistó**	po-lee ka-la, ef-cha-ree-**sto**
Pleased to meet you	**Chaíro polę**	**che**-ro po-lee
What is your name?	**Pós légeste?**	pos **le**-ye-ste?
Where is/where are...?	**Poú eínai?**	poo ee-ne?
How far is it to...?	**Póso apéchei...?**	**po**-so a-pe-chee?
I understand	**Katalavaíno**	ka-ta-la-**ve**-no
I don't understand	**Den katalavaíno**	then ka-ta-la-**ve**-no
Can you speak more slowly?	**Miláte lígo pio argá parakaló?**	mee-**la**-te lee-go pyo ar-**ga** pa-ra-ka-**lo**?
I'm sorry	**Me synchoreíte**	me-seen-cho-**ree** teh

Useful Words

big	**Megálo**	me-**ga**-lo
small	**Mikró**	mi-**kro**
hot	**Zestó**	zes-**to**
cold	**Kreyo**	kree-o
good	**Kaló**	ka-**lo**
bad	**Kakó**	ka-**ko**
open	**Anoichtá**	a-neech-**ta**
closed	**Kleistá**	klee-sta
left	**Aristerá**	a-ree-ste-**ra**

right	**Dexiá**	dek-see-**a**
straight	**Eftheía**	ef-**thee**-a
between	**Anámesa/ Metaxey**	a-**na**-me-sa/ Metaxý
on the corner....	**Sti gonía tou...**	stee go-nee-a too
near	**Kontá**	kon-**da**
far	**Makriá**	ma-kree-**a**
up	**Epáno**	e-**pa**-no
down	**Káto**	ka-to
early	**Norís**	no-rees
late	**Argá**	ar-**ga**
entrance	**I eísodos**	ee ee-so-thos
exit	**I éxodos**	eee-kso-dos
toilets	**Oi toualétes**	eee-kso-dos

Shopping

How much is it?	**Póso kánei?**	po-so ka-nee?
Do you...?	**Echete...?**	e-che-teh
Do you accept credit cards?	**Décheste pistotikés kártes**	the-ches-teh pee-sto-tee-kes kar-tes
Do you accept travellers' cheques?	**Déchesteh pistotikés travellers' cheques?**	the-ches-teh pee-sto-tee-kes travellers' cheques
What time do you open?	**Póte anoígete?**	po-teh a-nee-ye-teh?
What time do you close?	**Póte kleínete?**	po-teh klee-ne-teh?
this one	**Aftó edó**	af-**to** e-**do**
that	**Ekeíno**	e-kee-no
expensive	**Akrivó**	e-kree-**vo**
cheap	**Fthinó**	fthee-**no**
size	**To mégethos**	to me-ge-thos
white	**Lefkó**	lef-**ko**
black	**Mávro**	**mav**-ro
red	**Kókkino**	ko-kee-no
yellow	**Kítrino**	kee-tree-no
green	**Prásino**	pra-see-no
blue	**Mple**	bleh
antique shop	**Magazí me antíkes**	ma-ga-**zee** me an-dee-kes
bakery	**O foúrnos**	o **foor**-nos
bank	**I trápeza**	**I** trápeza
bazaar	**To pazári**	to pa-**za**-ree
bookshop	**To vivliopoleío**	o vee-vlee-o-po-lee-o
pharmacy	**To farmakeío**	to far-ma-kee-o
post office	**To tachy- dromeío**	to ta-chee -thro-mee-o
supermarket	**Supermarket**	"Supermarket"

Sightseeing

tourist information	**CTO**	CTO
beach	**I paralía**	ee pa-ra-lee-a
Byzantine	**vyzantinós**	vee-zan-dee-nos
castle	**To kástro**	to ka-stro
church	**I ekklisía**	ee e-klee-see-a
monastery	**moní**	mo-ni
museum	**To mouseío**	to moo-see-o
national	**ethnikós**	eth-nee-kos
river	**To potámi**	to po-ta-mee
road	**O drómos**	o thro-mos
saint	**ágios**	**a**-yee-os
theatre	**To théatro**	to the-a-tro

Travelling

When does the ... leave?	**Póte févgei to...?**	po-teh fev-yee to..
Where is the bus stop?	**Poú eínai i stási tou leoforeíou?**	poo ee-neh ee sta-see tou le-o-fo-ree-oo?
Is this bus going to...?	**Ypárche I leoforeío gia...?**	ee-par-chee le-o-fo-ree-o yia...?
bus ticket	**Eisitírio leoforeíou**	ee-see-tee-ree-o le-o-fo-ree-o?
harbour	**To limáni**	to lee-ma-nee
bicycle	**To podílato**	to po-thee-la-to
taxi	**To taxí**	to tak-see
airport	**To aero- drómio**	to a-e-ro-thro- mee-o
ferry	**To "ferry-boat"**	to fe-ree-bot

alternatives for a female speaker are shown in brackets

In a Hotel

Do you have a vacant room?	**Echete domátia?**	e-che-teh tho-ma-tee-a?
double room	**Díklino me dipló kreváti**	thee-klee-no meh thee-plo kre-va-tee
single room	**Monóklino**	mo-no-klee-no
room with bathroom	**Domátio me mpánio**	tho-ma-tee-o meh ban-yo
shower	**To douz**	To dooz
key	**To kleidí**	to klee-dee
I have a reservation	**Echo kánei krátisi**	e-cho ka-nee kra-tee-see
room with sea view	**Domátio me théasti thálassa**	tho-ma-tee-o meh the-a stee tha-la-sa
room with a balcony	**Domátio me théasti mpalkóni**	tho-ma-tee-o meh the-a stee bal-ko-nee
Does the price include breakfast	**To proïnó symperilamvánetai stin timí?**	to pro-ee-no seem-be-ree-lam-va-ne-tehsteen tee-mee?

Eating out

Have you got a free table?	**Echete trapézi?**	e-che-te tra-pe-zee?
I'd like to reserve a table	**Thélo na kratíso éna trapézi**	the-lo na kra-tee-so e-na tra-pe-zee
The bill, please	**Ton logariazmó parakaló**	tonlo-gar-yas-mo pa-ra-ka-lo
I'm a vegetarian	**Eímai chortofágos**	ee-meh chor-to-fa-gos
menu	**O katálogos**	o ka-ta-lo-gos
wine list	**O katálogos me ta oinopnevmatódi**	o ka-ta-lo-gos meh ta ee-no-pnev-ma-to-thee
glass	**To potíri**	to po-tee-ree
bottle	**To mpoukáli**	to bou-ka-lee
knife	**To machaíri**	to ma-che-ree
fork	**To piroúni**	to pee-roo-nee
spoon	**To koutáli**	to koo-ta-lee
breakfast	**To proïnó**	to pro-ee-no
lunch	**To mesimerianó**	to me-see-mer-ya-no
dinner	**To deípno**	to theep-no
main course	**To kyríos gévma**	to kee-ree-os yev-ma
starter	**Ta orektiká**	ta o-rek-tee-ka
dessert	**To glykó**	to ylee-ko
dish of the day	**To piáto tis iméras**	to pya-to tees ee-me-ras
bar	**To "bar"**	To bar
tavern	**I tavérna**	ee ta-ver-na
café	**To kafeneío**	to ka-fe-nee-o
wine shop	**To oinopoleío**	to ee-no-po-lee-o
restaurant	**To estiatório**	to e-stee-a-to-ree-o
ouzeria	**To ouzerí**	To ouzeri
kebab take-away	**To souvlatzídiko**	To soo-vlat-zee-dee-ko

Menu Decoder

coffee	**O Kafés**	o ka-fes
with milk	**me gála**	me ga-la
black coffee	**skétos**	ske-tos
without sugar	**chorís záchari**	cho-rees za-cha-ree
tea	**tsái**	tsa-ee
wine	**krasí**	kra-see
red	**kókkino**	ko-kee-no
white	**lefkó**	lef-ko
rosé	**rozé**	ro-ze
raki	**To rakí**	to ra-kee
ouzo	**To oúzo**	to oo-zo
retsina	**I retsína**	ee ret-see-na
water	**To neró**	to ne-ro
fish	**To psári**	to psa-ree

cheese	**To tyrí**	to tee-ree
halloumi cheese	**To chaloúmi**	
feta	**I féta**	ee fe-ta
bread	**To psomí**	to pso-mee
hummus	**To houmous**	to choo-moos
halva	**O chalvás**	o chal-vas
Turkish Delight	**To loukoúmi**	to loo-koo-mee loo-koo-mee
baklava	**O mpaklavás**	o bak-la-vas
kléftiko (lamb dish)	**To kléftiko**	to klef-tee-ko

Numbers

1	**éna**	e-na
2	**dyo**	thee-o
3	**tría**	tree-a
4	**téssera**	te-se-ra
5	**pénte**	pen-deh
6	**éxi**	ek-si
7	**eptá**	ep-ta
8	**ochtó**	och-to
9	**ennéa**	e-ne-a
10	**déka**	the-ka
100	**ekató**	e-ka-to
200	**diakósia**	thya-kos-ya
1,000	**chília**	cheel-ya
2,000	**dychiliádes**	thee-o cheel-ya-thes
1,000,000	**éna ekat-ommyrio**	e-na e-ka-to-mee-ree-o

Days of the Week, Months, Time

one minute	**éna leptó**	e-na lep-to
one hour	**mía óra**	mee-a o-ra
half an hour	**misí óra**	mee-see o-ra
a day	**mía méra**	mee-a me-ra
week	**mía evdomáda**	mee-a ev-tho-ma-tha
month	**énas mínas**	e-nas mee-nas
year	**énas chrónos**	e-nas chro-nos
Monday	**Deftéra**	thef-te-ra
Tuesday	**Tríti**	tree-tee
Wednesday	**Tetárti**	te-tar-tee
Thursday	**Pémpti**	pemp-tee
Friday	**Paraskeví**	pa-ras-ke-vee
Saturday	**Sávvato**	sa-va-to
Sunday	**Kyriakí**	keer-ee-a-kee
January	**Ianouários**	ee-a-noo-a-ree-os
February	**Fevrouários**	fev-roo-a-ree-os
March	**Mártios**	mar-tee-os
April	**Aprílios**	a-pree-lee-os
May	**Máios**	ma-ee-os
June	**Ioúnios**	ee-oo-nee-os
July	**Ioúlios**	ee-oo-lee-os
August	**Avgoustos**	av-goo-stos
September	**Septémvrios**	sep-tem-vree-os
October	**Októvrios**	ok-to-vree-os
November	**Noémvrios**	no-em-vree-os
December	**Dekémvrios**	the-kem-vree-os

alternatives for a female speaker are shown in brackets

English-Turkish Phrase Book

Pronunciation

Turkish uses a Roman alphabet. It has 29 letters: 8 vowels and 21 consonants. Letters that differ from the English alphabet are: **c**, pronounced "j" as in "jolly"; **ç**, pronounced "ch" as in "church"; **ğ**, which lengthens the preceding vowel and is not pronounced; **ı**, pronounced "uh"; **ö**, pronounced "ur" (like the sound in "further"); **ş**, pronounced "sh" as in "ship"; **ü**, pronounced "ew" as in "few".

In an Emergency

Help!	İmdat!	eem-**dat**
Stop!	Dur!	door
Call a doctor!	Bir doktor çağrın!	beer dok-**tor** chah-ruhn
Call an ambulance!	Bir ambulans çağrın!	beer am-boo-**lans** chah-ruhn
Call the police!	Polis çağrın!	po-**lees** chah-ruhn
Fire!	Yangın!	yan-**guhn**
Where is the nearest telephone?	En yakın telefon nerede?	en ya-**kuhn** teh-leh-**fon** neh-reh-deh
Where is the nearest hospital?	En yakın hastane nerede?	en ya-**kuhn** has-ta-neh neh-reh-deh

Communication Essentials

Yes	Evet	eh-**vet**
No	Hayır	h-**eye**'-uhr
Thank you	Teşekkür ederim	teh-shek-**kewr** eh-deh-reem
Please	Lütfen	lewt-fen
Excuse me	Affedersiniz	af-feh-der-se-neez
Hello	Merhaba	mer-ha-ba
Goodbye	Hoşça kalın	hosh-**cha ka**-luhn
Good morning	Günaydın	gewn-**eye**'-duhn
Good evening	İyi akşamlar	ee-yee ak-sham-**lar**
Morning	Sabah	sa-**bah**
Afternoon	Öğleden sonra	ur-gleh-**den son**-ra
Evening	Akşam	ak-**sham**
Yesterday	Dün	dewn
Today	Bugün	boo-gewn
Tomorrow	Yarın	ya-ruhn
Here	Burada	boo-ra-da
There	Şurada	shoo-ra-da
Over there	Orada	o-ra-da
What?	Ne?	neh
When?	Ne zaman?	neh za-man
Why?	Neden	neh-**den**
Where?	Nerede	neh-reh-deh

Useful Phrases

How are you?	Nasılsınız?	na-suhl-suh-nuhz
I'm fine	İyiyim	ee-**yee**-yeem
Pleased to meet you	Memnun oldum	mem-**noon ol**-doom
That's fine	Tamam	ta-**mam**
Where is/are …?	… nerede?	…**neh**-reh-deh
How far is it to …?	… ne kadar uzakta?	…**neh ka**-dar oo-zak-ta
I want to go to …	… a/e gitmek istiyorum	… a/eh geet-**mek** ees-**tee**-yo-room
Do you speak English?	İngilizce biliyor musunuz?	een-gee-**leez**-jeh bee-**lee**-yor boo-soo-nooz?
I don't understand	Anlamıyorum	an-**la**-muh-yo-room
Can you help me?	Bana yardım edebilir misiniz?	ba-**na** yar-**duhm** eh-deh-bee-**leer** mee-see-neez?

Useful Words

big	büyük	bew-**yewk**
small	küçük	kew-**chewk**
hot	sıcak	suh-**jak**
cold	soğuk	soh-**ook**
good/well	iyi	ee-**yee**
bad	kötü	kur-**tew**
open	acık	a-**chuhk**
closed	kapalı	ka-pa-**luh**
left	sol	sol
right	sağ	saa
straight on	doğru	doh-**roo**
near	yakın	ya-**kuhn**
far	uzak	oo-**zak**
early	erken	er-**ken**
late	geç	gech
entrance	giriş	gee-**reesh**

exit	çıkış	chuh-**kuhsh**
toilets	tuvaletler	too-va-let-**ler**

Shopping

How much is this?	Bu kaç lira?	boo kach lee-ra
I would like …	… istiyorum	… ees-**tee**-yo-room
Do you have …?	… var mı?	…**var** muh?
Do you take credit cards?	Kredi kartı kabul ediyor musunuz?	kreh-dee **kar**-tuh ka-**bool** eh-**dee**-yor moo-soo-nooz?
What time do you open/close?	Saat kaçta açılıyor/kapanıyor?	Sa-**at** kach-**ta** a-chuh-**luh**-yor/ka-pa-**nuh**-yor
this one	bunu	boo-**noo**
that one	şunu	shoo-**noo**
expensive	pahalı	pa-ha-**luh**
cheap	ucuz	oo-**jooz**
size (clothes)	beden	beh-**den**
size (shoes)	numara	noo-ma-**ra**
white	beyaz	bay-**yaz**
black	siyah	see-**yah**
red	kırmızı	kuhr-muh-**zuh**
yellow	sarı	sa-**ruh**
green	yeşil	yeh-**sheel**
blue	mavi	ma-**vee**
bakery	fırın	fuh-**ruhn**
bank	banka	ban-ka
cake shop	pastane	pas-ta-**neh**
chemist's/pharmacy	eczane	ej-za-**neh**
hairdresser	kuaför	kwaf-**fur**
barber	berber	ber-**ber**
market/bazaar	çarşı/pazar	char-**shuh**/pa-**zar**
post office	postane	pos-ta-**neh**
travel agency	seyahat acentesi	say-ya-**hat** a-jen-teh-**see**

Sightseeing

castle	hisar	hee-**sar**
church	kilise	kee-lee-seh
mosque	cami	ja-mee
museum	müze	mew-zeh
square	meydan	may-**dan**
theological college	medrese	med-reh-seh
tomb	türbe	tewr-**beh**
tourist information office	turizm danışma bürosu	too-**reezm** da-nuhsh-**mah** bew-ro-soo
town hall	belediye sarayı	beh-leh-dee-**yeh** sar-**eye**'-uh
Turkish bath	hamam	ha-**mam**

Travelling

airport	havalimanı	ha-**va**-lee-ma-nuh
bus/coach	otobüs	o-to-**bewss**
bus stop	otobüs durağı	o-to-**bewss** doo-ra-uh
ferry	vapur	va-**poor**
taxi	taksi	tak-see
ticket	bilet	bee-**let**
ticket office	bilet gişesi	bee-**let** gee-sheh-**see**
timetable	tarife	ta-ree-**feh**

Staying in a Hotel

Do you have a vacant room?	Boş odanız var mı?	bosh o-da-**nuhz** var muh?
double room	iki kişilik bir oda	ee-**kee** kee-shee-**leek** beer o-**da**
twin room	çift yataklı bir oda	cheeft ya-**tak**-luh beer o-**da**
single room	tek kişilik	tek kee-shee-**leek** with
a bathroom	banyolu bir oda	ban-yo-loo beer o-**da**
key	anahtar	a-nah-**tar**
room service	oda servisi	o-da ser-vee-**see**
I have a reservation	Rezervasyonum var	reh-zer-vas-yo-**noom** var
Does the price include breakfast?	Fiyata kahvaltı dahil mi?	fee-ya-**ta** kah-val-tuh da-**heel** mee?

Eating Out

Do you have a table	… kişilik bir masa	… kee-shee-**leek** for …people
The bill please	Hesap lütfen	heh-**sap** lewt-fen
I am a vegetarian	Et yemiyorum	et yeh-mee-yo-room
restaurant	lokanta	lo-**kan**-ta
waiter	garson	gar-**son**

menu	**yemek listesi**	ye-**mek lees**-teh-see
wine list	**şarap listesi**	sha-**rap lees**-teh-see
breakfast	**kahvaltı**	kah-val-**tuh**
lunch	**öğle yemeği**	ur-**leh** yeh-meh-**ee**
dinner	**akşam yemeği**	ak-**sham** yeh-meh-**ee**
starter	**meze**	**meh**-zeh
main course	**ana yemek**	a-**na** yeh-**mek**
dish of the day	**günün yemeği**	gewn-**ewn**
		yeh-meh-**ee**
dessert	**tatlı**	tat-**luh**
glass	**bardak**	bar-**dak**
bottle	**şişe**	shee-**sheh**
knife	**bıçak**	buh-**chak**
fork	**çatal**	cha-**tal**
spoon	**kaşık**	ka-**shuhk**

sebze	seb-**zeh**	vegetables
şeftali	shef-ta-**lee**	peach
şeker	sheh-**ker**	sugar
su	soo	water
süt	sewt	milk
sütlü	sewt-**lew**	with milk
tavuk	ta-**vook**	chicken
tereyağı	teh-**reh**-yah-uh	butter
tuz	tooz	salt
üzüm	ew-**zewm**	grapes
yoğurt	yoh-**urt**	yoghurt
yumurta	yoo-moor-**ta**	egg
zeytin	zay-**teen**	olives
zeytinyağı	zay-**teen**-yah-uh	olive oil

Menu Decoder

bal	bal	honey
balık	ba-**luhk**	fish
bira	**bee**-ra	beer
bonfile	**bon**-fee-leh	fillet steak
buz	booz	ice
çay	ch-'eye'	tea
çilek	chee-**lek**	strawberry
çorba	chor-**ba**	soup
dondurma	don-door-**ma**	ice cream
ekmek	ek-**mek**	bread
elma	el-**ma**	apple
et	et	meat
fasulye	fa-**sool**-yeh	beans
fırında	fuh-ruhn-**da**	roast
gazoz	ga-**zoz**	fizzy drink
kahve	kah-**veh**	coffee
karpuz	kar-**pooz**	water melon
kavun	ka-**voon**	melon
kayısı	k-'eye'-uh-**suh**	apricots
kıyma	kuhy-**ma**	minced meat
kızartma	kuh-zart-**ma**	fried
köfte	kurf-**teh**	meatballs
kuzu eti	koo-**zoo** eh-**tee**	lamb
lokum	lo-**koom**	Turkish delight
maden suyu	ma-**den** soo-**yoo**	mineral water
meyve suyu	may-**veh** soo-**yoo**	fruit juice
muz	mooz	banana
patlıcan	pat-luh-**jan**	aubergine (eggplant)
peynir	pay-**neer**	cheese
pilav	pee-**lav**	rice
piliç	pee-**leech**	roast chicken
şarap	sha-**rap**	wine

Numbers

0	**sıfır**	**suh**-fuhr
1	**bir**	beer
2	**iki**	ee-**kee**
3	**üç**	ewch
4	**dört**	durt
5	**beş**	besh
6	**altı**	al-**tuh**
7	**yedi**	yeh-**dee**
8	**sekiz**	seh-**keez**
9	**dokuz**	doh-**kooz**
10	**on**	on
100	**yüz**	yewz
200	**iki yüz**	ee-**kee** yewz
1,000	**bin**	been
100,000	**yüz bin**	**yewz** been
1,000,000	**bir milyon**	**beer** meel-**yon**

Time

one minute	**bir dakika**	**beer** da-kee-**ka**
one hour	**bir saat**	**beer** sa-at
half an hour	**yarım saat**	ya-**ruhm sa**-at
day	**gün**	gewn
week	**hafta**	haf-**ta**
month	**ay**	'eye'
year	**yıl**	yuhl
Sunday	**pazar**	pa-**zar**
Monday	**pazartesi**	pa-**zar**-teh-see
Tuesday	**salı**	sa-**luh**
Wednesday	**çarşamba**	char-sham-**ba**
Thursday	**perşembe**	per-shem-**beh**
Friday	**cuma**	joo-**ma**
Saturday	**cumartesi**	joo-**mar**-teh-see